Object Recognition
through Invariant Indexing

Object Recognition through Invariant Indexing

CHARLES A. ROTHWELL

Projet Robotvis
INRIA
Sophia Antipolis, France

OXFORD   NEW YORK   TOKYO
OXFORD UNIVERSITY PRESS
1995

Oxford University Press, Walton Street, Oxford OX2 6DP

Oxford New York
Athens Auckland Bangkok Bombay
Calcutta Cape Town Dar es Salaam Delhi
Florence Hong Kong Istanbul Karachi
Kuala Lumpur Madras Madrid Melbourne
Mexico City Nairobi Paris Singapore
Taipei Tokyo Toronto
and associated companies in
Berlin Ibadan

Oxford is a trade mark of Oxford University Press

Published in the United States
by Oxford University Press Inc., New York

A catalogue record for this book is available from the British Library

Library of Congress Cataloging in Publication Data
Rothwell, Charles A.
Object recognition through invariant indexing / Charles A.
Rothwell.
Includes index.
1. Computer vision.   2. Optical pattern recognition.   3. Image
processing—Digital techniques.   I. Title.
TA1634.R68   1994   006.3'7—dc20   94–24402
ISBN 0 19 856512 7

Typeset by the author using LaTeX
Printed in Great Britain by
Bookcraft (Bath) Ltd, Midsomer Norton, Avon

PREFACE

Lewis: I don't know, sir. I just get more confused the more I think about it.

Morse: It's easy when you think about it, Lewis.

— The Silent World of Nicholas Quinn (30)

Morse: But your brain, Lewis, it seems to get sharper every day.

Lewis: It must be working with you sir.

— The Riddle of the Third Mile (29)

This monograph describes some research into object recognition performed by the author over the last four or so years. Although I have attempted to be broad-minded with regard to the best approach to use for computerized object recognition, the reader will very quickly discover a strong bias towards the use of geometric invariance as the foundation for object description and shape recovery.

The enthusiasm for invariance is a product of a fruitful collaboration with three other researchers, David Forsyth, Joe Mundy, and Andrew Zisserman, which started at Oxford University but has now spread around the globe. Their influence on the following pages is unquestionable, and I would like to express my sincere gratitude for all of their efforts.

My principal intention for publishing a book on object recognition is to fill a void that appears to stretch beyond the wealth of theoretical studies in the field of computer vision. Although recent publications do not totally omit aspects of computer implementations, much of the literature comes under the aegis of mathematics. Therefore, the following chapters are written to be a complement to geometry texts (both old and new) that provides a sufficient level of theory to motivate recognition system design, but invests its main interest in aspects of system implementation. From an alternative point of view, this monograph has the intention of spanning the distance between the recent book edited by Joe Mundy and Andrew Zisserman (92) which contains a collection of reports on basic research into invariance, and that by Eric Grimson (53) which reviews object recognition in detail from the non-invariance standpoint. Briefly, by studying the real life problem of object recognition, we can bring theory from the former, and the practical aspects of the latter together.

Although not written as a textbook, my aim has been to provide both a sufficiently high level appreciation of the problem of object recognition, as well as a detailed discussion about the building of a pair of working recognition systems. Of course we have not yet succeeded in finding the ideal recognition algorithm (as yet, both robotic and surveillance recognition systems are rather primitive), but we can at least demonstrate a basic capability. Hopefully, by understanding the problems that were encountered during the research period covered by this book, we can go on to achieve something markedly better.

Obviously, a book that invests its main interest in the architectural aspects of computer vision can hope only to provide a snap-shot view of the state-of-the-art in its domain. No doubt we will soon learn how to tackle the problems in faster and more sophisticated ways, and so such a text will become rapidly outdated. I can make no apology for the fact that portions of this work are already obsolete, though I will be satisfied if any one part should survive for just a sixth of the time of Robert's thesis (106).

There are many people who have either directly, or indirectly assisted me during the writing of this book. The principal source of financial support was General Electric CRD. Most of the research was carried out whilst I was a member of the Oxford University Robotics Research Group. I have had many stimulating discussions with members of the group, of whom I would like to thank in particular Mike Brady, Paul Beardsley, Rupert Curwen, Doug McCowen, Steve Maybank, Ian Reid, David Sinclair, and Mike Taylor. I have also benefited from discussions with Tom Binford, Olivier Faugeras, Richard Hartley, and Luc Van Gool. Furthermore, I would like to express my gratitude to Pat Mundy for many untold favours.

I have also appreciated the efficiency and skill of those at Oxford University Press who brought this book from its initial draft form to the current state. Additionally, thanks are expressed to Mike Nugent who made a significant contribution to the clarity and presentation of the text.

Finally, and most importantly, I would like to express my thanks to three people. The first two are my parents who have always provided the necessary support whenever it has been needed. The third is Pippa, who has not only allowed me to sort out many problems of all magnitudes from afar, but who is also a close and loving companion.

Sophia Antipolis   C.A.R.
June 1994

CONTENTS

1

INTRODUCTION

From the point of view of computer implementations, object recognition was first studied by Roberts (106) in the early 1960s. Although the methods and the generality of the tasks have changed considerably since then, the goal is still the same:

The goal of an object recognition system is to take either a single image or a sequence of images of a scene and determine both the identities and locations of objects that are present.

Steadily, the aspirations of recognition researchers have developed so that now the objective is considered to be the ability to recognize three-dimensional objects from an arbitrary three-dimensional viewpoint. Essentially, recognition can be formulated as a search problem and as such has to be guided in a controlled manner. This monograph investigates a number of the search issues.

Note that the intention is generally to answer two distinct problems: *what* is present and *where*, Marr (78). It may appear to be odd to separate these two problems as humans solve them simultaneously. However, they can and will be treated as distinct tasks throughout the subsequent chapters. The principal reason for this is due to the specific architecture we use for recognition. In fact, we concentrate on the former and pay little attention to the computation of object pose. The rest of this introductory chapter will take the above definition of the general recognition problem and show how it can be developed into a far more specific task that can then be studied in detail. Subsequently, the rest of the monograph will describe a series of experiments in object recognition that make use of the more restricted domain. We shall not pretend to provide a general solution to the object recognition problem; that is still too far off as will be seen from current system abilities discussed in the second chapter.

No distinction will be drawn between the different application environments in which the algorithms can be deployed. Generally, computer-based object recognition has been investigated in robotics, surveillance, in medical and industrial inspection, and in other environments where precise measurements are required. The methods discussed in the sequel are applicable within any environment in which a sensor has to provide geometric information about object identities. Although recognition does not necessarily have to use geometric features, other cues such as surface shading, texture or colour do not as yet provide such a rich and accurate source of information as geometry. Therefore, we shall restrict the discussion only to the use of object geometry.

1.1   The architecture

The investigation will adhere to the *selection–indexing–correspondence* approach to recognition formulated by Grimson (53). This provides a concrete framework in which to develop the recognition techniques and allows the grounding of the ideas with plausible examples of recognition. It is our belief that recognition cannot be studied without a detailed architectural framework, or to use Marr's phraseology, the architecture provides a basis for a computational model (78).

The specific architecture discussed is called LEWIS: Library Entry Working through an Indexing Sequence.[1] LEWIS highlights the two main areas that we believe have recently required detailed analysis. These are:

1. What is the rôle of indexing within the process of formulating object hypotheses and the subsequent recognition conclusions? We will in practice concentrate on indexes formed out of geometric invariant measures.

2. Can sequential processing be used effectively for recognition, or are other architectures required?

The example in the following section sets invariant indexing into context. Geometric invariants are shape measures that remain constant under imaging. Most familiar shape descriptions change as one views an object from different positions. For instance, the boundary of the vase in Fig. 1.1 changes considerably between the two views shown. Consequently, any process designed to recognize the vase must account for this change in shape. In contrast, an invariant description for the same shape does not change between viewpoints and so the recognition process has to deal only with the variations between different objects, rather than those produced by viewing a single object. In fact, the value of the invariant measured on the object and in all images of the object should be constant. At this stage it is premature to describe the structure of invariants, but by the end of Chapter 3 it will be clear both what we mean by, and the significance of the term *invariant*.

The description of the sequential architecture will not be discussed until Chapter 4. The question being addressed with regard to architecture is how detailed the interactions between the different processes in a recognition system have to be. We have investigated an approach to recognition that passes information between distinct modules. In fact, the desire to employ

---

[1] The name is taken from the series of novels by Colin Dexter (29, 30). Lewis is the straightforward and occasionally successful assistant to the eponymous detective Morse.

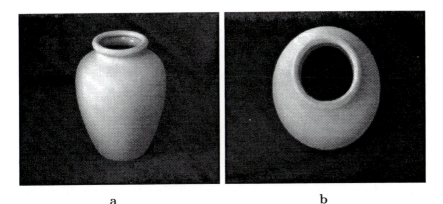

a   b

FIG. 1.1. The perceived outline of an object such as a vase changes significantly as one changes viewpoint. Shape cues such as invariants do not
change as the viewpoint is moved and are thus better for recognition
than more straightforward measures.

selection–indexing–correspondence effectively enforces modularity. Such a
design has the advantage that it is possible to effect minor changes in
a single process without complete system reconfiguration. However, there
are some disadvantages that will become apparent. LEWIS is a bottom-up
architecture, by which we mean that all the data flows from the original
image up to recognition hypotheses. The effectiveness of this approach will
become clearer throughout the following chapters, and will be discussed in
detail in the closing chapter.

Two variants of the recognition architecture, LEWIS1 and LEWIS2,
have been developed to recognize different classes of object. These have
been built and substantially tested over many sample images. Constructing
the systems has clarified how different processes communicate with each
other in recognition and also how varied object class descriptions might be
integrated into a single system.

1.2   A recognition example

We begin with a simple recognition example. First, some definitions are
made that are limited to this particular example. These define a model, an
image, and a view:

- *A model* is a description of an object. The objects that we wish to
  recognize are composed of a pair of line segments that are coincident
  at one of their endpoints. A sample model is shown in Fig. 1.2. The
  model description used for an object containing lines $\{\mathbf{L}_1, \mathbf{L}_2\}$ is $\mathbf{M} = \{\Theta_{12}, L_1, L_2\}$, where Θ_{12} is the angle between the lines and L_i is the
  length of the ith line. Nothing needs to be said about the units in
  which these quantities are expressed, just so long as the same units

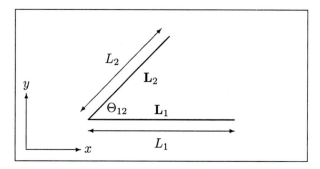

FIG. 1.2. A model consists of a pair of lines that have an endpoint in common. The model information is stored in the triple $\{\Theta_{12}, L_1, L_2\}$. The model may, or may not, include a local coordinate frame.

are used for all parts of the recognition process. If necessary, one may include a local coordinate frame within the model description, though $\mathbf{M}$ does not do this. Models are members of a model base which is a library of objects. A model base of n objects consists simply of a list $\mathcal{M} = \{\mathbf{M}_1, \ldots, \mathbf{M}_n\}$.

- *An image* is a view of a set of features. The features of interest are line segments. We are not concerned with how these are extracted from the sensor data. Rather, assume that the image consists of a list of line segments in a given coordinate frame. The five lines $\mathbf{l}_i$ $i \in \{1, \ldots, 5\}$ are represented by $\mathcal{I} = \{\mathbf{l}_1, \ldots, \mathbf{l}_5\}$ in the image shown in Fig. 1.3. As can be seen from the figure, the image has an associated Euclidean coordinate frame. Finally, some relationships between the lines may also be given (such as connectivity of $\mathbf{l}_1$ and $\mathbf{l}_2$).

- *A view* provides constraints between a scene containing the objects and the image features. In this case, a view is restricted to a plane Euclidean distortion of the object, so the only deformations of the model that are allowed are rigid planar translations, rotations and reflections. In the sequel, we will be concerned with measures that are invariant under the constraints provided by the view. In general, invariants are equal on an object in a scene and in any view of the object.

Given the above definitions, the recognition task is defined simply as:

Determine which models in $\mathcal{M}$ cause the features to be observed in an image $\mathcal{I}$.

Solution 1

The first solution is to take all possible pairs of lines $\mathbf{l}_i, \mathbf{l}_j \in \mathcal{I}$ and for each compute the triples $\mathbf{m}_{ij} = \{\theta_{ij}, l_i, l_j\}$. Then, compare each $\mathbf{m}_{ij}$ with every model $\mathbf{M}_k \in \mathcal{M}$. If the image triple matches a model, the model is supposed to explain the image data, and the object whose model is $\mathbf{M}_k$ is declared

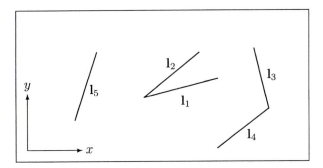

FIG. 1.3. A simple example of an image. The features in the scene are the
   five lines l_i, $i \in \{1,\ldots,5\}$, some of which have coincident endpoints.
   Note that there is also an intrinsic coordinate frame associated with
   the image.

to be recognized. The computational complexity of the approach can be
analysed quite simply for the case given in Fig. 1.3: for five image lines
there are ${}^5C_2$ possible line pairs. Let there be n models in $\mathcal{M}$. Therefore,
assuming that the correspondence process is tolerant to changes in ordering
of the lines, a total of ${}^5C_2 \times n = 10n$ different image-feature-to-model checks
have to be made.

   This is recognition in its simplest form, and demonstrates the use of
correspondence. There is little doubt that this approach will work. The
next step is to consider how to make it more efficient.

Solution 2

As stated in the definition of an image, it is possible to assert relationships
between image features. Figure 1.3 suggests that one relationship of use is
the coincidence of the line endpoints. Let us say that $\mathcal{I}$ can be structured
so that the task of determining whether a pair of lines is connected requires
negligible computation time. Now define the recognition algorithm so that
it selects only pairs of lines from $\mathcal{I}$ that are connected, and then performs
the comparison with $\mathcal{M}$ as in the first solution.

   This approach is again guaranteed to work as plane Euclidean transformations cannot disrupt the connectivity between pairs of object lines. It is
also true generally that the algorithm is more efficient than the first solution as fewer line pairs l_i,l_j are considered in the process. The difference in
performance can be quite substantial if there are many lines in the image.
Even for the example in Fig. 1.3 only two consistency checks have to be
made per model rather than ten as previously. Therefore, the number of
pairings that now have to be considered is $2n$. This use of image structure
to improve efficiency is termed *selection*.

Solution 3

The final improvement in efficiency involves a substantial restructuring of the model base. One can first construct $\mathcal{M}$ as a hash table perhaps using the value Θ_k as the hash key for each model $\mathbf{M}_k$. Recognition proceeds by computing all possible triples $\mathbf{m}_{ij}$ using selection, then hashing into $\mathcal{M}$ using θ_{ij}. Whenever $\mathbf{m}_{ij}$ scores a hit, compare each model triple found with the entire image triple. A recognition hypothesis is formed if they match. This approach is termed *indexing*, or in this case *invariant indexing* since the indexes are formed using invariants (the value of θ_{ij} is unaffected by the imaging process).

Knowledge of $\mathcal{M}$ is needed to judge how much more efficient the use of indexing makes recognition compared to the previous solutions. In the best case, if all of the models have different values for Θ, only two consistency checks will require evaluation between the image and the model base because recognition is achieved solely by computing θ_{12} and θ_{34}. In this situation, complexity depends only on the number of image feature configurations. Every time a pair of models share their value for Θ, the number of correspondence tests required increases by 2. In the worst case, if all of the models have the same Θ the overall complexity returns to $2n$.

This simple example has shown how the different phases of the selection–indexing–correspondence approach to recognition play off each other. It is hard to say which step is most important; one could argue that correspondence is in fact the only essential process as it is required to determine the compatibility of image and model features and can solve the entire task by itself (which it did in the first solution). However, relying solely on correspondence typically leads to implementations that are too slow to be useful because of the linear dependence on the number of models n.

The purpose of this monograph is to examine how each phase can be combined to produce reliable and efficient recognition systems. More importantly, we shall be studying how invariant indexing affects the performance of the other two processes and thus recognition as a whole.

1.3   A more realistic situation

Performing recognition from real images using the methods suggested in the previous section is rather optimistic. The following paragraphs examine how the different effects normally encountered in vision affect the performance of a recognition algorithm. The discussion will again centre around the simple example. However, all of the ideas introduced are actually motivated by problems encountered in real images.

1.3.1   *Error*

Features are never extracted perfectly from images. In practice, line segments become displaced from their correct positions and may also become fragmented. Displacements arise for many reasons, including: specularity; shadow; confusion of features due to three-dimensional proximity; and poor sensor performance. Alternatively, displacements may be introduced by earlier steps in the feature extraction process. The errors can be observed through a perturbation of the line segment endpoints. To a certain extent, fragmentation can also be described in this way, though the errors are much larger. More importantly, fragmentation leads to an increase in the number of scene features.

Generally, one wants to ensure that the performance of a recognition system degrades gracefully in the presence of error. At either limit, this is not possible. First, the case for tiny errors caused by incorrect location of features is very much harder than the ideal situation; and second, under excessive fragmentation one reaches a stage where recognition becomes impossible given the meagre image measurements (a void of reliable information is unlikely to lead to any meaningful conclusion). However, the area of most interest is the middle ground. Fortunately, something can be achieved in this domain. Adaptation to this region of operation is achieved by:

1. **Selection:** Error causes the topology of object features required for measuring connectivity to be disrupted. However, one might relax the need for incidence and insist only on proximity, that is, pair all lines whose endpoints are close into single groups. Note that as soon as error is introduced the number of image pairings requiring evaluation is likely to increase dramatically.

2. **Indexing:** Image θ values are affected by changing the positions of line endpoints, though only by a small amount. Consequently, the probability that a value of θ actually matches a model Θ becomes vanishingly small, so one has to adapt the model base access mechanism so that a key to the hash table still hits the right cell. In practice, this is done by quantizing the hash function using knowledge of the maximum expected error bound on each value of Θ. For the error-free case two models could be indexed by the same image features only if they had exactly the same values for Θ. However, with the inclusion of an error bound the possibility of hashing an incorrect model is introduced.

3. **Correspondence:** The original recognition algorithm matches a measurement point $\mathbf{m}_{ij}$ in a three-dimensional space to a model point $\mathbf{M}_k$. As with indexing, the introduction of errors means that the points will no longer coincide in correspondence space, but instead $\mathbf{m}_{ij}$ will only lie close to $\mathbf{M}_k$. Recognition must therefore proceed by accepting model-to-image matches that lie sufficiently close in the matching space. The upper bound on the acceptable distance between

$\mathbf{m}_{ij}$ and $\mathbf{M}_k$ for identification to be hypothesized requires an understanding of the types and sizes of errors expected by the recognition system. Introducing the error ball around each model point increases the opportunity for matching incorrectly. Additionally, if the wrong assumptions are made about the error model it is conceivable that matches will even be missed.

There are many causes of image error, and generally they are poorly understood. All three of the recognition stages must make various assumptions about the expected image errors so that the different tolerances required can be set (for instance the proximity measure used in selection must be assigned). However, correctly forming the error models is hard. One of the issues that we emphasize is the poor relationship drawn between most commonly used error models and the actual disturbances that are likely to arise in practice.

1.3.2   Occlusion

Occlusion is often considered to be a gross form of error in which feature locations are misplaced by larger amounts than would normally be expected by a sensor. Perhaps such a model is useful as it simplifies the requirement for a different analysis of occlusion and error. However, occlusion usually has two effects: first, there is a resultant reduction in the amount of object data provided by the sensor. Shape descriptors should be designed so this does not cause a catastrophic reduction in recognition performance. For instance, in the model description in the example above, the angle θ will remain unaffected by occlusion should both line segments remain visible, but the segment lengths l_i will become unreliable. Therefore, we can conclude that angle measures are a better shape descriptor than length. The choice of preferred shape measures is a very important theme in recognition and is often not as easy to determine as in the angle–length case.

The second effect of occlusion, which causes the incorrect positioning of image features, can often be modelled by error. The main problems arise from the actual endpoints of the features ceasing to be visible and so their locations are hypothesized incorrectly. Additionally, the process that extracts the feature from the sensor often confuses the object with the occluding shape and so the former is positioned incorrectly. Ultimately, the sizes of the error bounds introduced by occlusion are much larger than those caused by conventional errors and therefore must be treated differently.

1.3.3   Clutter

Clutter is the presence of unmodelled objects in the scene. It affects both the accuracy with which measurements are taken and also the overall complexity of recognition. We have already considered the first effect, as confusion between proximal scene features often results in measurements becoming either incorrect or lost totally. The second problem is that extraneous image features arising from background objects cause the complexity of recognition to rise dramatically. In the example above the complexity of the recognition system given by the first solution is $^kC_2n = O(nk^2)$ in the presense of k scene features. Obviously this complexity becomes unmanageable even if k becomes moderately large. We have already seen how selection can be used to reduce the number of feature groups under consideration, but a dependence on k will still result. Ultimately the rôle of selection is to reduce the effects of clutter by producing only feature configurations that come from single objects.

Finally, one can expect to observe clutter within most realistic recognition environments. Therefore, it is pointless to study cases in which the only observable scene features are known to come from single test objects. Even if a system is designed to work with single isolated objects, spurious features are frequently produced by shadows and specularity that add to the numbers of measurements taken in a scene. These cause similar distractions to those caused by clutter.

1.4 Shape description

A theme central to the discussions in this monograph is the desire for an efficient description of the geometric shape of objects. The correct choice of shape measure is possibly the most important issue in the design of a recognition system as it determines to what extent indexing can be used; an incorrect choice can lead to grossly inefficient implementations requiring complicated mathematical analysis.

We have chosen to use invariant shape descriptors. These have the benefit that they are not affected by the imaging process and so can be computed from image measurements without any initial reference to the model base (though such measures cannot always be measured directly in images but, as demonstrated in Chapter 8, sometimes require an intermediate reconstruction process). All three of the measures $\{\theta, l_1, l_2\}$ used in the example are invariants as their values are unaffected by the position of the object on the image plane. Very few descriptions are invariant; for example, under more general perspective viewing, Euclidean measurements such as angles and lengths cease to be constant. It was this observation that necessitated the contrast between *viewer centred* and *object centred* descriptions in the work of Marr (78); although the former are easier to measure, the latter are more often invariant to the imaging process and hence most useful.

Real cameras usually produce perspective object distortions and so we have employed projectively invariant shape descriptors within LEWIS. These descriptions will not change under projection to the image and are thus invariant. Using projective shape means that no Euclidean object information is required by any part of the recognition process and subsequently there is no need to compute object pose. This is how the *what* and *where* tasks become separated. This simplifies the earlier stages of recognition as we are trying to solve for fewer variables (only object identity and not its pose parameters). However, non-invariant pose measures can be employed during correspondence or verification processes which evaluate the recognition hypotheses, but this is not exploited heavily in LEWIS.

Invariant shape descriptors are well documented in the mathematics literature for transformations between spaces of the same dimension. For instance, invariants are well understood for plane-to-plane projective transformations (which are characteristic of imaging a planar object). However, little is known about the invariant properties for singular projections that map, say, three-dimensional points onto a plane. Therefore, describing planar objects using invariants has been a relatively simple task as the transformations they undergo are plane to plane; descriptions for 3D objects under imaging have been much harder. Understanding three-dimensional invariant descriptions (which are fundamental for the recognition of 3D objects by invariant indexing), represents a challenging research area that is driving current research in object recognition. This monograph reports on a number of recent advances in 3D invariant shape description that have occurred over the last few of years.

Another important research area has studied how local invariant shape descriptors can be tied together to form global object descriptions. One may ask what the best shape description in the example above would have been if a third line had been introduced into the model. Obviously, it seems wise to maintain descriptors only between pairs of lines so that we have some tolerance to occlusion, but then one would be able to measure a number of different cues that would not be initially consistent with a single object hypothesis. For example, if the lines where l_i, $i \in \{1, \ldots, 3\}$, and the values of θ_{12} and θ_{23} were measured in the scene, what would be the most efficient way to determine whether all three lines came from a single object instance or from two nearby instances of the same model? Within LEWIS a process called *hypothesis extension* is developed to achieve this task.

1.5 The domain

Now that a few of the issues that address object recognition in general have been introduced, we can look at specific examples of the application areas of the systems described in the following chapters. These systems are capable of recognizing both two-dimensional and three-dimensional objects from single scenes. Examples of the domains are shown in Figs 1.4 to 1.6. In all the cases we can measure invariants for the objects that are used to drive recognition. Although the maturities of the different systems are varied, the examples contain error, occlusion, and clutter. The following discussions contain a number of details connected to the recognition system design and some of the assumptions that we have made.

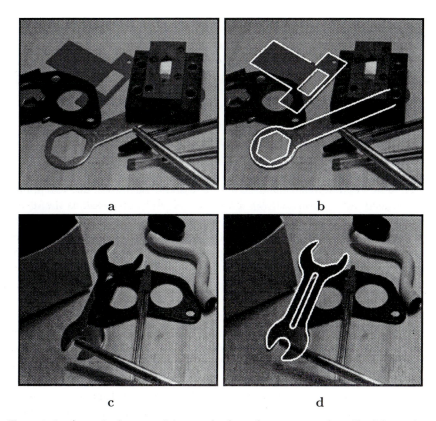

a   b

c   d

FIG. 1.4. A typical recognition task that the systems described later in
this monograph are capable of is the determination of which models
from a library of planar objects are present in a scene. (a) shows a
scene in which two objects, a spanner and a lock striker-plate, can be
recognized from a library of over thirty objects. The other objects in
the scene are not in the model library. The white outline depicted in
(b) demonstrates where the system believes the objects are located.
Another example for a different class of planar object is shown in (c);
again recognition is demonstrated in (d). Note that we are essentially
interested in recognizing well-defined rigid objects.

1.5.1 *The viewpoint*

The example recognition task given at the beginning of this chapter is very
restrictive and is not typical of many real applications. Normally, one does
not observe plane Euclidean distortions in images as such deformations result from cameras observing the world from very restricted viewpoints. In
the sequel, the domain of application is such that the objects to be identified
have complete translational and rotational freedom in the world, that is,

FIG. 1.5. Three-dimensional structure can be recovered for the points marked on the stapler from a single view. Such structure is useful for recognition as it contains (projective) details about the dimensions of the object rather than just information that can be measured in a scene. Different views of the reconstruction are shown in Fig. 1.6.

no assumption is made about their position or orientation with respect to the position of the camera in Euclidean 3-space. Such a viewing configuration produces perspective distortions of objects in the image to which both the shape descriptions we will use, and the recognition algorithms, must be tolerant. Our attention will be restricted to rigid objects. Such a task environment fits in with the generality now expected from object recognition systems. Examples of this type of imaging are demonstrated in Figs 1.4 and 1.5 where full perspective distortions are present, but furthermore, the distortions cannot be undone fully prior to recognition.

Only single greyscale CCD cameras will be used for sensing. Although many of the given algorithms are applicable to multiple image techniques (for instance stereo or motion sequences), range sensors and colour cameras, we have not made use of these. Furthermore, there is no issue of either using attentive or active vision; the system should be able to deduce conclusions from any scene with which it is presented.

1.5.2 The image

The input images are not already segmented into a list of lines as assumed in the example above. They are quantized intensity surfaces; the recognition features are extracted from this surface using a process called *segmentation*. We will restrict our attention purely to geometric features that either make up the boundaries of object surfaces, or are surface markings. These are observed most readily by searching the image for contrast changes (edges). The edges are best described using geometric tokens that are related to each other using topological properties such as line connectivity, or geometric ones such as proximity. Other geometric features that can be used apart from lines are points, conics, and higher-degree plane curves. Note that due to its planarity, it is most convenient in the image to describe the features

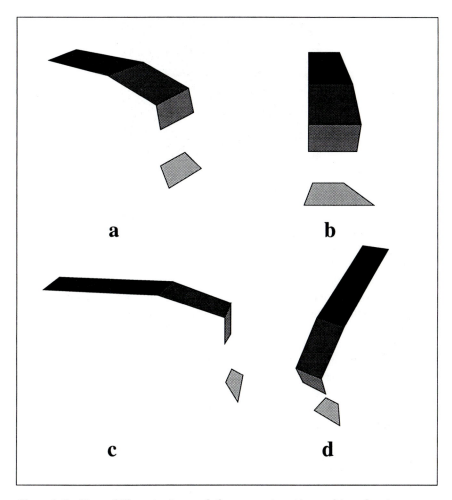

FIG. 1.6. Four different views of the reconstruction achieved using measurements taken from Fig. 1.5: (a) the viewpoint used to render the object is from a position close to that of the original camera view; (b) the observer has moved round to the front of the stapler; (c) and (d) are from other general viewpoints.

by planar tokens.

The completion of the feature extraction process does not mark the end of the utility of the intensity surface. The greyscale image is rich in information that reveals the associativity between different features that can aid selection, or may provide more detailed data about the nature of the object surfaces that underly the presence of a feature. However, we do not currently consider in detail the use of the intensity surface subsequent to edge detection.

1.5.3   *The model*

The use of object models immediately means that we must restrict our attention to the domain of model-based vision. Recognition is sufficiently difficult without the need to attempt to describe objects whose geometry or other properties fail to be bounded tightly; some such objects are trees, clouds or people. Associated with the use of model-based techniques is a restriction that there is no desire to recognize generic object classes, but rather to extract only specific object identities from images.

The desire to use invariant indexing places a number of restrictions on the models that we can use for the representation of objects. Principally, a model must contain information that allows both indexing and correspondence to be performed. An implicit relationship between these two pieces of data must also be defined. One of the themes of the research covered in the following chapters is how certain types of shape descriptor can be used to facilitate library access.

A final issue of concern to the design of the model-base is related to how new objects should be included in the library. A large body of researchers has paid significant attention to automatic model learning. Consequently, it is often a feature of reports on system building that a process must be available for automatic model acquisition. This is normally put in context by the desire for systems that can recognize large numbers of objects to have their model-bases expanded rapidly; however, such systems do not at present exist. Therefore, we have concentrated our efforts on trying to improve library access for larger model-bases and have postponed automated model learning until a later date. Perhaps this has also been motivated by the wish to have reliable and accurate models with which to work; assisted model acquisition can ensure the integrity of the model geometry written to the model-base.

The above topics represent the main issues for consideration during system building. There are, however, a number of brief points that must be addressed prior to a detailed investigation of the invariant indexing approach to recognition:

- **Context:** The purpose of context is to restrict the size of the recognition task. Essentially, context is controlled by choosing which models should be included within the model-base. In practice this may be instantiated by preventing objects that are unlikely to occur in the same scene being placed simultaneously in the object library. Figures 1.4 and 1.5 show the general context of the systems that we will describe; the application domain is for man-made objects of a restrictive type. Certainly, context is important in forming some type of priority list of evaluations, but really we have already determined the context through the use of a restricted model-base.

- **False positives and negatives:** Current recognition systems tend to achieve results that are far from perfect. Generally, the presence of either false negative (failing to register an object) or false positive (incorrectly assigning an identity to image features) conclusions are expected. The former may result purely from excessive occlusion preventing a reasonable number of object features being present, and the latter from excessively loose bounds on the correspondence constraints. Although we may strive to reduce both of these to zero, one should always consider which trade-offs are required to force either of the performance parameters to go to a certain level.

- **Pose versus identification:** The goal of a recognition problem is usually defined in such a way that there is a desire both to identify objects and to position them in space. Most systems conflate this *what* and *where* problem by combining the geometric constraints used to determine correspondence with the pose parameters. It is a feature of the invariant indexing approach to recognition that one can hypothesize which objects are in a scene prior to computing their pose. However, the distinction between the two tasks should not be drawn too strongly as it appears that pose information is crucial in distinguishing between false positives and correct interpretations.

- **Efficiency:** This should be played off very carefully with the ability to ensure the correctness of solutions. It is unwise to build a system that runs quickly but produces unreliable identification conclusions. Overall, greedy algorithms are of little use unless they are guaranteed to produce the right results. We concentrate our efforts on making reliable recognition systems run faster rather than making fast systems more reliable. The main concern in the sequel is enhancing efficiency with respect to the size of the model-base, though we intend to take care to achieve this without too great a cost to the selection or correspondence phases.

1.6   Chapter summaries

Chapter 2 provides a review of much of the current recognition literature, though it does not intend to be exhaustive. The three-phase recognition framework of *selection, indexing* and *correspondence* suggested by Grimson (53) is motivated by examples drawn from the literature. The real purpose of the chapter is to try and provide a picture of what research has, and has not, been done in the past. Principally, it motivates the need for a genuine indexing step. The second half of the chapter surveys some of the literature on invariant shape description so that it can be seen which invariant cues are available, and where more research is required. Generally, planar object shape descriptions are now common in the literature, three-dimensional ones less so.

Chapter 3 introduces the notation used throughout the subsequent chapters and covers most of the mathematical details required for the discussions. The first recognition system design, LEWIS1, uses planar algebraic invariant descriptions. After a brief introduction to projective invariance via the cross ratio, this chapter describes the planar algebraic invariants used in detail. It is not meant to be a substitute for the more mathematical treatise on projective geometry such as Semple and Kneebone (115) or Springer (124). Furthermore, the approach is not as broad as that given by Mundy and Zisserman (92), as we wish to cover only the descriptions used in LEWIS1. However, one extra detail of this chapter not normally considered is the way in which the performance of different formulations of the same invariant type are contrasted, and it is shown that the specific formulations affect the competence of the invariants as recognition cues. A system designer should always try to choose the optimal descriptors to be used from those that are available. Furthermore, although the plane projective group is frequently used as a model of the imaging process for planar objects, it is shown that only restrictive elements of the group actually correspond to real camera deformations.

Chapter 4 describes the LEWIS architecture used for invariant index-based recognition. The specific variant of the architecture called LEWIS1 that uses planar algebraic invariants is portrayed in detail, together with some references to more general architectural issues. The system has been evaluated extensively over a broad range of images; details of the tests are given both with recognition examples and sample statistics for general scenes. For instance, the flow of data between the modules is reported as the numbers of scene features are turned into indexes and then hypotheses for testing by the correspondence stage. The goal of this chapter is to see how the invariant indexing approach can be brought to life and then judged by its effectiveness. Even at this stage of development we begin to see the strengths and weaknesses of the approach emerging.

Chapter 5 introduces a novel construction that provides an invariant description for objects containing smooth planar curves. The method exploits a *canonical frame*, Marr (78). The features of the construction are reviewed before it is shown how to integrate the method into the LEWIS architecture in the form of LEWIS2. Although many parts of the system are identical to that of LEWIS1, an analysis of the system working independently is provided. The two systems can, however, be made to run side by side working off the same image. Again, examples of LEWIS2 working over a range of images are given with detailed statistics that have been gathered empirically.

Chapter 6 reviews the necessary segmentation and grouping algorithms used in the two recognition systems. The descriptions given in Chapters 4 and 5 exclude details of how the basic features (such as lines, conics, and higher-degree smooth plane curves) are extracted from the image so as not to cloud the essential issues involved in designing an index-based recognition system. Algorithms are presented that provide the data required for invariant index formation. Although the methods are based on approaches that are familiar in the recognition literature, practical observations due to their use with invariants have led to improvements of both the numerical performance and efficiency of the algorithms when coupled with the LEWIS architecture.

Chapter 7 lists the criteria that a shape descriptor which is useful for recognition should have in light of the results gained in building LEWIS1 and LEWIS2. Frequently, the useful properties of shape measures are supposed, without any direct relationship to a working system. In this monograph, shape description is approached from the opposite viewpoint, that is, we see what is effective for simple examples and then use the results to guide further research in shape description. There are distinct similarities with some of the concepts previously described in the literature; however, other criteria become almost redundant in light of developments in invariant shape description.

Chapter 8 looks ahead to shape descriptors that can be used within a three-dimensional object recognition system. Although a reliable recognition system for these cues has not been built based on the invariant indexing approach, it is necessary to determine how the descriptors are to be extracted from the scenes for such systems. Recent contributions to invariant theory are reviewed that demonstrate how 3D projective shape can be recovered from single images and then invariant indexes extracted from the reconstructions. However, the approach raises many questions as to how these descriptors may be employed within the LEWIS recognition framework.

Chapter 9 sums up the invariant indexing approach, and summarizes the contributions provided by the LEWIS architecture towards producing reliable and efficient recognition systems. We then look forward to see how the three-dimensional descriptors of Chapter 8 may be integrated into the systems and finish by suggesting adaptations that are necessary for the production of the next generation of recognition system.

2

OBJECT RECOGNITION

The task of recognizing objects using computers has been investigated fairly broadly since the earliest days of research into machine vision. However, very few reliable systems exist; those that actually work do so in very specific environments and adapt poorly to other circumstances. Until systems are built which can recognize large numbers of objects from realistic scenes, any claims of success should be treated with caution by an independent observer. There is also a unilateral failure to test systems properly over a large number of varying images and conditions. This may be because the complete system building process takes so long, but it is certainly true that a more concerted effort is required to produce consistent methods of testing by which we can judge our efforts.

The aim of this book is to investigate the rôle of indexing within the context of the selection, indexing, and correspondence recognition paradigm. Principally the study has been made using single greyscale images, but the scope of this chapter is a little more general in that approaches to recognition that use either multiple images or sensing modalities other than greyscale CCD are reviewed, as many of their methods are relevant. Discussion of many other recognition techniques such as character recognition or consideration of functionality such as in the work of Sutton, et al. (128), have been excluded deliberately.

Detailed reviews already exist that describe the host of different vision algorithms available for recognition, for example the book by Grimson (53), and papers by Besl and Jain (7) and Flynn and Jain (38). However, existing systems have not been reviewed properly within the light of the improvements in the understanding of the application of invariant theory within computer vision. This chapter contrasts the opinions expressed in the above surveys with those of the author in light of that knowledge.

A further feature that concerns recognition, shape representation, has been reviewed by Marr (78) and Brady (15), and is discussed in Chapter 7. There are also other issues that should be considered important for good system design, though these do not actually find a place within this book. These cover some of the weak links within the computerized visual process, many of which are within the stages of *early vision*. The systems reported in this book demonstrate that recognition is possible even when image geometry is unreliable due to poor segmentation (this is also demonstrated for example in (53)).

At this stage a bench-mark should be established on the abilities of current recognition systems that recognize objects from a database of real models in actual scenes. Very few systems exist that can recognize more than one object reliably in cluttered occluded scenes. A proportion of those that can, do so very slowly. Although some systems can identify larger numbers of objects under realistic imaging conditions, there should be no interest in building systems that recognize objects from synthetic model bases.

2.0.1   *The recognition framework*

Current understanding of the recognition process divides recognition into three phases (Grimson (53), p. 33):

1. **selection:** what subset of the data corresponds to the object?
2. **indexing:** which object model corresponds to the data subset?
3. **correspondence:** which individual model features correspond to each data feature?

None of these stages can be considered as entirely separate, but rather as modules within a feedback loop. However, the general structure yields a good framework for studying recognition. Later in this chapter research expended within each phase will be studied, though this will not be done in the order given above. The reason for this is that the correspondence process has always been seen (incorrectly) as the key to producing reliable recognition systems, and so has experienced the most research effort. It will therefore be considered first. Next, in order of decreasing attention comes selection, and finally indexing. However, the three steps are described briefly below so that the general framework can be understood.

The aim of selection (also called *perceptual organization* (71), *grouping*, or *figure–ground discrimination*) is to provide a grouping of features that are likely to have come from a single object in a scene. The features may be of a number of different varieties: edgels; corners; texture; algebraic features such as lines and conics; smooth curves represented as splines; or a host of others. Although the efficient extraction of these features is itself a hard (unsolved) problem due to the inadequacy of early vision, the rest of this chapter will take their availability as read (note however that all systems described in the literature that work on real images have had to go some distance towards solving this problem).

Second comes indexing. Before model features can be paired with image features a model must be selected from the model database. The brute force way to do this is to test every model in the library in turn, that is, use a linear search through the database. This approach is typical of current recognition systems (see Section 2.1); if there are a large number of objects in the model base then progress will be slow. A better method would be to choose potential models from the library based on the observed image features, that is, image measurements are used to *index* into the model base. Although many researchers have failed to use this approach, it can potentially provide a vast increase in recognition efficiency by pruning a large amount of the search at an early stage.

The final stage is correspondence. Selection and indexing have hypothesized a match between an object and a small number of image features. Before the hypothesis can be accepted a confidence level must be calculated. This is done by searching for image features that have not been used to form the hypothesis that may also come from the same object (these are features that may have been missed by the grouping stage). The more features that can be found the more likely it is that the initial hypothesis is correct. Once all possible correspondences have been accepted or ruled out a conclusion as to the identity of an object can be made.

2.1   Correspondence

The correspondence between model and image features can be framed as a search in three different ways. These are using *interpretation trees, hypothesize and test,* and the *generalized Hough transform.* Each of these are considered in turn, though it should be emphasized that the review is intended to be brief. The interested reader should follow up many of the references through (53).

Most of the correspondence algorithms have been used to try and achieve recognition through a single process. It is the belief of the author that this approach will not succeed; each algorithm may be useful within an entire system, but they should occupy only modules within it. Therefore one should always try to envisage how each contribution fits into a hybrid recognition architecture.

2.1.1   *Interpretation trees*

Interpretation trees frame the search for legitimate pairings between image and model data as a tree search where each node of the IT represents a set of image and model feature pairings. This is both the simplest way to do the search and also the most expensive. A different tree is created for each model to be matched. The first pairing constructed is of the first image feature with the first model feature. If this represents a feasible match (in a sense determined by the precise details of the search algorithm), a second scene feature is matched to the first model feature, and so on. This approach of matching more than one image feature to a single model feature ensures that features broken during imaging are still useful (for example, if in Fig. 2.1 feature 1 had been broken into 1*a* and 1*b* it must be possible to match both pieces against model feature *a*). If a match is not feasible the image feature is matched against the next model feature, etc. A 'null' model feature is used so that an image feature does not have to come from the object model under test. The basic method expands the entire tree,

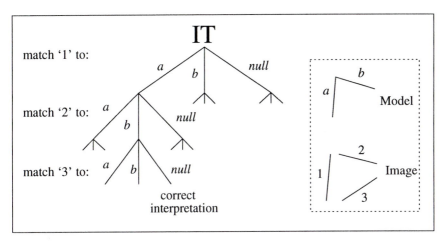

FIG. 2.1. A simple IT implementation: the model to be matched has two features, lines a and b. These are matched in turn to the image features $1, 2$ and 3. The correct correspondence is shown, $\{1, 2, 3\} \rightarrow \{a, b, null\}$. The key to an IT implementation is preventing search to the other leaves.

matching all image features against a model or null feature, and forming a recognition hypothesis based on the leaves reached.

2.1.1.1 *Geometric constraints* The inefficiency of the IT algorithm becomes apparent when all of the paths to the leaves of the tree have to be expanded; such a search has exponential cost. The key to a tractable implementation is to prevent this. The basic ways to achieve control of the search were given by Grimson and Lozano-Pérez (50), who built a recognition system capable of recognizing complex planar parts under plane Euclidean actions (translation and rotation). They suggested the use of *geometric constraints* between features to test feasibility and so prune large portions of the tree. These constraints are invariants that must take the same values between image features as they do for model features. There are *unary* constraints that apply to single features, and *binary* constraints between pairs of features. Under plane Euclidean actions the constraints are simple: the unary constraint of size; and the binary ones of angle and distance. Extending to other environments requires invariants to more general transformations, and so more complex search trees. It is probably because of this, and the associated increase in exponential complexity, that ITs have not been applied directly to other imaging environments. However, the LEWIS system has successfully employed an IT search strategy to test for the satisfaction of projective constraints after initial model and image correspondences have been made.

2.1.1.2 *Search cut-off* Geometric constraints have only a limited effect at controlling the search. Although they are very good at determining local consistency, they do not signify when a global solution has been reached and so the search continues for longer than necessary. An effective way to terminate the search is by *search cut-off* (50): as soon as it is clear that expanding the current path will not produce a satisfactory solution, the entire path should be pruned. Grimson and Lozano-Pérez also used search cut-off to decide when a sufficiently good match hypothesis had been found, at which time it would be verified and the search terminated. The problem with this winner-takes-all strategy is that it fails catastrophically for false negatives. If cut-off is to be used to prevent every path of the tree being expanded, then there is a chance that good matches will be missed. This also raises questions about how the generation of multiple hypotheses for the same model due to repeated object instances should be handled. Ignoring potential matches makes the search space smaller, but leaves absolutely no room for backtracking. Tolerating false positives is a far more conservative and wiser approach. Furthermore, a large part of the IT will have to be expanded for each model in the library that does not have a scene instance and so in these cases the process becomes exceptionally slow.

Even with cut-off the search remains exponential under occlusion (this is due significantly to the use of the null feature match). However, it is better than complete exploration of the search space. Under more restrictive conditions, such as no occlusion or clutter, the search becomes polynomial in the number of image features[2] (quadratic for the planar Euclidean case), though such a situation is not typical of many imaging environments. It also should be realized that an exponential tree search is executed for every model in the model base, and so there is also a multiplicative linear expense in the number of objects in the library. This fact is important if a large number of models can potentially be matched to a scene. It is this deficiency that motivated the use of indexing which is a process central to the themes in this book.

If image data provides 3D constraints then the IT paradigm can be adapted to locate and identify 3D objects. Generally such information cannot be provided by single greyscale images, but alternatives are available: range data (50); data recovered from motion reconstruction as by Murray and Cook (94, 95); and stereo data as within the TINA system (100) or that of Ayache and Faugeras (4). Essentially the paradigm works in the same way for 3D as 2D, but 3D rather than 2D Euclidean invariants are

---

[2]As there is no clutter, the numbers of model and image features are approximately equal; any discrepancy is due to the fragmentation of model features into multiple image features.

required.

2.1.1.3 *Subparts* The two main drawbacks of the IT are its exponential complexity in the number of features, and the linear cost with respect to the number of models in the model base. Most of the work on ITs has been to reduce the first term, with very little on the second. One interesting exception is the use of *subparts* by Ettinger (34). A subpart is simply a smaller part of an object that can be recognized independently of the whole; there are likely to be a number of subparts within each object (Section 7.3 reviews the link between subparts, which are local descriptions, and more global measures). The algorithm proceeds by recognizing subparts and then using these as larger features within a hierarchical IT system.

The reasons for the subpart approach being more efficient are two-fold: the first is that the objects that are being recognized by the IT are simpler, and so the exponential component of the search will be reduced; secondly, and more importantly, the structure of the model base has been changed as subparts are being recognized rather than objects. If there are fewer subparts than objects (and so the same subparts occur frequently in many objects), the model base used to drive the IT will be smaller. Therefore, the linear complexity term is reduced, and is *sublinear* in the number of actual objects in the library (though still linear in the number of subparts).

Ettinger successfully demonstrated such a scheme working on a model base of road signs. The basic features used to form the subparts were the components of the *curvature primal sketch* (2); using higher-order features than just points provides a further check on consistency as a *unary constraint*, and so further improves efficiency. Unary constraints can be used to good effect as *focus features* (11), an idea that is developed in Section 2.1.2.

The general concept of a subpart is a very useful one, and reappears later in this book. Although both Ettinger's work and the LEWIS systems use a two-layer hierarchy (subpart and object), many different levels could be used. However, the problem with the approach of Ettinger is still that the IT used to identify each subpart is inefficient, and the sublinear behaviour in the number of models is restricted by the number of subparts.

2.1.1.4 *Parametrized objects* It is also possible to use the IT strategy to cope with more complicated transformations than plane Euclidean, for example similarity, or for parametrized objects. There are two ways to do this:

1. Use another implementation of subparts where local feature groups are recognized, and then hypotheses are joined together using parametrized geometric constraints. This was demonstrated by Grimson (51, 53), and to a certain extent by Ettinger (34).

2. The geometric constraints used can be relaxed in the sense that they do not have to take single values (with a small error bound), but instead can vary within a range. Such an approach to recognition was followed by Brooks (17), Fisher (37) and more recently by Reid (104). This allows far more general recognition algorithms than those provided by the plane Euclidean IT paradigm, but they all still suffer from high complexity and also often from ambiguous results.

A different angle on the problem of parametrized shape description has recently appeared in a paper by Moons, *et al.* (87). This throws light on the effects that different types of deformation (both through parametrization and the imaging process) have on invariant descriptions that can be recovered.

Although a number of different variants exist for the IT algorithm (most of them are given in (53)), they all suffer from two severe drawbacks. Both are due to inefficiency: under normal realistic imaging situations (occlusion, clutter and noise), the search is exponential; and the almost total disregard for indexing means that for large model bases recognition is slow. Even when indexing is used to hypothesize the identity of an object in the scene the exponential correspondence phase will still exist. However, as is shown in the next section, if indexing is used prior to a *hypothesize and test* scheme the whole process can be made to have polynomial complexity (under occlusion and clutter) with regard to the number of model or image features.

2.1.2 *Hypothesize and test*

Hypothesize and test algorithms are implemented in two stages: the first is an alignment phase; and the second a search for hypothesis support. The difference between hypothesis and test and an IT paradigm is that alignment is used first to bootstrap the search within a region of the image, and then IT search is used, rather than using more random IT search for the whole process.

Again, it should be realized that indexing is generally performed poorly for hypothesis and test algorithms, and so in much of the published material there is still the linear complexity with respect to the number of models in the model library.

2.1.2.1 *Alignment*   The alignment phase registers a hypothesized model in a scene before starting an interpretation tree search to find further image support. Essentially alignment provides the matches required for the first few levels of the IT. A simple form of the algorithm was given by Huttenlocher and Ullman (57, 58), in which an affine imaging model was used. Although it was stated earlier that extensions to more general imaging models than plane Euclidean is hard (at least for interpretation trees), aligning the model in the image means that any imaging distortion has been removed and so simpler Euclidean constraints can be used.

For planar objects under affine imaging, three points can be used to align the model in the image. The alignment process is simple: compute the affine transformation between three chosen points on the model and in the image, and then project the whole model to the image. If the match is correct, the model should have the same Euclidean shape as the image features. In its basic form such an algorithm will have a polynomial complexity of $O(m^3 n^3)$ for m model features and n image features.

Using the linear grouping strategy of (58) the complexity can be reduced to $O(mn)$. This is done by making use of connectivity between inflection points that are used to define the affine map; grouping strategies are discussed in more detail in Section 2.2. The use of grouping can be employed further so that a variety of more complex scene structures can be employed rather than just points. Three basic improvements in efficiency become apparent when this is done:

- Compared to the scenario of points, there are fewer higher-order features on the models and in images, so m and n will be relatively lower.

- The types of feature groups used to affect the alignment must be the same, and so the type can be used as a unary constraint.

- Fewer features are required to compute the model-to-image transformation (ideally a single measured feature), and so fewer levels of the IT will have to be expanded during the hypothesis support phase.

The benefits realized when these considerations are used result in the *feature focus* approach to recognition; this term was coined within the system of Bolles and Cain (11).

2.1.2.2 *Hypothesis support* Once an object location has been hypothesized within a scene using alignment, an IT search is initiated to increase its image support. The IT search is, however, framed in a different way to make the process more efficient. As the model location has been predicted within the image, the location of features which have not been used in the alignment phase can be hypothesized. Thus, correspondences are achieved by searching regions local to the expected feature locations. As each model feature finds a match, the model-to-image transformation can be refined, the model reprojected, and the tree expanded further. Therefore, each level represents an attempt to match a model feature to all of the potential image features, rather than the converse which is true of Grimson's algorithm (50). Again, search cut-off can be used to terminate path expansion and so reduce the search.

Hypothesize and test algorithms have been implemented for a variety of data formats and feature types: Ayache and Faugeras (3); 3DPO by Bolles and Horaud (12), Faugeras and Hebert (35) and Lowe (72). Specialized approaches have also been suggested by Goad (48). In fact, extensions to 3D curved surfaces have even been created: Dhome, et al. (31); and Kriegman and Ponce (67). The extent to which feature focus and alignment are used varies between the algorithms, and so does the range of transformations under which they work, but all have the same basic framework. One can even envisage an ideal framework in which the alignment phase is entirely replaced by indexing, and then a hypothesis support scheme employed to determine the correspondences for other model features.

One of the overriding benefits of using higher-order features results from the differing stabilities and amounts of information that each one has. The search can actually be directed so that the most discriminating features are searched for first, rather than using arbitrary priorities. Such a model-based approach makes the hypothesis and test IT superior[3] to the image-driven version of Section 2.1.1. Hypothesis and test algorithms may be considered to be IT searches driven by grouping in which there is feedback and feedforward between the two processes. Features missed during the initial alignment phase are found using intelligent selection based on hypothesizing their positions. This emphasizes the fact that the three-stage recognition process cannot be treated as having three separate phases, but is rather a more complicated feedback loop.

There is an interesting extension to the hypothesize and test paradigm that attempts to construct a single tree for the whole model base, and models are pruned from the search as paths are expanded. These methods essentially perform selection, indexing and correspondence within a single framework, but as yet there has not been sufficient demonstration of their success on real data. In this vein a couple of similar approaches have been suggested: *prediction hierarchies* by Burns and Kitchen (18); and *decision trees* by Swain (127).

2.1.3   *Generalized Hough transform*

The generalized Hough transform hypothesizes model matches by accumulating votes for feature group matches within pose space: given a hypothesized object, the transformation mapping each object feature group to every image group is computed (if one exists), and a vote cast at the corresponding point in a quantized pose parameter space. For a rigid object, all of the correct model matches should be mapped to the image using the same transformation (modulo noise), and thus have the same pose. There will therefore be a peak in the parameter space at a given pose corresponding to these matches. This approach is frequently called *pose clustering*.

The paradigm proceeds by creating hypotheses wherever there is a peak of a size over some predefined threshold in the accumulator. The size of the

---

[3]Though due to the structure of the search tree it is impossible to match a single model feature to multiple scene features.

threshold depends on the number of feature groups on the models, and the amount of occlusion allowed. There are of course problems with image clutter: random votes cast by incorrect matchings can lead to false peaks. However, as all of these pairings are geometrically consistent, they would also be produced by both the interpretation tree and hypothesize and test algorithms, and so the generalized Hough will produce no extra false matches. The differences are in efficiency, the way that errors are handled due to the quantization of the pose space, and also in how adaptable the paradigms are to parallel architectures that may enhance their performances.

2.1.3.1 *Decomposition of pose space*   The major drawback of the generalized Hough paradigm is that within a 3D environment a six-dimensional accumulator space is required (three to represent 3D Euclidean rotations and three for translations). This makes the method memory intensive and it also becomes inefficient to search for peaks once the voting process is complete. Thompson and Mundy (133) suggested that decomposing the pose space into orthogonal directions is an effective way to overcome this. This means that voting is done over only a small subset of the parameters at any one time, and then elements that contribute to peaks in each lower-dimensional space are used to vote in the space corresponding to the next parameter, and so on. The actual decomposition used in (133) is to cluster over slant and tilt, then rotation about the camera axis, translation in the image plane, and finally scale of the object (translation along the optical axis). In this way, accumulation is never performed in anything greater than a two-dimensional space.

Grimson and Huttenlocher claim that the decomposition eliminates very few matches at each stage, and so potential matches tend to be carried through to the final accumulation space (52). In (53), it is claimed that only 1% of the matches are eliminated in the first accumulation stage, and only a few per cent are removed over all of the stages. However, the analysis was done for the case of plane similarity transformations with uniform clutter assumptions. One should therefore be cautious of the claims for two particular reasons: the first is that it is *not* clear how the analysis extends to 3D; and second, real images contain structured features and *not* homogeneous texture elements.

A proper understanding of the situation can be gained only from studying real image data. Mundy and Heller (91), in their *vertex pair* matching system which has been thoroughly tested over a number of years (26, 92, 133), find that there is still a thousand-fold data reduction when clustering is used. Perhaps this result throws light on the importance of comparing theoretical and experimental results. Theoretical investigations usually provoke the notion of how vision problems may be solved, but such considerations should seldom be given weight without supporting experimental evidence.

2.1.3.2   *Adaptive generalized Hough transform*   An alternative way to reduce the size of the accumulator space is to use a hierarchical decomposition of the pose space. Stockman (125) suggested that each dimension of the pose space should initially be sampled coarsely, and then resampled in the region of any peaks to improve accuracy and disambiguate merged hypotheses. This approach can actually be extended into the framework known as the *adaptive Hough transform*, and can be made relatively efficient (see for example the work of Illingworth, *et al.* (61)).

2.1.3.3   *Non-rectangular quantization*   Although the complexity of generalized Hough algorithms is polynomial in the numbers of model and image features, the discreteness of the accumulator space can lead to a number of inefficient implementations due to the requirement that noise should not reduce peak sizes. Noise in the image measurements means that compatible pose estimates actually end up in adjacent, rather than the same cells, in the accumulator space. One way to overcome this is to vote for multiple cells in the pose space. An alternative method is to use a continuous parameter space, but to bound regions of consistent pose with algebraic surfaces (say planes). When this is done, only those (continuous) poses that actually correspond to the match will receive a 'vote'. Accumulation is then done over the bounded regions rather than individual cells. Cass (23) implemented such a system, and was able to maintain a polynomial recognition complexity.

2.1.3.4   *Hypothesis verification*   The generalized Hough algorithm also forms the basis of the verification procedure suggested by Grimson (53). Once a number of model-to-image feature correspondences have been hypothesized (by IT, hypothesize and test, or generalized Hough), a test for pose consistency (say using the algorithm of Cass (23)) is found, and the hypothesis confirmed or rejected. It should be noted, however, that this approach requires a large number of model and image matches (at least twenty or thirty) before sufficient confidence levels can be achieved. Both of the LEWIS systems use a different method for verification because the objects generally have few features and so high confidence levels could not the achieved through the Hough approach. The method used is backprojection which is a form of hypothesize and test.

2.1.4   *Summary*

Before considering the effects that selection can make on recognition efficiency it should be emphasized that all of the IT, hypothesize and test and Hough paradigms can be used to good effect within a single recognition system, though only after indexing has been used to hypothesize a model identity. First, alignment should be used to register an indexed model in an image, then a search for hypothesis support should be made using an IT, before finally doing verification by checking for consistency of the model and image features in pose space using an approach similar to that of Cass (23).

Indexing is required because all of the correspondence algorithms have to assume the model to be matched to the scene. In practice, without indexing every model has to be tested during the processing of each image and so the time spent during analysis will be proportional to the number of models in the model base. For large model bases the processing time subsequently becomes excessive.

2.2   Selection

A large reduction in the recognition search space can be achieved if features from individual objects are associated prior to recognition. This process is hard as it represents an instance of the 'chicken and egg' paradox: recognition cannot be done without grouped features, and features cannot be grouped without knowing object identity and pose. Again the requirement for feedback within recognition is highlighted. Without knowledge of identity a single guiding constraint remains: *in the absence of other evidence, assume...* (9).

Binford (9) suggested that accidental relationships are unlikely to happen, and so should be used to flag the occurrence of structure. Structure in an image immediately evokes connectivity and hence the presence of a single object. He defined a number of grouping criteria which vary in strength; they all make use of *invariant* or *quasi-invariant* (a term coined by Binford and Levitt (10)) properties of the data. Invariance relations are always valid, for example coincidence and planarity, and the quasi-invariant measures apply under a range of 'normal' viewing conditions: parallelism in a scene implies parallelism in the world; a vertical scene line implies a vertical world line, etc. Lowe extended these ideas to list a large number of viewpoint invariant conditions (71)(p. 78), and then went on to exploit these within the SCERPO recognition system. Dickson (32) reformulated these ideas within a Bayesian framework (specifically for collinearity and parallelism), and emphasized that the main problem with selection is that it generally has a high complexity. Consequently grouping can be used to reduce the complexity of the indexing and correspondence stages, though only at the cost of expending a large amount of effort early on in the recognition process.

Similar grouping constraints (connectivity and proximity) have been exploited within this book, and also by Huttenlocher (58). However, these and the work of Binford and Lowe all exploit token information extracted from a process such as the *primal sketch* (78). One can also question how selection or grouping would progress in the absence of this information (if the scene is composed of either distinct edgels or short chains of edges).

This problem was solved in part by Canny (22) using *hysteresis*, though further advances have been made by Sha'ashua and Ullman (116), and Cox (27). Both of these approaches again make use of the *in the absence of other evidence, assume...* grouping heuristic in expecting minimal curvature changes between grouped features.

As yet no entirely satisfactory solution has been found to the selection problem; a number of open questions still need to answered:

- How often do the invariance assumptions break down in realistic imaging environments? Secondly, how likely are 'random' feature configurations to satisfy the assumptions (for example due to textures)?

- When is it most efficient to invoke feedback within the recognition framework to drive grouping?

- Can knowledge of non-geometric information such as contrast or texture be exploited to provide grouping cues?

We should not, however, be too disheartened by the problems posed by segmentation and grouping. Current systems successfully use the output from the above algorithms to recognize objects. The whole of Chapter 6 is devoted to showing how they can be integrated into the index-based recognition architecture of LEWIS.

2.3   Indexing

The fundamental drawback in the way that the algorithms of Section 2.1 are framed is that they have a linear complexity with respect to the number of objects in the model base. Generally, this inefficiency has not been noticeable due to the small numbers of models used in implemented systems, however, if such systems are ever going to be used in world environments one requirement may well be that they must cope with much larger model bases. Recognition systems might have to recognize hundreds of objects, which is a couple of orders of magnitude more than at present. This would make the linear algorithms prohibitively slow.

As suggested by a number of authors, algorithmic speed can be increased if parallelism is exploited. One can simply connect together a few hundred processors, and then the recognizer will work at a similar speed for large model bases to that for single objects. However, the objection to this approach is the same one suggested for improving any algorithmic complexity: certainly improved hardware will speed up the process, but frequently adapting the underlying algorithm can have more marked effects on the efficiency. Furthermore, the use of a parallel architecture opens up many unanswered questions with the problems of processor communication; recognition architectures cannot be implemented as pipelines, but involve complex feedback loops that overcome deficiencies in the connected processes.

Generally, the best way to improve performance is not to alter the system hardware, but rather to reduce algorithmic complexity. The best way to improve performance for large model bases is to use indexing. Indexing hypothesizes model identities in a scene from only image measurements. The *value* of a measure for a set of features is used to index into the library without the need for a sequential search. Indexing is defined in detail later in Section 4.1. Once indexing has been achieved a hypothesize and test paradigm can be used to group other object features and so accept or rule out the initial model hypothesis. Then, verification is done using a Hough clustering technique or backprojection.

Efficient indexing functions are based on invariants (indexing functions can be constructed that do not exploit invariance, for example see Jacobs (62), but it appears these compromise efficiency to gain freedom from invariance). Different types of invariants can be used; this book deals almost exclusively with projective indexing functions, though affine invariants have been used to good effect (68, 136, 140). Alternatively, topological invariants can be used; these are the output of processes such as the *curvature primal sketch* (2). In fact, these were exploited by Ettinger (34) to form subparts. Conceptually, other cues such as colour can be used, for example as employed by Syeda-Mahmood (129), though these have not yet proved sufficiently robust to be considered viable for general indexing tasks.

One must realize that invariant indexes are the key to effective recognition algorithms rather than just invariants themselves. A number of researchers have used invariants to construct *invariant signatures* (very much along the lines of Turney, *et al.* (135)), but have then failed to compute indexes from them. This results in a template matching problem, which in its basic form still requires a linear search through the model base and is similar to many classical pattern recognition tasks.

It has also been argued frequently that indexing does not provide any speedup because the probability of finding a clash in the index space is too high. However, as can be seen from the argument in the next section, this probability can be made arbitrarily small by increasing the dimensions of the indexing space. Obviously, increasing the dimension of the index space will exponentially increase its size, though as the index space is implemented as a hash table this will not be a problem.

2.3.1 *Complexity*

A major concern with the effectiveness of an indexing function is the probability that an image measurement taken from background clutter actually indexes a model. Often, it is suggested that the number of clashes produced within the hash table is important, but this is not the case. The hash table is simply an implementation of the index space, and should be designed so that only objects with matching image measurements are returned rather than those having only matching hash key values.[4]

Here an informal argument is given that determines the likelihood that a random measurement will index an actual model; it shows that the indexing paradigm is (non-asymptotically) constant time, or at least can be made so with judicious use of the indexes. Consider a measure for a set of features that forms an n-dimensional index; assume that each dimension has the same behaviour. Let each index cover a segment on the real line from i_0 to $i_0 + L$ (Fig. 2.2), and the quantization along the line be δ, a constant quantity over the line segment.[5] There are $b = L/\delta$ buckets along the line, and so for n indexes and *assuming* that the measured invariants have a constant PDF over the invariant space,[6] the probability of hitting any cell at random is $1/b^n$. If there are λ models in the library, each with α shape descriptors, and each invariant can be measured up to an error of $\pm\delta\epsilon/2$, $\epsilon \in \mathbb{N}$ (the set of natural numbers), there will be $\alpha\epsilon\lambda$ entries in the table.[7] If it is assumed that these entries are spread uniformly over the hash table, the chances of indexing a model through noise is $(\alpha\epsilon\lambda)/b^n$.

This analysis means that there is an algorithmic complexity of $O(k_1 + k_2\alpha\epsilon\lambda/b^n)$, where k_1 is the cost of edge detection, feature extraction and grouping (essentially constant), and k_2 is another constant dependent on the form of the invariants, etc. It can be seen immediately that by making n large, the term dependent on the number of models, λ, becomes arbitrarily small, and so recognition time tends towards k_1, a constant.

There are two problems associated with making n large:

1. For algebraic invariants there is little control over n. If a minimal feature group is used there is no control, but by using larger structures n can be increased. However, the grouping task may then become harder. Alternatively one could index using less discriminatory invariants and then group using results of this first indexing stage before forming higher-order invariants and indexing a second time. For the invariants of other structures, such as the plane curves of Chapter 5, n can be made large (subject to the noise present in the curve).

2. Making n too large means that the problem of finding an efficient hashing function is much harder. The best method of choosing a

---

[4]The function mapping index values onto hash keys is many-to-one.

[5]More exactly a logarithmic scale should be used as the errors in invariant indexes tend to be proportional to the invariant values (42).

[6]This claim is a current topic of research, and should be compared to the work of Hopcroft, *et al.* (92) and Maybank (82). However, the actual form of the PDF does not affect the underlying result of this section.

[7]For efficiency reasons during recognition only a single cell will be read. Models are not stored in single cells, but in as many as defined by the range $\delta\epsilon$ which is the expected measurement error. This contrasts with storing models in single cells and then indexing over a range.

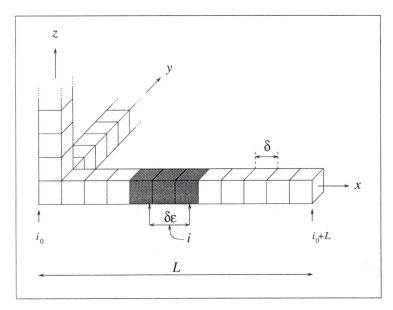

FIG. 2.2. Although the index space is multidimensional, it can loosely be assumed to be isotropic in all directions. Considering only the x direction: the index space ranges from i_0 to $i_0 + L$, with bucket quantization of size δ. On measurement of an index i in a scene, all the buckets within a range $\pm \delta \epsilon / 2$ must be searched in the index space. These cells are shaded grey.

  hash function has not been studied closely up till now as many software packages are available that make the table construction process transparent to the user.

As an example of the above argument, during the development of LEWIS1 it was found that an invariant composed of a conic and two lines gave insufficient discrimination between objects. However, when an extra line was used to make $n = 3$ rather than $n = 1$ the invariant increased in utility. This demonstrates that the underlying theory is supported in practice, a result that has also been observed by Mao, *et al.* (76).

2.3.2 *Invariant types*

A range of different invariant types is becoming commonplace within the computer vision literature; a summary of many of the known methods is given in the book by Mundy and Zisserman (92). Most of them apply to plane-to-plane mappings and have been derived from some of the more traditional aspects of geometry. More recently, invariants of 3D structures that can be measured in a single image have been discovered that enable the recognition of a wider class of objects.

2.3.2.1 *Algebraic invariants* These are the simplest invariants to form. Their existence and properties have been understood for a long time within the mathematics community, though they have only recently been applied to computer vision, Forsyth, *et al.* (42). Generally, they have been used to describe planar objects, and so traditional methods of plane projective geometry can be used (texts such as Semple and Kneebone (115) or Springer (124) are ideal studies to assist in the understanding of the relevant geometry). One of the earliest machine vision implementations of algebraic invariants was by Lei (70), who used the *cross ratio* (also given in Duda and Hart (33)), the simplest of all the invariants, to recognize polygonal shapes. Another important contributor was Weiss (141).

Other early work of note was that of Nielsen (97) who used area ratios to form invariants. Areas and volumes can easily be expressed as determinants of geometric configurations and so yield simple algebraic expressions. An early demonstration of indexing (using geometric hashing) was in the series of papers by Lamdan, *et al.* (68). Other references of note are by Mohr, *et al.* (85), Hopcroft, *et al.* (55), Reiss and Rayner (105), and others. Chapters 3 and 4 in this book are based entirely on the use of algebraic invariants for recognition.

2.3.2.2 *Moment invariants* Traditional moment invariants are global and hence sensitive to occlusion. Therefore they are not good shape descriptors for most of the scenes that we shall consider. They are in fact comparable to Fourier descriptions of shapes. Reviews of recent global moment invariant work can be found in the papers by Taubin and Cooper (130), or Reiss and Rayner (105). Moment descriptors can be made local, and hence more useful, if small shape regions can be segmented reliably from image data as shown by Åström (1). The segmentation methods are comparable to those discussed in Chapter 5 for the construction of a *canonical frame*.

2.3.2.3 *Differential invariants* Invariants can be formed for points lying on a curve at a single point if a sufficient number of derivatives of the curve can be computed. From the mathematical standpoint one such invariant is due to Halphen and is reported by Wilczynski (144). It is invariant under plane-to-plane projective deformations. However, it requires the accurate measurement of a point location and seven curve derivatives at the point. This is impossible in practice for discrete noisy curves and so the invariant is not useful in vision.

To form invariants under simpler imaging models, such as an affine one, fewer derivatives are needed (only five), though this is still too many. Under realistic imaging situations it seems unlikely that measurement of any more than the second derivative of a curve is possible, and so the only differential invariant that can be formed is curvature. As this is applicable under only plane Euclidean actions it is not really a useful descriptor of shape.

Weiss has suggested alternative ways of computing differential invariants at a single point that do not rely on taking high-order derivatives. His method relies on locally fitting different types of curve to the image data (142), and using parameters of the fit to provide a frame for measurement of the invariant. However, with regard to noise, there is very little difference between local fitting and computing derivatives, and so it is unlikely that sufficient stability will be realized in real images for these measurements to be taken accurately.

2.3.2.4 *Semi-differential invariants* Algebraic invariants require a relatively large number of points for their formation, and differential invariants need too many derivatives at a single point. A compromise situation exists for which invariants can be formed from a few low-order derivatives at a small number of points. This fact motivated the construction of the *semi-differential* invariants of Barrett, *et al.* (5) and Van Gool, *et al.* (136). Although many examples exist, and are given in (92), it is worth considering what is likely to be the fewest number of points that can be used to compute a stable semi-differential invariant. As second-order derivatives are the highest order that may be computed reliably, computing these at two different points makes it possible to form a full projective invariant. Affine invariants can also be computed using semi-differential constructions with fewer points or derivatives.

Semi-differential invariants do not just use any points along the curve, but must employ *distinguished points*. These points are covariant to the imaging process; such points are those derived from different orders of incidence (curve crossings, tangency, inflection, etc.). Measuring the invariant at an arbitrary point does not give sufficient discrimination between different curves as most curves will possess at least one point with a given invariant value. Other curve points can, however, be used to form invariant signatures (136), though it should be remembered that these are not immediately useful for indexing.

2.3.2.5 *Canonical frames* Curve signatures can be used as a starting point for recognition if indexes can be extracted from them. This is the motivation behind the canonical frame construction used in LEWIS2. Canonical frames have been used to form invariant indexes for arbitrary plane curves. An early example of the construction of signatures was demonstrated by Turney, *et al.* (135), who extracted $\theta - s$ (slope versus arc-length) representations for plane curves. Such representations can easily be made invariant to Euclidean actions by a suitable choice of the starting angle and starting point of the $\theta - s$ plot.

An alternative approach for deriving signatures for plane curves under Euclidean actions was taken by Kalvin, *et al.* (63), who computed invariant *footprints*. This work was extended by Lamdan, *et al.* (68), and recently by

Wolfson (146), to yield footprints under plane affine transformations. The method works well for non-convex shapes, but application to convex ones is harder. The extension to the projective case demonstrated in Chapter 5 shows how to construct a stable signature, and then the route that should be taken to form useful invariant indexes is given.

For convex curves, normalization to a canonical frame is still relatively easy for plane Euclidean or similarity transformations. Under affine maps, compactness can be used as demonstrated by Brady and Yuille (16, 33), and an extension to the projective case has been implemented by Sinclair and Blake (120).

2.3.2.6 *Three-dimensional invariants*   Classical invariant theory does not cover the construction of invariants from perspective views of 3D objects (which are singular transformations), and so the construction of indexing functions for such objects has required a substantial research effort. However, a number of 3D invariant shape descriptors have recently appeared in the literature; some of these are the focus of Chapter 8. Two different scenarios exist for the measurement of such invariants:

1. single perspective views;
2. multiple perspective views.

The existence of invariants for the first case should be contrasted with a common misinterpretation of a result presented by Burns, *et al.* (19) and also given by Clemens and Jacobs (24), Moses and Ullman (89), and Huttenlocher and Kleinberg (60). The correct statement for the theorem is: *Non-trivial invariants cannot be formed from single views of 3D point sets in general position.* The incorrect interpretation of the theorem is that *invariants cannot be formed for any 3D structure from a single view. General position* is defined more precisely as follows (19):

Definition 2.1 *A set of 3D points are in general position if there are no constraints assumed for the set.*

This definition applies to a very unstructured set of points; one that is not really of interest in practice. Invariants can be measured as soon as structure is available; frequently one encounters constraints such as collinearity, planarity or symmetry in the world. However, these are not the only constraints that are useful; invariants can be formed for points lying on a host of constraint curves or surfaces of which twisted cubics and quadrics are simple examples.

The incorrect belief can be dispelled by example:

- Surfaces that are projectively equivalent to solids of revolution possess invariants based on the cross ratio, see Forsyth, *et al.* (43, 73).
- Algebraic surfaces can be reconstructed projectively from single non-degenerate views, and invariants measured as shown by Forsyth (44).

- Extruded surfaces or ruled surfaces can be reconstructed up to a projective transformation of three-space and any surface markings can be mapped from the image onto the reconstructed surface, Forsyth and Rothwell (45).

- Invariants can be computed for classes of *canal surface,* Zisserman, *et al.* (150).

- Under single scaled orthographic views invariants can be extracted for sets of four points that form an orthogonal basis, Wayner (140).

- 3D point sets that lie on the vertices of polyhedra possess invariants. These are derived using a projective reconstruction similar to that of Sugihara (126), and is reported by Rothwell, *et al.* (112), and in Chapter 8.

- Exploitation of symmetry can lead to the measurement of invariants from single views. One example is given in Chapter 8 and other cases have been examined by Mundy (93).

There has been a much broader base of research into invariants for multiple views of unconstrained point sets. 3D affine reconstructions were first demonstrated by Koenderink and Van Doorn (66), and then adapted by Quan and Mohr (102), and Demey, *et al.* (28). The most general methods are capable of producing projective, or uncalibrated stereo: Faugeras (36), and Hartley, *et al.* (54) have demonstrated that a 3D projective representation of features can be reconstructed from two independent views. Once reconstructed, invariants can be measured in a manner similar to that shown later in Chapter 8.

If constraints exist on the data set, say there exists a set of four coplanar points, then the measurement of invariant indexes can be done in the image without a full 3D projective reconstruction. This has been demonstrated by Mohr, *et al.* (86) and Beardsley (6). This type of invariant is also demonstrated in Chapter 8 when symmetry is exploited from a single view to enable the measurement of indexes using multiple-view invariant theory.

2.3.3 *Summary*

The requirement for indexing is unquestionable. Invariants also appear to provide the most efficient route to indexing once they have been constructed from image data. Prior to a use of invariants in the creation of indexes one should pose the following two questions: first, does a sufficiently rich library of invariants exist so that every object which will be encountered can be represented geometrically? and second, is the invariant formation process in itself efficient?

The second question is answered in part by the chapter on segmentation and grouping (Chapter 6), where for at least the planar case it is shown how invariants should be computed from image data. A more complete answer cannot be given until further concentrated attempts have been made to build three-dimensional recognition systems that use invariants. The first question is a much harder one to respond to, though considering the rapid progress that is being made at finding three-dimensional invariant descriptions one should at least be open minded if not optimistic.

2.4   Conclusions

This chapter has briefly reviewed the literature covering some of the contributions made to computer-based object recognition. The discussion has focused on the emphasis placed on the different phases of the selection, indexing and correspondence paradigm, but we have seen that almost all of the working systems have exclusively used correspondence to do the larger part of the work.

Correspondence definitely has a rôle to play in recognition as it is the process that finally concludes whether an object is actually present in a scene. However, correspondence should not drive recognition. This is because it cannot determine efficiently which models may be present in a scene (that is all models must be tested). Indexing overcomes this as models are ruled out without expending significant effort; only those models that possess the same shape cues that are measured directly in the scene need to be considered.

Computing these cues is of course a non-trivial task and relies heavily on the reliability of the selection process. Indexing has perhaps been ruled out in the past because the combined indexing and selection process has appeared intractable; the rest of this book describes two recognition systems that use this process and still have reliable recognition performances.

3

PLANE ALGEBRAIC PROJECTIVE INVARIANTS

This chapter provides a sufficient level of theoretical background material in projective geometry and algebraic invariant theory for the understanding of the planar algebraic invariant shape descriptions used in LEWIS1. Algebraic invariants are just one example of how indexing functions can be computed for real shapes and so this chapter paves the way for Chapter 4 to achieve its goal, namely to prove by experiment that indexing is one of the key steps to producing an efficient recognition algorithm.

The intention of this chapter is not to provide a complete and formal review of projective geometry or algebraic invariant theory, for that the reader should refer to texts such as Semple and Kneebone (115) or Springer (124). A simpler account of some of the same material can be found in Maxwell (80), or for a review more closely related to aspects of computer vision the appendix of (92) by Mundy and Zisserman is appropriate. In fact only a very small number of plane invariants are covered in the following sections; namely the *cross ratio* due to its fundamental importance in invariance, and the three invariants actually used in LEWIS1.

The following discussions do examine the properties of each invariant in more detail than in the above texts, especially with respect to the invariants being used as shape descriptors for objects. More than one formulation is given for each type of invariant, and it is shown that the different forms are not equivalent. Furthermore, there are certain properties desirable in a shape descriptor that are reviewed in more detail in Chapter 7; a couple of these are considered ahead of their time and are defined in this chapter. These are notions such as *completeness* and *stability* to measurement error.

A final issue that is touched upon in this chapter is the relationship between the mathematical transformations that are used to develop the invariance properties (in this case projectivities), and the actual deformations that arise during imaging onto a camera. In fact the latter form only a subset of the former and so the mathematics being used it too general. A topic that is currently arousing much interest is how to limit the generality of the mathematical transformations to those that can be observed by real cameras.

3.1 Notation

Homogeneous coordinates are useful representation for points as they permit projective maps to be modelled by linear transformations and therefore by matrices. They also provide a convenient representation for lines lying in the plane; conics are represented by symmetric matrices.

Throughout the rest of this book the typewriter font denotes matrices and bold letters denote vectors. Furthermore, where necessary large letters will be used to denote world objects and small letters image objects. Therefore C and $\mathbf{X}$ are world objects (a matrix and a vector respectively), and c and $\mathbf{x}$ their images.

3.1.1 Homogeneous coordinates and duality

This section principally describes plane homogeneous coordinates, though their use extends to spaces of any dimension. Their definition uses a convenient representation that removes the mystique associated with points at infinity in either the Euclidean or affine plane; this is essential because under projection all points must be treated equally (for a planar world the horizon line is the projection of a line that lies at infinity in the Euclidean world coordinate frame, but although it is an everyday occurrence it cannot be handled by Euclidean coordinates). The definition will also lead to an important property used in projective geometry, that is the notion of duality of geometric features.

Definition 3.1 *Homogeneous points on the projective plane are represented by the triple* $\mathbf{x} = (x, y, z)^T$, *where at least one element of* $\{x, y, z\}$ *is non-zero. The Euclidean coordinates of a point on the plane are found from the ratios* $(x/z, y/z)$.

From this definition two important facts emerge:

1. Points at infinity are represented by points with $z = 0$. The definition is natural within the projective plane as points of the form $(x, y, 0)^T$ define the line at infinity. This line is commonly the pre-image of the horizon. Using a Euclidean representation the line incorrectly appears as an *undefined single point* (∞, ∞).

2. The point $(\lambda x, \lambda y, \lambda z)^T$ is equivalent to $(x, y, z)^T$ for $\lambda \neq 0$. The point $\lambda = 0$ is the *only* one that is not defined within a homogeneous representation.

Points on the projective line are represented by the pair (y, z) in a similar manner. The point $z = 0$ is the unique point at infinity or *ideal point* of the line. The projective plane is made up of a two-parameter family of projective lines.

A common representation of the projective plane uses a *ray space*. This space is three-dimensional, the same dimension as the homogeneous coordinates. Rays through the origin represent plane points; a point $(x, y, z)^T$ lies on the same ray as $\lambda(x, y, z)^T$. The only point not defined in the ray space is the origin. Any point on a ray can be used to parametrize the space.

Lines on the plane are represented by planes through the origin in ray space. This is intuitive as a line can be defined by pairs of points, and a plane through the origin can be identified by a pair of rays (that is the plane that contains both rays). In fact any ray on the plane in ray space can be realized as a point on the projective line. Similarly, a pair of different planes passing through the origin in ray space always intersect in a unique ray, the projective plane analogy is that a pair of lines intersect in a point. These observations lead to the duality of points and lines in projective space:

The *principle of duality* in the projective plane means that any result that is true for a set of points has a dual form that is true for a set of lines. The principle applies equally to mixed configurations of points and lines.

One of the simplest applications of the principle can be stated using the following dual remarks:

1. A line is defined by a pair of points; it must pass through both points.
2. A point is defined by the intersection point of a pair of lines.

Incidence is, however, the simplest dual relationship. Consider the familiar homogeneous line equation:

$$ax + by + cz = 0,$$

or, if $l = (a, b, c)^T$:

$$l^T x = 0. \tag{3.1.1}$$

This is saying no more than that a point lies on a line, and that a line passes through a point. The obvious symmetry of eqn 3.1.1 is a result of the duality of points and lines. Frequently, lines will be represented by their homogeneous coordinates l, and will be treated in exactly the same manner as points.

There are many situations in which duality arises. One applies to the measurement of a cross ratio which is the fundamental *projective invariant*. A set of four points on a line define a cross ratio (see Section 3.3). Similarly a set of four lines through a point also yields a cross ratio. Any set of lines through a single point is called a pencil; a pencil is a one-parameter family of lines which is dual to a line. Coordinates along a pencil behave in exactly the same way as the coordinates along a line. If l_1 and l_2 are any members of the pencil, then $l_3 = \lambda l_1 + \mu l_2$ is also on the pencil and has homogeneous coordinates $(\lambda, \mu)^T$. Incidentally, l_1 has coordinates $(1, 0)^T$ and l_2 is represented by $(0, 1)^T$.

Both homogeneous points and duality extend to projective spaces of any dimension, for example projective 3-space uses coordinates $x = (x, y, z, t)^T$. In three dimensions points and planes are dual, and the dual of a line is a line. Three-dimensional homogeneous coordinates and their corresponding transformations are considered in Chapter 8 of this book.

3.1.2   Conics

Conics can also be represented in a homogeneous form. A conic is the set of points (x_i, y_i) that satisfy:

$$ax_i^2 + bx_iy_i + cy_i^2 + dx_i + ey_i + f = 0, \tag{3.1.2}$$

and so each conic is represented by a point $(a, b, c, d, e, f)^T$ in projective 5-space. From this we see that a conic has five degrees of freedom. A more convenient representation uses a planar homogeneous point $\mathbf{x}$ and a quadratic form C:

$$\mathbf{x}^T C \mathbf{x} = 0, \tag{3.1.3}$$

where:

$$C = \begin{bmatrix} a & \frac{b}{2} & \frac{d}{2} \\ \frac{b}{2} & c & \frac{e}{2} \\ \frac{d}{2} & \frac{e}{2} & f \end{bmatrix}. \tag{3.1.4}$$

From eqn 3.1.3 it is clear that kC is the same curve as C ($k \in \mathbb{C} - \{0\}$, where $\mathbb{C}$ is the set of complex numbers). This highlights a problem that can be encountered when homogeneous coordinates are used, that is care must be taken in making the correct choice of scale or normalization for the coordinates when they are used as parameters to functions. Different choices of k will produce different function values as is shown in the following examples.

Example 3.2 If the scaling k is chosen so that the resulting conic has the property $|C| = 1$ (where $|\ |$ is the determinant operator), and if C is an ellipse, then the function $\Delta(C) = ac - b^2/4$ returns the area contained within the curve. However, if the conic $k_1 C$ is used the function returns $\Delta(k_1 C) = k_1^2(ac - b^2/4)$ which is k_1^2 times the area. Subsequently, if we are to use $\Delta(C)$ to compute the area of an ellipse we must first ensure that $|C| = 1$.

Example 3.3 The *algebraic distance* of a point from a conic is defined as $q(x_i, C) = ax_i^2 + bx_iy_i + cy_i^2 + dx_i + ey_i + f$. The algebraic distance is frequently used as a cost for fitting an algebraic curve to a data set (it is used later in Chapter 6), and was used in the frame invariant fitting technique described by Forsyth, *et al.* (39). However, $q(x_i, 2C) = 4q(x_i, C)$, and so to make the algebraic distance meaningful one must apply a constraint to C. In the case of (39) the normalization $|C| = 1$ was used.

Both of the above examples normalize the conics so that $|\mathsf{C}| = 1$ and this normalization will be used for many of the examples in this book. However, such a scaling means that pairs of straight lines (which are degenerate conics) cannot be represented as they have the property that $|\mathsf{C}| = 0$. Unfortunately, each scale one might care to use has some disadvantage (as described by Bookstein (13)), e.g.:

1. $a = 1$ prevents use of some parabolas, for instance $y^2 - 1 = 0$.
2. $b = 1$ makes it impossible to fit circles.
3. $f = 1$ makes it impossible to fit curves that pass through the origin.

The determinant normalization is used because degenerate conics can be represented by lower-order features (lines or even points), and so it does not exclude any generic conics.

Rather than requiring the normalization process, an alternative way to overcome the scaling problem is to include the conic scale within any function definition. For example, in Example 3.2 above all constraints on the conic normalization could be removed if the expression for computing the area of an ellipse took the form:

$$\text{Area}(\mathsf{C}) = \frac{ac - b^2/4}{|\mathsf{C}|^{\frac{2}{3}}}.$$

Conics are self-dual in the projective plane; this means that the dual of a conic is also a conic. The dual of C ($|\mathsf{C}| \neq 0$) is $\mathsf{C}_e = \mathsf{C}^{-1}$. As C_e is non-singular and symmetric it also represents a well-defined conic. The interpretation of the dual conic is as follows: normally $\mathbf{x}$ lies on C if $\mathbf{x}^T \mathsf{C} \mathbf{x} = 0$, likewise the line $\mathbf{l}$ is tangent to C if $\mathbf{l}^T \mathsf{C}_e \mathbf{l} = 0$. From this definition the alternative names for C_e arise, that is the conic envelope or the line conic.

3.1.3   Projective transformations

Using a pinhole perspective camera, planar world points map to the image by a plane projectivity T represented by a 3×3 matrix acting on plane homogeneous coordinates. This is a result of the following theorem proved in Appendix A:

Theorem 3.4 *A pinhole perspective map between a set of homogeneous planar world points* $\mathbf{X_i} = (X_i, Y_i, 1)^T$ *and their images* $\mathbf{x_i} = (x_i, y_i, 1)^T$ *is represented by a plane projectivity.*

A homogeneous representation of points means that only ratios of matrix elements are significant, and consequently T has 8 degrees of freedom. Under imaging, this transformation models the *composed* effects of 3D rigid rotation and translation of the world plane (camera extrinsic parameters), perspective projection to the image plane, and an affine transformation of the final image (which covers the effects of changing camera intrinsic parameters). The effects of radial distortion due to the camera lens are not modelled, though these effects can be removed using the techniques of Slama (121). Clearly, all of these separate transformations cannot be recovered uniquely from a single 3×3 matrix, since there are 6 unknown pose parameters, and 4 unknown camera parameters (camera centre, focal length and aspect ratio). There are therefore 10 unknowns with 8 constraints. However, for most applications solving for T is often sufficient and the Euclidean pose parameters are not needed. Subsequently there is frequently no requirement to know the camera parameters and so calibration is not necessary.

The mapping of four points, of which no three are collinear, between a pair of planes is sufficient to determine the transformation matrix T linking the planes. Each point provides two linear constraints on the parameters of T and therefore four independent points provide the $4 \times 2 = 8$ constraints that define the map uniquely. The projective transformation $\mathbf{x} = \mathbf{TX}$, ($|\mathbf{T}| \neq 0$) is expressed:[8]

$$k_i \begin{pmatrix} x_i \\ y_i \\ 1 \end{pmatrix} = \begin{bmatrix} T_{11} & T_{12} & T_{13} \\ T_{21} & T_{22} & T_{23} \\ T_{31} & T_{32} & 1 \end{bmatrix} \begin{pmatrix} X_i \\ Y_i \\ 1 \end{pmatrix}, \qquad (3.1.5)$$

where k_i is an arbitrary non-zero scalar. Eliminating k gives eight simultaneous equations linear in the parameters of the map; the form of the solution is given in Appendix B.1.

T is a linear mapping on homogeneous points, as can be seen from the following identities:

$$\mathbf{T}(\lambda \mathbf{x}) = \lambda \mathbf{T}\mathbf{x} \qquad \text{and} \qquad \mathbf{T}(\mathbf{x} + \mathbf{y}) = \mathbf{T}\mathbf{x} + \mathbf{T}\mathbf{y}.$$

The proof of these expressions follows directly from the linearity of matrix operations on vectors. One result of linearity is:

Theorem 3.5 *Lines in the world map to lines in the image.*

Proof   A line through $\mathbf{X}_1$ and $\mathbf{X}_2$ can be parametrized by $\mathbf{X} = \lambda \mathbf{X}_1 + \mu \mathbf{X}_2$. Its image is:

$$\mathbf{x} = \mathbf{TX},$$

---

[8]With this form for T, the complete space of projectivities cannot be represented; one is unable to use a projectivity with $T_{33} = 0$. However, as can be seen from Appendix A this form of T is realized only when the world coordinate frame lies in the camera plane $z = 0$ (that is the z component of translation is zero). This scenario is unlikely to occur. Note also from this definition that points at infinity cannot be used to determine T as ideal points have the third homogeneous component equal to zero. However, this is not a problem as such points are not within the bounds of the finite image plane and the object coordinate frames can be designed so that the object does not pass though the ideal line.

$$= T(\lambda \mathbf{X}_1 + \mu \mathbf{X}_2),$$
$$= \lambda T \mathbf{X}_1 + \mu T \mathbf{X}_2,$$
$$= \lambda \mathbf{x}_1 + \mu \mathbf{x}_2,$$

which is a line. □

Note that (non-singular) projective actions inherit all of the group properties possessed by matrices, most importantly:

- The inverse map which takes the image back to the world is always well defined.
- Concatenation of projective transformations is effected by multiplication of matrices, and such transformations are also projectivities. Consequently pictures of pictures are also related by a plane projectivity.

3.1.3.1 *Plane affine and Euclidean maps* If T in eqn 3.1.5 takes the form:

$$T_{31} = 0 \quad \text{and} \quad T_{32} = 0,$$

then T is an *plane affine map*. This transformation has the property that the ideal line is mapped onto itself. If further constraints are applied such that:

$$T_{11} = T_{22},$$
$$T_{21} = -T_{12},$$
$$T_{11}^2 + T_{12}^2 = 1,$$

then T becomes a *plane Euclidean map*.

3.1.3.2 *Projectivities on lines* As a consequence of the duality of points and lines the following result can be derived which relates world and image lines by projective transformations:

Theorem 3.6 *Under the point projectivity* T *the world line* **L** *maps to* l *in the image by* $l = T^{-T}L$, *where* T^{-T} *is the inverse transpose of* T.

Proof From the world line–point constraint equation:

$$\mathbf{L}^T \mathbf{X} = 0,$$

and the point projectivity $\mathbf{x} = T\mathbf{X}$ we have:

$$\mathbf{L}^T T^{-1} \mathbf{x} = 0.$$

Compare this to the image line–point constraint $\mathbf{l}^T \mathbf{x} = 0$:

$$\Rightarrow \quad \mathbf{1}^T = \mathbf{L}^T \mathbf{T}^{-1},$$
$$\Rightarrow \quad \mathbf{1} = \mathbf{T}^{-T} \mathbf{L}.$$

□

3.1.3.3 *Projectivities on conics*

Theorem 3.7 *Under the point projectivity* $\mathbf{T}$ *the world conic* $\mathbf{C}$ *maps to* $\mathbf{c}$
by:

$$\mathbf{c} = \kappa \, . \, \mathbf{T}^{-T} \mathbf{C} \, \mathbf{T}^{-1}. \qquad (3.1.6)$$

In effect $\mathbf{T}^{-1}$ strips the effect of the coordinate transformation. The
scaling $\kappa = |\mathbf{T}|^{\frac{2}{3}}$ ensures the normalization $|\mathbf{c}| = 1$ when $|\mathbf{C}| = 1$.

Proof From the world conic–point constraint equation:

$$\mathbf{X}^T \mathbf{C} \, \mathbf{X} = 0,$$

and the point projectivity $\mathbf{x} = \mathbf{T}\mathbf{X}$ we have:

$$\mathbf{x}^T \mathbf{T}^{-T} \mathbf{C} \, \mathbf{T}^{-1} \mathbf{x} = 0.$$

Compare this to the image conic–point constraint:

$$\mathbf{x}^T \mathbf{c} \, \mathbf{x} = 0,$$
$$\Rightarrow \quad \mathbf{c} = \mathbf{T}^{-T} \mathbf{C} \, \mathbf{T}^{-1},$$

where $\mathbf{c}$ is not normalized.   □

Constraints on $\mathbf{T}$ for different algebraic configurations such as mixtures
of points, lines and conics, are considered in more detail in Appendix B.
Although the earlier chapters of this book are concerned only with planar
shapes and hence plane projectivities, it should be noted that projective
transformations on the line are represented by 2×2 matrices and between
points in three-dimensional projective space as 4×4 matrices.

3.2   Plane projective invariants

The following sections introduce the three invariants used within LEWIS1.
These invariants are formed for configurations of: five coplanar points; a
pair of coplanar conics; and a conic and a pair of coplanar points. Invariants
can also be formed for the dual configurations.

First however, the properties of an invariant function are to be defined
(Mundy and Zisserman (92)):

Definition 3.8 *An invariant,* $I(\mathbf{P})$*, of a geometric structure described by a
parameter vector* $\mathbf{P}$*, subject to a linear transformation* $\mathbf{T}$ *of the coordinates*
$\mathbf{x} = \mathbf{T}\mathbf{X}$*, is transformed according to* $I(\mathbf{p}) = I(\mathbf{P})|\mathbf{T}|^w$*. Here* $I(\mathbf{p})$ *is the
function of the parameters after the linear transformation, and* $|\mathbf{T}|$ *is the
determinant of the matrix* $\mathbf{T}$*.*

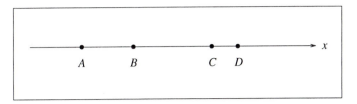

FIG. 3.1. Four collinear points define the simplest projective invariant: the cross ratio.

Throughout this book we shall be concerned mainly with *scalar* invariants; these are invariants for which $w = 0$.

The invariant functions will be defined in a number of different forms. Principally this is to demonstrate that both geometric and algebraic approaches can be used for their formation. However, it will be shown that although there are frequently similarities between the different formulations of the invariants, they can often behave differently. The emphasis of this book is also on the use of projective invariants rather than of those to other group deformations. Some of the example below will contrast projective invariants with affine ones (affine transformations provide only an approximation to the pinhole camera imaging deformation) to contrast the accuracy of the two approaches.

Although the cross ratio is not used directly in LEWIS1, it is introduced first as its properties are important within the derivations of the other invariants.

3.3 The cross ratio

The cross ratio is the simplest projective invariant, and is often considered to be the *classic* invariant. Proof of its invariance has been covered extensively in geometry texts such as (115, 124), and more recently in computer vision books such as (92). It has been applied to machine vision tasks in its raw form by a number of researchers, for example by Lei (70) and Mohr and Morin (85).

The cross ratio τ is defined for four points on a line (see Fig. 3.1). It is also defined for four lines in a *pencil*. This results follows from the *duality* of points and lines in the plane. The simplest definition of the invariant uses ratios of lengths, for example if the distance between points A and B is denoted by AB, τ is given by a ratio of ratios of distances:

$$\tau = \frac{AC}{BC} \cdot \frac{BD}{AD} = \{A, B : C, D\}. \tag{3.3.7}$$

As this expression is homogeneous in the distances between the points, the units used to record the distances are irrelevant. An alternative definition uses a homogeneous coordinate system defined on the line. The choice of the coordinates is arbitrary:

$$\tau(\mathbf{X}) = \frac{|\mathbf{X}_A\ \mathbf{X}_C|}{|\mathbf{X}_B\ \mathbf{X}_C|} \cdot \frac{|\mathbf{X}_B\ \mathbf{X}_D|}{|\mathbf{X}_A\ \mathbf{X}_D|}. \tag{3.3.8}$$

Here $\mathbf{X}_i$ is the homogeneous coordinates of the point i. There is a similarity between eqns 3.3.7 and 3.3.8 in that $PQ = -|\mathbf{X}_P\ \mathbf{X}_Q|$ when the second components of $\mathbf{X}_P$ and $\mathbf{X}_Q$ are set to unity. Note also that the expression for $\tau(\mathbf{X})$ is formed from determinants of matrices. This makes proof of invariance under linear transformations simple. If a projective transformation of the line $\mathbf{T}$ is considered, described by a 2×2 matrix, the point $\mathbf{X}$ maps to $\mathbf{x}$ by $\mathbf{x} = \mathbf{TX}$. Therefore:

$$\begin{aligned}
\tau(\mathbf{x}) &= \frac{|\mathbf{x}_A\ \mathbf{x}_C|}{|\mathbf{x}_B\ \mathbf{x}_C|} \cdot \frac{|\mathbf{x}_B\ \mathbf{x}_D|}{|\mathbf{x}_A\ \mathbf{x}_D|}, \\
&= \frac{|T.\mathbf{X}_A\ T.\mathbf{X}_C|}{|T.\mathbf{X}_B\ T.\mathbf{X}_C|} \cdot \frac{|T.\mathbf{X}_B\ T.\mathbf{X}_D|}{|T.\mathbf{X}_A\ T.\mathbf{X}_D|}, \\
&= \frac{|T.[\mathbf{X}_A\ \mathbf{X}_C]|}{|T.[\mathbf{X}_B\ \mathbf{X}_C]|} \cdot \frac{|T.[\mathbf{X}_B\ \mathbf{X}_D]|}{|T.[\mathbf{X}_A\ \mathbf{X}_D]|}, \\
&= \frac{|T|.|\mathbf{X}_A\ \mathbf{X}_C|}{|T|.|\mathbf{X}_B\ \mathbf{X}_C|} \cdot \frac{|T|.|\mathbf{X}_B\ \mathbf{X}_D|}{|T|.|\mathbf{X}_A\ \mathbf{X}_D|}, \\
&= \frac{|\mathbf{X}_A\ \mathbf{X}_C|}{|\mathbf{X}_B\ \mathbf{X}_C|} \cdot \frac{|\mathbf{X}_B\ \mathbf{X}_D|}{|\mathbf{X}_A\ \mathbf{X}_D|}, \\
&= \tau(\mathbf{X}),
\end{aligned}$$

and so τ for the image points $\mathbf{x}_i$ is the same as that for the original points $\mathbf{X}_i$. The proof is not in fact as simple as it appears because of the arbitrary scaling that can be applied to homogeneous coordinates: $\mathbf{x}$ and $\lambda\mathbf{x}, \lambda \neq 0$, describe exactly the same image point. The proof of invariance is therefore completed by observing the effect of the scaling:

$$\begin{aligned}
\tau_\lambda(\mathbf{x}) &= \frac{|\lambda_A\mathbf{x}_A\ \lambda_C\mathbf{x}_C|}{|\lambda_B\mathbf{x}_B\ \lambda_C\mathbf{x}_C|} \cdot \frac{|\lambda_B\mathbf{x}_B\ \lambda_D\mathbf{x}_D|}{|\lambda_A\mathbf{x}_A\ \lambda_D\mathbf{x}_D|}, \\
&= \frac{\lambda_A\lambda_C\ |\mathbf{x}_A\ \mathbf{x}_C|}{\lambda_B\lambda_C\ |\mathbf{x}_B\ \mathbf{x}_C|} \cdot \frac{\lambda_B\lambda_D\ |\mathbf{x}_B\ \mathbf{x}_D|}{\lambda_A\lambda_D\ |\mathbf{x}_A\ \mathbf{x}_D|}, \\
&= \frac{|\mathbf{x}_A\ \mathbf{x}_C|}{|\mathbf{x}_B\ \mathbf{x}_C|} \cdot \frac{|\mathbf{x}_B\ \mathbf{x}_D|}{|\mathbf{x}_A\ \mathbf{x}_D|}, \\
&= \tau(\mathbf{x}).
\end{aligned}$$

As the expression for the cross ratio is homogeneous in each term, any scaling factor will automatically cancel out and the function will be invariant.

The requirement for the elimination of any dependency on the scaling is directly analogous to the normalization problems encountered with conics in Section 3.1.2.

One fact that becomes clear is that using determinants eases the proof of invariance of many of the geometric expressions. In fact, a large part of projective geometry can be explained using the axioms of linear algebra. However, geometric reasoning often suggests instances when invariants can be formed and so an understanding of both the geometric and algebraic methods is useful.

An important concern with the application of an invariant function in machine vision is completeness. A formal definition of completeness is:

Definition 3.9 *An invariant function I acting on objects x and y under a group of transformations T is complete iff $I(x) = I(y) \Rightarrow y = T(x)$.*

The full implications of non-completeness are given in Section 7.7; here it is sufficient to state that completeness is desirable because it means that knowledge of the invariants of a set of features uniquely defines their geometric shape.

Completeness of a projective invariant I acting on a geometric structure **P** can be tested in the following way:

1. Constrain enough degrees of freedom in **P** so that a projective representation is defined for **P**. For example, if **P** is a set of collinear points three points must be fixed as these define a projective representation on the line (115, 124). Four points must be fixed if **P** is a set of coplanar points.

2. Then, given a value I_0 for I determine the coordinates of any other point in the frame given by the fixed points. In general the process involves substituting I_0 and the coordinates of the fixed points into the expression for I and solving for the coordinates of any other point.

3. The invariant is complete if the coordinates of all of the other points are defined uniquely.

Completeness for τ is therefore determined in the following way: the cross ratio is measured on the line so three points must be fixed. Assign the coordinates $\mathbf{X}_A = 0$, $\mathbf{X}_B = 1$ and $\mathbf{X}_C = \infty$. If $\mathbf{X}_D$ is assigned the coordinate x, τ is given by:

$$\tau = \{0, 1 : \infty : x\},$$
$$= \frac{\infty}{\infty} \cdot \frac{x-1}{x},$$
$$= 1 - \frac{1}{x}, \qquad (3.3.9)$$

which is sketched in Fig. 3.2. Conversely x can be computed for any given value τ_0 (that is τ is invertible), and so the cross ratio is complete. This

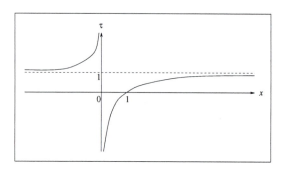

FIG. 3.2. The value of the cross ratio for a point x, as it moves from $-\infty \to \infty$ with $\tau = \{0, 1 : \infty : x\}$.

observation leads to a more fundamental result of the projective geometry of the line:

Given the projective coordinates of the first three points, a one-to-one map exists between the coordinates of the fourth point and the cross ratio of the four points.

So far the assumption has been made that the points on the line are ordered, that is $\mathbf{x}_i$ corresponds to $\mathbf{X}_i$. It is frequently believed that this assumption is not always true in vision applications as the correspondence problem may not have been solved. By permuting the four points, the following six different values of the cross ratio are obtained (the reader might care to verify these using eqn (3.3.9)):

$$\tau, \quad 1 - \tau, \quad \frac{1}{\tau}, \quad 1 - \frac{1}{\tau}, \quad \frac{1}{1 - \tau}, \quad \frac{\tau}{\tau - 1}.$$

In these situations one must form a *symmetric function* of τ that is ordering independent.[9] Symmetric projective invariants are also invariant to permutation actions on their features. One such function is the j-invariant described by Maybank (81):

$$j(\tau) = \frac{(\tau^2 - \tau + 1)^3}{\tau^2(\tau - 1)^2}. \tag{3.3.10}$$

If the representation of eqn 3.3.9 is used the j-invariant can be expressed as:

$$j(\tau) = \frac{(x^2 - x + 1)^3}{x^2(x - 1)^2}. \tag{3.3.11}$$

[9]If f is a symmetric function, and $i \neq j$, $i, j \in \{0, \ldots, n\}$, the following result holds: $f(x_0, \ldots, x_i, \ldots, x_j, \ldots, x_n) = f(x_0, \ldots, x_j, \ldots, x_i, \ldots, x_n)$.

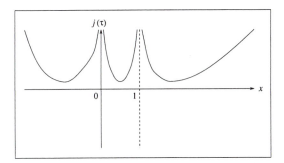

FIG. 3.3. The value of the j-invariant is plotted for $-\infty < x < \infty$. Note that the inverse of the function is not single valued.

This is plotted in Fig. 3.3. Note that $\mathbf{X}_D$ can no longer be determined uniquely given τ and the coordinates of the other three points. Therefore the j-invariant is not complete. If the j-invariant were to be used for recognition one may find that a number of (projectively) different objects have the same invariant, and so inter-object discrimination has been reduced (the objects will be projectively equivalent under a permutation of the points).

3.3.1 Pinhole camera projectivities

Real vision applications are not subject to the full permutation group. This can be seen from Fig. 3.4. The ordering of points along a line can only change cyclically or be reflected, that is, the topology of the line is preserved. The proof of this follows from the preservation of the topology imposed by the pencil of lines passing through the focal point. Consequently, if the points on L_0 are projected through the focal point and onto line L_1 an ordering of $\{d, c, b, a\}$ results (reversal). Alternatively the projection can be done onto L_2 and yields $\{b', c', d', a'\}$ (cyclic permutation). As all line-to-line projectivities can be defined as a sequence of up to two perspectivities, Semple and Kneebone (115), it can been seen that the property holds under projectivities as well.

The implications of this on the cross ratio can be seen using two results from Springer (124), p. 15, with $\tau = \{A, B : C, D\}$:

1. interchanging $A \leftrightarrow B$ or $C \leftrightarrow D$ yields

$$\{B, A : C, D\} = \{A, B : D, C\} = \frac{1}{\tau},$$

2. and changing $A \leftrightarrow D$ or $B \leftrightarrow C$ gives

$$\{D, B : C, A\} = \{A, C : B, D\} = 1 - \tau.$$

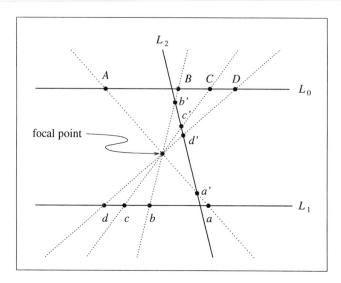

FIG. 3.4. Under a perspective projection the ordering of points on a line can only be changed by up to a reflection or a cyclic permutation. For example projecting L_0 onto L_1 maps $\{A, B, C, D\} \Rightarrow \{d, c, b, a\}$, or mapping to L_2 yields $\{b', c', d', a'\}$. As a line-to-line projectivity is a combination of at most two perspectivities, a projectivity can only change the ordering on a set of points by a reflection or a cyclic permutation.

Now considering how the cross ratio changes under real projectivities the following results become apparent:

$$\{A, B : C, D\} = \tau,$$
$$\Longrightarrow \{B, A : C, D\} = \frac{1}{\tau},$$
$$\Longrightarrow \{B, C : A, D\} = 1 - \frac{1}{\tau},$$
$$\Longrightarrow \{B, C : D, A\} = \frac{1}{1 - \frac{1}{\tau}} = \frac{\tau}{\tau - 1}, \qquad [1]$$

and that:

$$\{C, D : A, B\} = \tau, \qquad\qquad [2]$$
$$\{D, A : B, C\} = \frac{\tau}{\tau - 1}, \qquad [3]$$
$$\{D, C : B, A\} = \tau. \qquad\qquad [4]$$

From this it can be seen that under real projectivities the only values of the cross ratio that can be measured are τ and $\tau/(\tau - 1)$. Symmetric functions

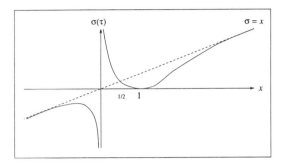

FIG. 3.5. Here, σ varies over the choice of the fourth point $\mathbf{X}_D$. Again the
value of the invariant does not define x uniquely.

of these two values can be constructed as follows:

$$\sigma(\tau) = -(\tau + \frac{\tau}{\tau - 1}) = \frac{\tau^2}{1 - \tau},$$

or,

$$\sigma(\tau) = -(\tau \times \frac{\tau}{\tau - 1}) = \frac{\tau^2}{1 - \tau}. \tag{3.3.12}$$

Both of these expressions are equal. Using the result $\tau = 1 - 1/x$ from eqn
3.3.9, both invariants take the form:

$$\sigma(x) = \frac{(x - 1)^2}{x}, \tag{3.3.13}$$

which is sketched in Fig. 3.5. Note that σ is not complete, but takes only
two values for each given value of x compared to the six different values
when the j-invariant is used.

It is very easy to evaluate the expression for the σ invariant. First
calculate τ, and then substitute it into eqn 3.3.12. Alternatively, though
less efficiently, the form in eqn 3.3.13 could be used directly, though that
would mean transforming the three basis points to the reference frame
$\{0, 1, \infty\}$.

It will be seen in Section 3.7 that if the line segment containing the
four points cannot pass through the plane parallel to the image plane that
contains the focal point, then even cyclic permutations of the points cannot occur (a real camera can observe only a finite solid angle centred on
the optical axis and so this constraint is always true). Therefore, the only
value of the cross ratio that needs to be measured is τ, and so a complete
invariant equal to τ can be used again. This demonstrates an instance of
when understanding the physical domain of the application simplifies the
complexity of the required shape descriptor. Benefits are often reaped by

marrying the actual physics of the situation with the mathematics; frequently just studying the mathematics does not provide a sufficiently tight bound on what can be observed in the world.

Another property of an invariant that should be studied is how errors in the measurement of parameters affect the observed value of the invariant. Errors are plentiful in imaging, and although frequently hard to model correctly, one must have an understanding of their effects. The error behaviour (say for τ) can be studied by looking at the way the invariant changes with respect to perturbations in the coordinate x (see also a recent paper by Maybank and Beardsley (83)):

$$\frac{d\tau}{dx} = \frac{1}{x^2} \qquad \text{and} \qquad \frac{d\sigma}{dx} = 1 - \frac{1}{x^2}.$$

From this we see that both τ and σ have poor noise performance, often called *stability*, when $x = 0$ (D is close to A). In contrast to this, both forms of the invariant have poor discrimination as $x \to \infty$ (D close to C) because the derivatives tend to 0. The trade-offs between discrimination and noise are studied in more detail in Chapter 7.

Studying error in the above way provides only a local measure of the invariant performance under errors. It does not really apply when the errors become large. For that more detailed analysis is required which unfortunately requires a complete model of the errors that will be encountered; as demonstrated later in Section 4.3.1 it is frequently hard to model the errors analytically. As a consequence of this much error analysis is done empirically.

Now that the cross ratio has been discussed in detail we can study the different forms of the three invariants used later in LEWIS1. As the different formulations for each invariant are introduced one should bear in mind questions as to which version would be easiest to implement, which has the best completeness properties, and how would the error analysis be performed most readily?

3.4   Five coplanar points

The first invariant used in the system is for five points in *general* position in the plane. Points in general position will have no triple collinear. Using the counting argument given in Forsyth, *et al.* (42) that allows one to estimate the number of independent invariants for a given feature group, we see that two projective invariants can be computed for five points:

For a geometric configuration with s parameters under the action of a group with t degrees of freedom, there are $n \geq s - t$ independent invariants. If there is no isotropy[10] present the '$\geq$' becomes an '$=$'.

Each point in a plane is described by two parameters, and so for five points $s = 5 \times 2 = 10$. The plane projective group has 8 degrees of freedom and so generically there are $n = 10 - 8 = 2$ invariants. Using the duality of points and lines five coplanar lines in general position also yield two invariants.

There are a number of ways of forming the invariants; these are described in the following sections.

3.4.1   *Geometric construction: using a cross ratio*

Many algebraic invariants can be measured using geometric constructions which entail the formation of a cross ratio. Here a construction similar to the ones employed by Mohr, *et al.* in (85) is used. There are frequently many similar constructions that can be used to derive the invariants; for brevity a few examples only will be given.

For the set of five points whose invariant is to be computed, form four concurrent lines through the first point to each of the other four points (see Fig. 3.6). Four lines on a pencil are described projectively by a cross ratio (see Section 3.3). A second independent cross ratio can be measured by constructing a similar configuration of four lines from the second point. The five-point configuration is therefore described by the pair of cross ratios $\mathbf{I} = (\tau_1, \tau_2)$.

If there is an ordering on the points the invariant $\mathbf{I}$ is complete. This can be seen to be true for two different circumstances:

1. Four points must be fixed to constrain the projective representation in the plane. Initially, fix the first two points, and any two of the last three. Without loss of generality fix the third and fourth points, which leaves the coordinates of the fifth point to be determined. Now, construct the pencil of lines concurrent on the first point. Pick the three lines in the pencil that pass through the second, third and fourth points, and using these determine the line in the pencil that yields a cross ratio τ_1 with the first three lines. As τ is a complete invariant (see Section 3.3), the fourth line is determined uniquely, and the fifth point lies on this line. Repeat the process using τ_2 and a pencil through the second point to find a second constraint line

---

[10] If an isotropy exists, there is a group of transformations (a non-trivial subgroup of the entire transformation group), that leaves configuration unchanged. There are a number of ways to determine whether a configuration yields an isotropy group. The preferred 'formal' method seems to be the computation of the Lie algebra (98) for the configuration and the action, however a more straightforward geometric method can be used for many configurations. This simply involves computing the group of actions that leaves the geometric configuration unchanged; an isotropy exists if the group contains more than the identity element.

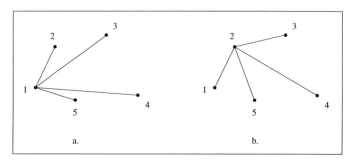

FIG. 3.6. For five coplanar points a pair of cross ratios can be constructed
as follows: draw lines from the first point to the other four to form four
concurrent lines (a). These four lines lie on a pencil and so are described
projectively by a cross ratio. From the second point construct a similar
set of lines and hence an independent cross ratio (b).

on which the fifth point lies. Intersect the two lines to determine the
location of the fifth point uniquely.

2. The positions of all except one of the first two points are defined;
   again, without loss of generality assume the first point is unknown.
   Using τ_1 construct the locus of the first point, this is the vertex of
   the set of lines through the four known points with cross ratio τ.
   Using Chasles' theorem (115) this locus is a conic through the four
   points. Then, using τ_2 constrain the first point to lie on a line through
   the second point. The unknown point lies on both the conic and the
   line. Two points satisfy this constraint, though as one of them is the
   second point, and the first and second points must be distinct, the
   location of the first point is defined uniquely.

One problem with this formulation is that the construction can fail for
certain non-general configurations. Should three points become collinear it
will be impossible to assign a non-singular value to one of the invariants;
this is because $s = 9$ for such a configuration. However, if the first two
points become collinear with any of the other points, it will be impossible
to form any invariants. This is because the construction is biased towards
the first two points. One way round this problem would be to use five
(dependent) invariants instead of the two, each one constructed using a set
of four lines at each different point.

The overall advantage of using the geometric construction to compute
the invariants for five coplanar points is that it is easy to observe the existence of the invariants, and to do limited reasoning about them. However,
without algebraic arguments it is very hard to determine which invariants
are independent, and which not.

3.4.2 *Canonical frame*

A canonical frame[11] construct can be used to form the invariant pair for
a set of five coplanar points. It makes use of the property that complete
invariant measures are isomorphic to the projective coordinates of points. A
simple version of the construction was used in eqn 3.3.9 where coordinates
were assigned to three of the points, and the fourth point had a projective
coordinate x (also invariant). The method of measurement of the invariant
in the planar case is to project four of the points to standard points in a
standard frame, and then measure the coordinates of the fifth point. The
map to the new frame uses the theory given in Section 3.1.3.

3.4.2.1 *Mapping to the canonical frame* As four points define a projec-
tive mapping between two frames, the first four points of a configuration
can be used to define the map between the image frame and a standard
measurement or *canonical* frame. The fifth point can then be mapped to
the new frame and its coordinates used as projective invariants. To ensure
that the coordinates really are invariant the first four points must always
be mapped to a standard set of four reference points in the canonical frame.
The choice of these points is arbitrary: the corners of the unit square may
be used (as in Fig. 3.7), or for example, the basis used in eqn 3.4.15. As
with the construction in Section 3.4.1 it is clear that this method of forming
the invariants is biased because if any three of the reference points become
collinear, or nearly so, the construction will fail. However, as with the cross
ratio, the invariant is complete if an ordering is imposed on the points.

There are practical considerations required for using the canonical frame
to measure invariants (these arise out of error effects). The most important
one is studied in more detail in Chapter 5 where the canonical frame is
used to measure invariants for planar curves. It considers the necessity of
taking care in placing the four reference points in the canonical frame.
Although it is hard to lay down firm rules for the locating of the points
certain obvious constraints are available, for example, no two points should
be placed too close together compared to the spacings of the other points.
There are also issues about how to choose the reference points from a data
set in an efficient and reliable manner.

The canonical frame does have one overriding advantage over algebraic
approaches in that it can often be used to determine at a glance when
invariants can be measured. Frequently it can even reveal how many invariants can be measured independently (for the case of five points the only
parameters that have not been fixed are the two coordinates of the fifth
point in the canonical frame).

---

[11] A canonical description is independent of vantage point used to observe the object,
Marr (78).

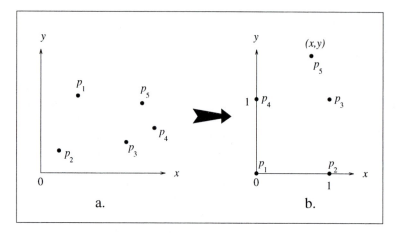

FIG. 3.7. One way of measuring the invariants of five coplanar points in a image (a) is to compute the map of four of the points $p_i, i \in \{1, \ldots, 4\}$ to reference points in the canonical frame (b). In this case the projection is to the corners of the unit square, though this is not the only configuration that could be used. Once this map is known p_5 can also be transformed to the new frame and its coordinates (x, y) used as invariants.

3.4.3   Algebraic construction: using determinants

As with the cross ratio, the invariants for five coplanar points can be defined using determinants. The proof of invariance follows in exactly the same way as that for the cross ratio. Given the five points in homogeneous form, $\mathbf{x}_i, i \in \{1, \ldots, 5\}$, two independent invariants are defined as:

$$I_1 = \frac{|M_{421}||M_{532}|}{|M_{432}||M_{521}|} \qquad \text{and} \qquad I_2 = \frac{|M_{421}||M_{531}|}{|M_{431}||M_{521}|}, \qquad (3.4.14)$$

where $M_{ijk} = [\mathbf{x}_i, \mathbf{x}_j, \mathbf{x}_k]$. Note that the invariants tend towards a singularity as any of the determinants in the denominators tend to zero. This may at first seem to be a problem, but a proper understanding of the error (stability) performance of the invariants can draw attention to such events; Section 4.3.1 demonstrates how to estimate the error. In fact the determinant becoming zero means that the three points contained in M_{ijk} are collinear, and so the algebraic invariant formulation responds to this specific configuration in a similar manner to the geometric and canonical frame forms.

The determinant formulation yields a very simple geometric interpretation of the invariants. $|M_{ijk}|$ is proportional to the area of the triangle with vertices $\{\mathbf{x}_i, \mathbf{x}_j, \mathbf{x}_k\}$, and so the invariants are formed from ratios of ratios of areas, or in fact from cross ratios of areas.

The determinant formulation of the invariants is the one actually used in LEWIS1. This is because it is far more *accessible* (easy to compute) than either the cross ratio or canonical frame formulations. However, it is hard to locate points with a sufficient degree of accuracy in an image for the invariants to be stable using just corner detectors (for example that of Wang, *et al.* (139)), or from high curvature points as found through the curvature primal sketch (2). Instead they have to be found by intersecting fitted features such as lines. As lines are dual to points in the plane a pair of invariants can be formed for a set of five lines, therefore rather than intersecting the lines and computing point invariants one can compute invariants directly with the lines. The result of this is that invariants are computed for sets of lines rather than points in LEWIS1.

Examples of the invariants computed for real image distortions are demonstrated in Fig. 3.8, and the invariant values given in Table 3.1. The fact that the values remain constant over a change in viewpoint demonstrates the stability of the invariants under image noise. In a recognition system the invariant values measured in the image would be used to *index* into the model base and subsequently *hypothesize* the presence of any object with an (approximately) matching invariant in the scene.

Two affine invariant values for each of the same images are also given in Table 3.1. These affine invariants are computed from the ratios of the areas of the triangles defined by the four intersection points of pairs of adjacent lines. Note that although the affine invariants remain reasonably constant between the object, the similarity and affine views, they change significantly for the perspective view. Therefore the invariant values could not be used reliably to index into the model base and are not suitable shape descriptions.

3.4.3.1 *Equivalence of the invariants and projective coordinates*   The

points $\mathbf{x}_i, i \in \{1, \ldots, 4\}$ can be assigned the following coordinates to form a projective basis in a canonical frame:

$$\mathbf{x}_1 = \begin{pmatrix} 1 \\ 0 \\ 0 \end{pmatrix}, \quad \mathbf{x}_2 = \begin{pmatrix} 0 \\ 1 \\ 0 \end{pmatrix}, \quad \mathbf{x}_3 = \begin{pmatrix} 0 \\ 0 \\ 1 \end{pmatrix}, \quad \mathbf{x}_4 = \begin{pmatrix} 1 \\ 1 \\ 1 \end{pmatrix}. \quad (3.4.15)$$

If the coordinates of $\mathbf{x}_5$ in this frame are set as $(x, y, z)^T$, it emerges after simple algebraic manipulations that:

$$I_1 = x/z \qquad \text{and} \qquad I_2 = y/z. \qquad (3.4.16)$$

Hence the coordinates of $\mathbf{x}_5$ that would be measured in a canonical frame with this choice of basis (that is the projective coordinates of $\mathbf{x}_5$) are exactly

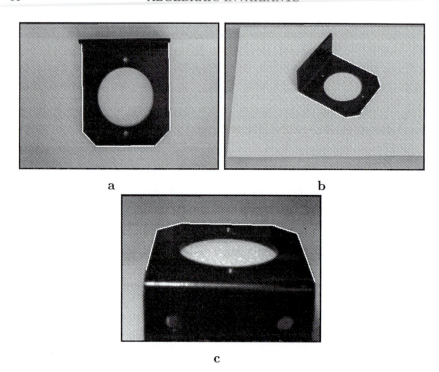

FIG. 3.8. These three views show similarity, affine and perspective distortions of a bracket. For each view the lines used to compute the invariants
are marked in white. A pair of five-line invariants are computed using
the determinant formulation for five points given in this section. The
principle of duality ensures that the invariants work for lines as well
as points. The invariant values for the images, and those actually measured on the object are shown in Table 3.1. The fact that they remain
essentially invariant demonstrates the stability of the invariants under
real imaging conditions.

the same as the invariants that would be measured using the determinant
formulation.

3.4.3.2 *Completeness* The five-point invariant formulated using determinants is also complete. Completeness can be seen algebraically for two
different cases: first, if the invariants (I_1, I_2), the coordinates of $\mathbf{x}_i, i \in \{1, 2\}$ and those of two other points are known (without loss of generality
$\mathbf{x}_i, i \in \{3, 4\}$), then the coordinates of $\mathbf{x}_5$ can be determined uniquely due
to the equivalence of the invariants and coordinates shown in eqn 3.4.16.

The second case assumes that the coordinates of either the first or
second point are unknown, but those of the four other points and (I_1, I_2)
are known. Again without loss of generality assume that $\mathbf{x}_1 = (x, y, z)^T$ is

Table 3.1 I_1 and I_2 are five-line invariants computed for the similarity, affine and perspective views of the bracket shown in Fig. 3.8. The fact that the values are consistent with those measured on the object, and do not change with viewpoint supports the theory that they are actually invariant. Affine invariants I_{a1} and I_{a2} have also been computed for the same configuration; it is clear that as perspective distortion is introduced the affine invariants no longer remain stable and so could not be used reasonably to describe the object shape. Details of how the affine invariants are computed is given in the text.

	I_1	I_2	I_{a1}	I_{a2}
object	0.840	1.236	0.739	1.083
similarity	0.842	1.234	0.706	1.051
affine	0.840	1.232	0.743	1.066
perspective	0.843	1.234	0.623	0.949

unknown. The first invariant in eqn 3.4.14 provides a linear constraint on $(\frac{x}{z})$ and $(\frac{y}{z})$:

$$(a_1(\frac{x}{z}) + b_1(\frac{y}{z}) + c_1)I_1 = a_2(\frac{x}{z}) + b_2(\frac{y}{z}) + c_2,$$

where the coefficients take known values that are functions of $\mathbf{x}_i, i \in \{2, \ldots, 5\}$. This constraint is derived by taking the expression for I_1 and multiplying through by the determinant of the right-hand side. Furthermore, I_2 can be rewritten as a function including I_1:

$$I_2 = \frac{|M_{531}||M_{432}|}{|M_{431}||M_{532}|} I_1.$$

Subsequently, the second invariant also provides a linear constraint on $(\frac{x}{z})$ and $(\frac{y}{z})$:

$$(d_1(\frac{x}{z}) + e_1(\frac{y}{z}) + f_1)I_2 = (d_2(\frac{x}{z}) + e_2(\frac{y}{z}) + f_2)I_1,$$

with the coefficients functions of $\mathbf{x}_i, i \in \{2, \ldots, 5\}$. Satisfying these two linear constraints determines $(\frac{x}{z})$ and $(\frac{y}{z})$ uniquely, and so the invariant (I_1, I_2) is complete.

3.4.3.3 *Singularities* A major problem with the determinant formulae given in eqn 3.4.14 is that both invariants are undefined or zero if either the points $\{1, 2, 4\}$ or $\{1, 2, 5\}$ become collinear, or nearly so; this is because the determinants tend to zero. However, one should still be able to form a single invariant with a non-zero or non-infinite value.[12] The simplest way to ensure that at least one of the invariants will be well defined is to replace the second invariant with:

$$I'_2 = \frac{|\mathbf{M}_{123}||\mathbf{M}_{145}||\mathbf{M}_{345}|}{|\mathbf{M}_{245}||\mathbf{M}_{134}||\mathbf{M}_{135}|}.$$

Now I_1 and I'_2 share no common determinants and so if only three points become collinear one of the invariants will still be meaningful. If four or more points become collinear it is possible that both invariants will be undefined, but in this case one should use the cross ratio on the line containing the points as an invariant descriptor. Unfortunately there is no way to form an invariant composed of products of pairs of determinants that is both independent of I_1, and behaves differently at degeneracies. Generally, the more complicated the structure of an invariant the less likely it is to be complete. As a result of this there is a desire to attempt to form invariants using pairs of products before triples, and so on.

An interesting issue is how to form the invariants so that they are independent and also behave well for special configurations. The process used to derive eqn 3.4.16 is one way of determining independence of the invariants; if I_2 turned out to be a function of I_1 only, then the invariants would have been functionally dependent. Fortunately lists of known independent projective invariants are given in text books such as Weyl (143), though such books do not tell us about the properties of new invariants.

3.5   Two coplanar conics

Using a further application of the counting argument a pair of conics yields two independent projective invariants (each conic has five degrees of freedom, therefore $n = 2 \times 5 - 8 = 2$). The invariants can be constructed using both geometric and algebraic methods.

3.5.1   *Geometric construction: using the cross ratio*

Two conics generically intersect in four points.[13] These points, $\{A, B, C, D\}$ are shown in Fig. 3.9 for a situation in which all of the intersections are real. Using Chasles' theorem, a conic is defined by four points and a cross ratio.

---

[12]In the current implementations grouping is used to prevent both situations arising, and so at least one of the values of I_1 and I_2 can always be used. Using the grouping paradigm given in Chapter 6 only the points $\mathbf{x}_i, i \in \{1, 3, 5\}$ can become collinear (or dually in the actual implementation, lines concurrent). As there is no determinant of $\mathbf{M}_{135}$ in I_1, it will always be well formed, though I_2 will go to zero.

[13]These intersections may be real or complex. In the sequel, no conceptual difference exists between cases in which algebraic objects intersect at real or complex points.

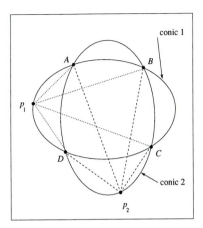

FIG. 3.9. Four intersection points can always be formed for a pair of conics.
For the conics in this figure these points are real. From any other point
on each conic a pencil of lines can be constructed as shown, and the
cross ratios $\tau_i, i \in \{1, 2\}$ measured. By Chasles' theorem the values of
τ_i are independent of the choice of p_i.

Put another way, for the four points $\{A, B, C, D\}$, the locus of points p_1
through which the four lines shown in Fig. 3.9 have a cross ratio τ_1 is conic
1. Developing this further, the four intersection points lying on the conic
1, and the conic itself, yield an invariant τ_1. Similarly a second invariant
τ_2 can be formed for the four points and conic 2.

When the intersections are real there is an ordering imposed on the
points (each conic is isomorphic to the projective line). Therefore the invariants should be expressed in the form of the symmetric function $\sigma(\tau)$
given in eqn 3.3.13.

If the intersections are complex (or a real and complex conjugate pair),
care must be taken to reduce the ambiguity of the shape of the configuration for a given invariant value. This is because the σ invariant no longer
applies, though a different symmetric function can again be constructed.
The intersections will always be in complex conjugate pairs, say $\{a, \bar{a}\}$
and $\{b, \bar{b}\}$. From these pairs eight different combinations of the cross ratio
can be computed: $\{a, \bar{a} : b, \bar{b}\}, \{\bar{a}, a : b, \bar{b}\}, \ldots, \{\bar{b}, b : \bar{a}, a\}$ (more details
are given in Appendix B). Using the results of Springer (124), p. 15, only
two different cross ratios can be measured for these combinations, that is
$\{a, \bar{a} : b, \bar{b}\} = \tau$ or $\{\bar{a}, a : b, \bar{b}\} = \frac{1}{\tau}$. A symmetric function is therefore
defined in τ: $\rho(\tau) = \tau + \frac{1}{\tau}$, which, when each conic is considered to be
isomorphic to the projective line, gives:

$$\rho(x) = \frac{2x^2 - 2x + 1}{x(x - 1)}.$$

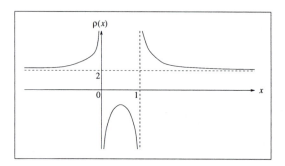

FIG. 3.10. The cross ratio for the intersection points for a pair of conics
and a conic locus (one of the two conics). The parameter x is the coordinate of the fourth point when the conic is mapped to a line, and the
other three points fixed to lie at $0, 1$ and ∞.

This function is plotted in Fig. 3.10. As the inverse of the graph is not
single valued the invariant is not complete.

3.5.2 *Algebraic construction: eigenvalue decomposition*

For a pair of conics $C_i, i \in \{1, 2\}$, two projective invariants can be formed
using an eigenvalue decomposition:

$$I_1 = \frac{\text{Trace}[C_1^{-1}C_2] \cdot |C_1|^{1/3}}{|C_2|^{1/3}} \qquad \text{and} \qquad I_2 = \frac{\text{Trace}[C_2^{-1}C_1] \cdot |C_2|^{1/3}}{|C_1|^{1/3}}.$$

If the conics are normalized so that $|C_i| = 1$ the invariants take on the
simpler forms of:

$$I_1 = \text{Trace}[C_1^{-1}C_2] \qquad \text{and} \qquad I_2 = \text{Trace}[C_2^{-1}C_1].$$

These invariants are complete for conics with real curve segments on the
plane as has been shown by Maybank and Beardsley (83).

The dual of a conic is a conic, or more precisely a *conic envelope*: the
dual of C is C^{-1}. This means that the dual construction for the invariants
of conic envelopes takes exactly the same form.

These invariants have been tested extensively in an object recognition
system and have been found to have good noise characteristics. A simple
example showing the measured invariants for similarity, affine and perspective views of the computer tape shown in Fig. 3.11 are given in Table 3.2.
The small deviation of the invariants demonstrates their stability; more
complete results are given in (42). Note that in this case the values of the
two invariants are very similar. This is not generally the case and is a result of using an object containing a pair of concentric circles of a similar
size. The conic pair invariant does provide sufficient discrimination between
objects to be a useful shape descriptor in a recognition system.

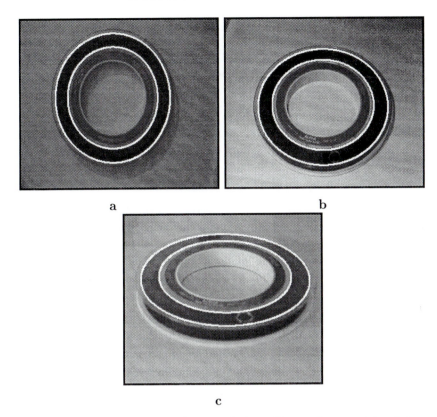

FIG. 3.11. These three views show similarity, affine and perspective distortions of a computer tape with the conics used to compute the invariants marked in white. The invariant values are given in Table 3.2.

There has also been a rigorous mathematical treatise done by Quan, *et al.* (103) showing the relationship of the invariants to the eigenvalues of the matrices $(C_1^{-1} C_2)$ and $(C_2^{-1} C_1)$.

The conic pair invariant provides one example of an algebraic invariant that out-performs a geometric one. The invariant formed through the use of the cross ratio is not complete, unlike the one that is a function of the eigenvalues of the conic matrices, and so it would be expected to provide less discrimination within a recognition system.

3.6   A conic and two points

3.6.1   *Geometric construction*

There are two simple geometric constructions that demonstrate the measurement of a single invariant for a conic and a pair of points. The first one (Fig. 3.12a) intersects the conic with the line AB and computes the

Table 3.2 *The conic pair invariants computed for the similarity, affine and perspective views of the computer tape shown in Fig. 3.11. Note the stability of the measured values with respect to change in viewpoint.*

	I_1	I_2
object	3.073	3.082
similarity	3.074	3.082
affine	3.072	3.080
perspective	3.070	3.078

cross ratio $\{A, B : C, D\}$. If the intersections of the line and the conic are complex the cross ratio can still be computed.

The second construction is more interesting because it shows how to construct a cross ratio for the configuration of a conic and a pair of lines (the dual of a conic and a pair of points). Using Fig. 3.12b, compute the polar lines[14] of the points A and B, and form the four intersection points of the polars with the conics, $p_i, i \in \{1, \ldots, 4\}$. These points then form a cross ratio $\{p_1, p_2 : p_3, p_4\}$ as in Section 3.5.1. Note that there are ordering ambiguities for both of the constructions as points C and D can be interchanged, or p_1 with p_2 and p_3 with p_4. Ideally this is overcome using symmetric forms of the cross ratio.

Both of the constructions can easily be shown to produce incomplete invariants. For the first case, consider when point A and the conic are defined. Then, defining the line through A on which B lies defines the full eight degrees of freedom of the projective representation: completeness is satisfied if the location of B is determined uniquely on the line. C and D are defined by the intersection of the line with the conic, though only up to an ambiguity (that is C and D can be exchanged). This therefore results in a two-fold ambiguity in the location of B, one for each ordering of C and D, and hence the invariant is incomplete (choosing B to satisfy the cross ratio with one choice of C and D, and then swapping C and D will produce the reciprocal cross ratio).

The second case is similar: again define A and the conic, but this time also p_3. Given the value of the cross ratio there is a two-fold ambiguity in the location of p_4 (as p_1 and p_2 can be swapped), and so B is not defined uniquely.

---

[14]The equations of the polars are given by $\mathbf{l}_i = \mathbf{C}\mathbf{x}_i$. The polar of a point (a pole) can be constructed as follows: determine the two lines through the point that are tangent to the conic. The polar passes through the points of tangency of the lines to the conic.

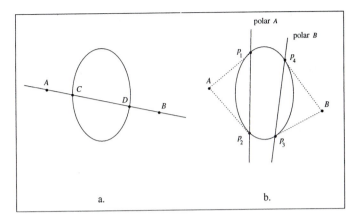

FIG. 3.12. Two sample constructions for finding the invariant of a conic
and two points. From (a), intersect the line joining the two points (AB),
and the conic to give C and D. Then use the value of $\{A, B : C, D\}$
as the invariant. Alternatively from (b), compute the polars of A
and B and intersect these lines with the conic to give the points
$p_i, i \in \{1, \ldots, 4\}$. The invariant is then given by $\{p_1, p_2 : p_3, p_4\}$. From
this second construction it becomes apparent how to form an invariant
for a conic and a pair of lines.

3.6.2 *Algebraic construction*

For a conic C and two points $\mathbf{x}_i, i \in \{1, 2\}$ the invariant can be represented
algebraically as:

$$I_{12} = \frac{(\mathbf{x}_1^T \mathsf{C} \mathbf{x}_2)^2}{(\mathbf{x}_1^T \mathsf{C} \mathbf{x}_1)(\mathbf{x}_2^T \mathsf{C} \mathbf{x}_2)}.$$

This form of the invariant can immediately be seen to be incomplete: if I_{12},
C and $\mathbf{x}_2$ are given, $\mathbf{x}_1$ is constrained to lie on the conic:

$$\mathbf{x}_1^T [\, (I_{12} \, \mathbf{x}_2^T \mathsf{C} \mathbf{x}_2) \, \mathsf{C} - \mathsf{C} \, \mathbf{x}_2 \mathbf{x}_2^T \, \mathsf{C} \,] \, \mathbf{x}_1 = 0.$$

Defining the conic and the second point constrains only seven out of eight
degrees of freedom of the projective representation; constraining the eighth
parameter, say by assigning a value to the x coordinate of $\mathbf{x}_1$, will mean that
the y coordinate can take two values and so the invariant is not complete.

As in Section 3.4 this form of the invariant has been computed for
the similarity, affine and perspective image sequence of the bracket. The
formulation is for the dual construction of a conic and two lines. This
is shown in Fig. 3.13, with the invariant values in Table 3.3. Again the
stability of the invariant form is demonstrated by the lack of change of the
measured values under change in viewpoint.

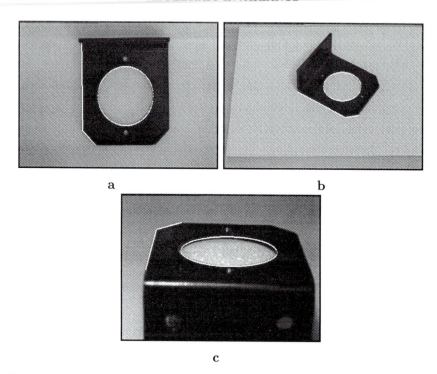

FIG. 3.13. These three views show similarity, affine and perspective distortions on a bracket with the conic and two lines used to compute the
invariants marked in white. The invariant values are given in Table 3.3.

An affine invariant has also been computed for the configuration and it
fails clearly for the perspective case. The affine invariant is computed from
the ratio of the area of a triangle and the conic. The triangle is formed
from the intersection point of the two lines, and the points of tangency to
the conic of lines passing through the intersection point.

The conic and line-pair invariant was used in an early form of LEWIS1.
It was found, however, to produce moderately little discrimination between
the objects in the model base. This was partly due to the fact that this
invariant is the only one that is not complete out of the three used in the
implementation. Note also that all objects containing a conic and a pair of
lines are mapped onto a single line parametrized by I_{12}. Due to this there is
a likelihood that a number of objects (when error bounds are included) will
overlap. As a consequence of the complexity argument in Section 2.3.1 it
was decided that an invariant with a higher-dimensional index space should
be tried. This is an invariant formed by a conic and three lines and takes
the form (I_{12}, I_{23}, I_{31}). Now objects are mapped into a three-dimensional
space and are less likely to coincide. In practice the approach worked and

Table 3.3 *The conic and line pair invariants computed for the similarity, affine and perspective views of the bracket shown in Fig. 3.13. Note the stability of the measured values with respect to change in viewpoint. Again an affine invariant I_a has been computed for the configuration to demonstrate the superiority of the projective invariant.*

	I	I_a
object	1.33	0.398
similarity	1.33	0.389
affine	1.31	0.403
perspective	1.28	0.437

far more discrimination was provided by the invariant.

3.7   Physical camera projectivities

One can build on the observation that topology is preserved under real imaging conditions discussed in Section 3.3.1. In fact, a much stronger constraint can be applied to objects in the image:

For a real camera, ordering is not only preserved on the projective line, but also the image of an object cannot pass through an ideal point on the image.

This statement has a meaning only when the object is continuous and of finite size (that is it does not apply to isolated points). This is explained geometrically in Fig. 3.14. If any points on an object project to a point at infinity on the image line, then the object must pass through the line Π. As this is within the camera, in real images such a situation cannot arise. Extending from the line case to the plane is trivial.

The existence of this result places limits on the region of the projective transform space that can actually be used, and is used during recognition hypothesis verification (see Section 4.2.6). Generally only a restricted region of the eight-dimensional projective space that describes a plane-to-plane projectivity can be encountered in practice. The shape of this region can be understood by studying the form of the projectivity given in Appendix A, though the bounds on the region are not of a simple nature.

An alternative approach is to consider what restrictions can be placed on the shape of the object in the image by realizing that the object must lie within a cone centred on the optical axis. Again this bound is somewhat awkward to consider from the general viewpoint (that is without actual knowledge of the camera set-up), but it can be helpful. For example, one property that is somewhat meaningless in the projective plane is that of the convex hull of a set of features. However, using the argument used in Fig. 3.14 one can prevent any part of the object from passing through the ideal

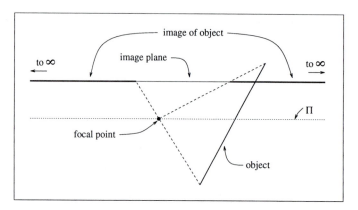

FIG. 3.14. Objects that project to infinity on the image line must pass through the line Π. The image line and Π are parallel. For a real camera this situation cannot arise, and so a restriction can be placed on the valid set of object-to-image projectivities. Note that the mathematically correct, though physically unrealistic situation is shown where the focal point is behind the image plane rather than in front.

line in the image, and so no part of the convex hull of the object defined in its own Euclidean plane can project to a point at infinity in the image. Subsequently, the convex hull computed on the (Euclidean) image plane is the projection of the convex hull on the object, and so the same features (object or projected) will lie on the perimeter of the hull in both cases. This process can be formalized by saying that under *allowable* projections, the number of points on the convex hull of a shape is invariant. This property is exploited during the verification of hypotheses in Section 4.2.6.

3.8   Conclusions

This chapter has provided the background theory required for the rest of this book. A brief introduction to projective geometry has been given, though the interested reader is encouraged to look at the book by Mundy and Zisserman (92), and possibly those by Semple and Kneebone (115) or Springer (124). The notation that will be used has also been introduced and some familiarity gained with respect to the way that points, lines, conics and projective transformations are represented and manipulated.

After an introduction to projective invariants using the cross ratio, the three invariants used in the index-based recognition system LEWIS1 were discussed, and their dual forms considered. The invariants are: two invariants for five coplanar lines; two invariants for a pair of coplanar conics; and an invariant triple for a conic coplanar with three lines (built on the conic two-line invariant).

Each of the invariants were reviewed using a number of different formulations that varied between being totally algebraic and totally geometric. The different versions frequently have contrasting performance characteristics, of which one, completeness, was discussed in detail. In practice the algebraic formulations have been used as they are generally more likely to be complete. They are also easy to implement using simple algebraic expressions. Examples of the algebraic invariants being computed for real images were shown and comparisons drawn with affine invariants computed for the same features. In all cases the projective invariants were more stable than the affine ones because the imaging process is modelled most precisely by a projective distortion; an affine distortion is only an approximation, valid only for restrictive viewing configurations such as a narrow field of view or for a small object depth with respect to viewing distance.

Finally, the observation was made that the projective group is too general a deformation model for real imaging situations, though it is the smallest enveloping group. In fact the only deformations that occur are a small subset of the projective group which is unfortunately hard to parametrize. However, by studying which effects can be observed one can hope to improve the performance of the invariant shape descriptors that are used.

4

THE RECOGNITION ARCHITECTURE: ALGEBRAIC INVARIANTS: LEWIS1

This chapter describes the LEWIS recognition system built around the three-phase selection–indexing–correspondence paradigm. In particular, the indexes are constructed from the plane algebraic invariants discussed in the previous chapter, and so the details given in this chapter are most relevant to a specific implementation called LEWIS1 that recognizes objects containing sets of coplanar lines and conics. The emphasis is very much on the value of the indexing stage, that is whether it is beneficial to the efficiency of the entire recognition process in contrast to a linear search through the model base. However, all of the different steps of the recognition process from edge detection through to verification are described in detail.

The architecture is not only useful for describing objects of an algebraic nature. The system is principally of a modular design that allows processes to be swapped in and out depending on the precise application. Therefore, LEWIS can be modified to account for the invariants based on smooth plane curves as will be shown in Chapter 5 in a similar system LEWIS2. One should consequently bear in mind that this chapter is not just presenting a single recognition system, but is also proposing a modular framework by which to do recognition for any class of object for which invariant shape descriptions are available.

First, the concept of an *indexing function* is introduced in Section 4.1. Then, the recognition architecture is described in detail in Section 4.2. This reviews the processes of extracting Canny (22) edge data from images and fitting algebraic forms (lines and conics) to the edgels (the details of the fitting processes are not given in this chapter but in Chapter 6). Then, the algebraic features are grouped together and invariants computed. These invariants are used to form *indexes* that index into the model base and form *hypotheses*. Then a novel algorithm is described that allows the merging of hypotheses into *joint hypotheses* which are confirmed or rejected by projecting the model to the image. This final process is called verification and is equivalent to correspondence.

Prior to giving examples of LEWIS1 being tested on a number of different images, and an analysis of its performance made, the procedure for building up the model base is given. Due to the projective nature of the shape descriptors model acquisition can be achieved entirely from images and Euclidean models are not required. This process essentially follows the recognition procedure, but the model base is written to rather than read. This is described in Section 4.3. Included in this section are details of experiments used to determine the error characteristics of the invariants; comparisons are made between the experimental results and theory.

Many lesson were learned whilst building LEWIS1. In fact, it can be seen clearly that the proposed architecture is not the final answer for solving more general recognition problems. However, most of the modules would have to be changed little to incorporate them within a more successful framework. The end of the chapter concentrates on describing the short-comings of the current approach and proposes some alternatives that should be investigated.

4.1 Indexing functions

The primary purpose of this book is to demonstrate how the efficiency of a recognition task can be enhanced when models are indexed from a library without the requirement for search. The indexing step is achieved through the use of *indexing functions*. An indexing function is a measure of scene features that is consistent with a measure on the object model.

We propose that the preferred indexing functions for use in recognition are also invariant to the imaging process, and so they are also invariants. However, the following facts should be realized:

1. Invariant functions are not necessarily indexing functions. For instance, a curve signature of a two-dimensional plane curve (which is also a plane curve) is an invariant, but it can in no way be used to index into a model base. An index is a finite-dimensional numeric vector (generally the elements take real values or are integers resulting from a quantization of the real numbers). Indexing functions can take either scene features or measured invariants as their arguments, but their outputs are always vectors; for the algebraic invariants described in Chapter 3 the indexing functions simply return measured invariants as vectors, and thus the invariants themselves could be used as indexes. However, for smooth plane curves (as will be described in Chapter 5), the index functions are more complicated as they have to return vectors from curve signatures.

2. Index functions need not be invariant to the imaging process. Jacobs (62) derived functions of image measurements whose values change with viewpoint. However, these values are guaranteed (up to image noise) to lie in a low-dimensional space that in some manner represents all possible views of the model features. Therefore, the indexing process tests whether an image measurement lies within the low-dimensional space, and if so creates a recognition hypothesis.

3. Indexing functions may not always be derived using constructions formulated in the image. For instance, indexing functions for three-dimensional shapes are frequently derived from their 3D invariants.

Often these invariants cannot be measured in an image, but must be determined through a reconstruction process.[15] Examples of this are given in Chapter 8.

The concept of the (invariant) indexing function can be developed formally as follows: the index is considered to be a vector, $\mathbf{M}$, which selects a particular model from the library. Furthermore, the index is a function only of the invariants of a set of imaged model features. If the model features are $\mathbf{F}$, we denote the set of invariants by $\mathbf{I}(\mathbf{F})$. The features may be those observed in any projection of the model object, or they may be features recovered from the image through a reconstruction process (this is particularly true for the invariants of three-dimensional shapes). However, we stress that $\mathbf{F}$ and subsequently $\mathbf{I}(\mathbf{F})$ can be measured without any prior knowledge of the object identity to which they belong.

As a result of this, $\mathbf{M}$ can be computed from any image projection of the model features; the practical consequence of this is that models can be constructed simply by acquiring one or a few image views of the object in isolation. If $\mathbf{F}_{\text{model}}$ is the set of features actually on an object, and T is the transformation representing both the imaging process that takes an object in an arbitrary pose onto the camera and the following derivation of the vector $\mathbf{F}$, then using the definition of a (scalar) invariant given in Section 3.2:

$$\mathbf{I}(T(\mathbf{F}_{\text{model}})) = \mathbf{I}(\mathbf{F}_{\text{model}}),$$

or, $\mathbf{I}_{\text{image}} = \mathbf{I}_{\text{model}}$. An indexing function can then be defined as follows:

Definition 4.1 *If* $\mathbf{M}$ *is an invariant indexing function, then:*

$$\mathbf{M}(\mathbf{I}_{\text{image}}) = \mathbf{M}(\mathbf{I}_{\text{model}}),$$

or, more completely:

$$\mathbf{M}(\mathbf{I}(T(\mathbf{F}_{\text{model}}))) = \mathbf{M}(\mathbf{I}(\mathbf{F}_{\text{model}})).$$

Directly one can see that $\mathbf{M}$ is also a scalar invariant under T, and so the value of an index function for a set of object features does not change with viewpoint.

The definition above assumes that both the indexes for the model and for the object can be measured perfectly in a scene. In practice, the mea-

---

[15]Often the 3D structure can be computed from the image without an explicit reconstruction process. However, one can argue that the measurements taken in the image are identical to those that would have been recovered through a reconstruction process, and so in fact an implicit reconstruction has been achieved. Note however, that in other cases the two sets of measurements may not be equivalent.

surements are imprecise due to both modelling and imaging errors.[16] The index is therefore quantized, as is the index space, to account for this error:

$$\mathbf{Q}(\mathbf{M}(\mathbf{I}_{model}) + \mathbf{E}_{model}) = \mathbf{Q}(\mathbf{M}(\mathbf{I}_{image}) + \mathbf{E}_{image}).$$

Note that the quantization function $\mathbf{Q}$ is the same for both the model and the image. This is a direct result of being able to acquire models from images, and so the error characteristics $\mathbf{E}_{model}$ and $\mathbf{E}_{image}$ are assumed to be the same.

In the results reported in this chapter the index functions are invariant to projective transformations of the image plane. Each element of the index vector $\mathbf{M}$ is an invariant measure computed from a group of model features such as conics, lines, points and plane curve segments. Ideally, the index function should uniquely label a model from the library, but in practice due to noise one should be satisfied if a small number of models are retrieved with the same index. Generally, the numbers of models retrieved will be significantly less than the number of models in the library and so a benefit has been realized without an exhaustive search of the library.

Indexing functions are becoming a familiar tool for recognition. Many examples are already available in the literature: Forsyth, *et al.* (42), Nielsen (97) (both projective), Lamdan, *et al.* (68) Wayner (140), Clemens and Jacobs (24), Huttenlocher (59), Taubin and Cooper (130) (all affine).

4.2 The recognition process

An outline of the recognition architecture is given in Fig. 4.1. Note the modular design with a simple flow of control implemented as a pipeline that takes an input image and outputs recognition hypotheses. The structure of LEWIS1 is very similar to those of the systems reviewed in Chapter 2, except for the presence of two modules: the indexing phase; and the hypothesis merging step. The former is obviously present to conform with the invariant indexing paradigm, the latter was introduced to enhance efficiency further within the system. Its purpose and workings will be described in detail later in the chapter.

Note also the common architecture for the acquisition and recognition stages. This is a direct result of using a projective representation for the shape of planar algebraic objects. Section 4.3 describes acquisition through the use of some simple examples.

The same architecture has been used for a number of different invariants, including those for three-dimensional objects. Therefore, one should bear in mind that although this chapter concentrates on the use of plane

---

[16]This is not just due to image noise which is often considered to be the sole cause of error, but also due to poor segmentation that is caused by distractors and shadows. Section 4.3.1 considers this further.

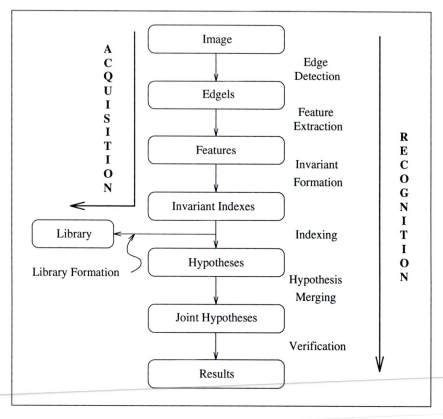

FIG. 4.1. LEWIS has a single greyscale image as input and the outputs are verified hypotheses with associated confidence values. The content of the boxes are the data structures available at any one moment during the recognition cycle; the processes (or modules) are listed on the right-hand side and show how one data structure is mapped to another. Many of the processes are shared by the acquisition and the recognition paths. The recognition system is similar to more conventional recognition systems in all but the indexing and hypothesis formation stages.

algebraic invariants other invariants and their related indexing functions can be substituted as required. As a result, when other invariants are discussed in the following chapters of this book and examples of recognition provided, there will be little discussion of the actual system used to do the recognition as most of the details are in this chapter.

One significant module that has been omitted here is that for feature extraction. Although very specific to the use of algebraic invariants the module has been described separately in Chapter 6 as it is concerned very closely with implementation details rather than more general architectural issues. Chapter 6 also includes the details of the feature grouping process which interacts fundamentally with the efficiency of recognition. It is likely that the reader will have to move back and forth between the two chapters to really understand the process in its entirity.

4.2.1 Edge detection

The shape descriptors used for recognition within this book and in most other recognition systems are geometric. Geometric information from the world is observable most accurately, though it would be untrue to say exclusively, through studying *changes* in the intensity distribution in an image. Generally, physical edges and surface markings in the world (which are all of the features we are interested in) are characterized by the boundaries between regions of different contrast in the image.

Edge detectors attempt to localize these boundaries through a number of different techniques. There are a large number of different edge detectors available; every result in this book was produced using a Canny (22) edge detector with full hysteresis. The Canny filter takes a greyscale image as input, and has as output linked edgel chains. An edgel has both a (floating point) location and an orientation.

The actual implementation we use is based on a transputer array which makes it both fast and efficient.[17] Even with this, edge detection is still the slowest part of the whole recognition process: the Canny process takes about 1 second on the transputer array with communications to a Sparc2 taking about 15 seconds for a 512×341 image;[18] segmentation takes 5 seconds; matching less than a second; and verification normally about 2 seconds. These times are typical of recognition performance measured over hundreds of images with varying complexities.

An example of the output of the Canny edge detector when applied to a simple recognition scene is shown in Fig. 4.2. Note that shadows and specularities cause problems for scenes even as simple as this one. A typical object from the model base is in the centre-right of the image.

4.2.2 Feature extraction

Continuous edge curves are extracted from the subpixel-accuracy edge image, then lines and conics are fitted using incremental fitters (see Chapter 6 for details). As stated in Section 3.4.3, points are not used to form the algebraic invariants because they cannot be located with sufficient accuracy. The only way that they can be located sufficiently well would be through the intersections of lines, but this would result in the invariants formed using the points being dependent on similar invariants for the lines.

---

[17]Implemented by Han Wang.

[18]If the Canny is run entirely on a Sparc2 it takes 25 to 30 seconds.

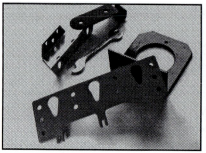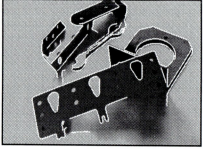

a   b

FIG. 4.2. The Canny edgels superimposed on a grey-level image of a scene. Note that the edge detector has not been able to characterize accurately all of the object boundaries in the image due to effects such as shadows and specularities.

The lines and conics are grouped into configurations for which invariants can be computed (groups containing sets of five lines, a conic and three lines, and conic pairs). These are the groups denoted by the vector $\mathbf{F}$. The grouping process used to form $\mathbf{F}$ for lines exploits continuity provided by the Canny edge chains, and conics are grouped by proximity in the scene. Full details are given in Chapter 6. The grouping process is efficient and is linear with respect to the number of lines (note that a naive grouping procedure would form ${}^{l}P_5 = O(l^5)$ line groups in an image containing l lines). Therefore, it does not form an excessive number of groups which would slow down the recognition process. However, there are of course problems encountered with using continuity as the sole grouping cue, these and possible extensions are discussed in Chapter 6.

An example of the output from the feature extraction phase is shown in Fig. 4.3; the conics and lines were fitted to the edge data shown in Fig. 4.2. Many more examples of the segmentation process are shown in Section 6.1.1.

If invariants are to be constructed from different types of feature sets then an alternative segmentation algorithm can be substituted for the one used for lines and conics. For example, should the model base contain objects characterized by smooth plane curves (as in LEWIS2) one should use the segmentation technique given in Section 6.2. For three-dimensional objects a variety of different segmentation methods are required, though the examples in Chapter 8 all require either the straight line fitting or the smooth plane curve segmentation routines in Chapter 6. The point to remember is that the modular design of the recognition architecture means that the feature extraction module (or in fact any module) can be replaced without significant effect on the rest of the system.

FIG. 4.3. Lines and conics are fitted using efficient incremental fitting procedures described in Section 6.1.1. The edge data used for the fit is shown in Fig. 4.2.

4.2.3 *Invariant formation*

An invariant vector $\mathbf{I}(\mathbf{F})$ is computed for each feature group $\mathbf{F}$ produced by the feature extraction process. For algebraic invariants $\mathbf{I}$ is calculated directly by applying the theory in Chapter 3 to the algebraic forms found through fitting. The components of the vector are the different invariants. $\mathbf{I}$ always has the following dimensions:

1. two dimensions for the five-line invariant;
2. two dimensions for the conic-pair invariant;
3. three dimensions for the conic and three-line invariant.

Note that in general $\mathbf{I}$ need not necessarily be a vector; for certain feature configurations it may be a curve signature or in fact any property of an object that is invariant under imaging.

4.2.4 *Indexing*

The invariant $\mathbf{I}$ is mapped into an index vector $\mathbf{M}$ and used to index into the model library. $\mathbf{M}$ is computed without any knowledge of which object caused the image data. This is why indexing enhances the efficiency of the recognition process: without making any assumptions about which object is in a scene, one can produce a list of recognition hypotheses.

For plane algebraic invariants the function $\mathbf{M}$ applied to $\mathbf{I}$ could be considered to be the identity operator. However, one can also include a quantization procedure within $\mathbf{M}$ that immediately derives an index to an integer index space (which is a space parametrized by the integers). The form of $\mathbf{M}$ is therefore:

$$\mathbf{M}_i(\mathbf{I}_i) = \mathbf{Q}\left(\frac{\mathbf{I}_i - \mathbf{I}_{\min}}{\delta_i}\right),$$

where the subscript i denotes the ith component of a vector, $\mathbf{I}_{\min}$ some minimum expected value of the invariant for the model base, $\mathbf{Q}$ a rounding function, and δ_i a quantization parameter. δ_i is really the most interesting element in the indexing function, though it is also the hardest to describe. Its value depends on the specific invariant being used and the expected errors that are to be observed in a scene. It also depends on the separation of the models in the model base and can only really be determined by observing the invariant distributions for the objects to be recognized.

Ideally δ_i should be as large as possible to keep the index space small, but small enough so that a single object occupies only near complete cells and does not just fringe into neighbouring cells. Generally, we have found that δ_i should be up to an order of magnitude smaller than the expected errors in the invariant. Both experimental and analytic bounds can be put on the size of the expected invariant error. Details are given in Section 4.3.1. The size of this bound must be known when the indexing space is constructed.

The indexing function does not always take such a simple form. For smooth plane curves the process of deriving an index is more complicated, as is true for the invariant formation process of Van Gool, *et al.* (136). This is because the invariants for these features are curve signatures rather than a finite set of numeric values. Details of how indexes are computed for this form of invariant are given in Section 5.2.

For all forms of invariant, each object feature group is represented by a collection of points that define a region in index space. The size of the region depends upon the expected error in the measurement of the invariant and the quantization δ_i. A complete object is represented by a number of these regions in (perhaps) different indexing spaces; this is because a single object is frequently described by a number of different invariant configurations (for example the bracket shown in Figs 3.8 and 3.13 can be described by five coplanar lines, or a conic and three lines). Indexing proceeds by matching the measured invariant vector to a point in the invariant space. This process is made more efficient using a hash table that allows simultaneous indexing on all of the elements of the measurement vector. Each index into the library produces a list of (possibly empty) hypotheses. These are then merged and verified using techniques described below. Note that the hash table is only an implementation of the indexing space, and it is clashing within the latter that causes the problems in recognition (instantiated as false positives). The problem of choosing an optimal hashing function has not been investigated within LEWIS1 because commercially available hashing libraries have high performances.

It is conceivable that at this stage any of the correspondence algorithms reviewed in Chapter 2 could be used to verify the hypotheses reached through indexing; so far we have effectively replaced the linear search through a model library used by these algorithms with an efficient indexing step which has little dependence on the number of models in the library. In fact, indexing has made an association between a small number of model and image features and so one could immediately initialize a hypothesize and test scheme such as those of Bolles and Horaud (12) or Lowe (72) which search for more model support in the image. For various reasons a slightly different route to verification is taken which is described below. However, first an intermediate processing step is described that substantially improves both recognition performance and the understanding of the scene that can be derived through recognition.

4.2.5 Hypothesis merging

So far LEWIS1 has used only *semi-local* shape cues to form recognition hypotheses. These use only a fraction of the object boundary to form invariant indexes. A distinction can be made between three scales of shape description:

1. **Local:** the shape is described at a single point on the object, for example the differential invariant of Halphen (144).

2. **Semi-local:** a description is provided by a number of proximal points, for example the semi-differential invariants in (5, 136), or the algebraic invariants used here.

3. **Global:** the entire object shape is used in the description. This is typical of Fourier methods (137), moment invariants (130), or isoperimetric normalization techniques (120).

The reason for using either local or semi-local description is that one can achieve a reasonable level of tolerance to occlusion. Should any small part of an object be either occluded, or simply not observable due to poor segmentation, then a global measure will fail. More details about the trade-offs between global and local (or semi-local) description are given in Chapter 7; here it is sufficient to say that the latter are preferable so long as redundancy is available. Redundancy in a description means that there are a number of shape cues spread around the boundary of an object (and so the pathological case of a single descriptor being occluded is prevented). Consequently, from any normal viewpoint one would expect to observe a number of descriptors (generally more than one), and so recognition is possible.

At the lowest level a full understanding of object geometry is not recovered using non-global structures. For example, given the scenario in Fig. 4.4, one would form two independent recognition hypotheses from the different five-line feature groups shown in (b) and (c) using the processing steps of LEWIS1 described so far. Given these, it would be impossible prior to verification to determine whether they came from the same object instance, or from different objects. The goal of hypothesis merging, or *extension,* is to combine these two hypotheses together if they really come from the same object and so gain a better geometric understanding of the scene. The result of extension is the formation of *joint hypotheses.* Through forming joint hypotheses we can derive a global object descrip-

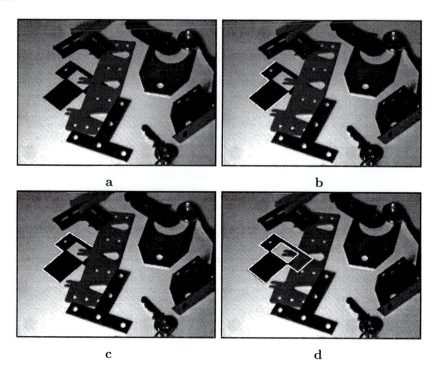

a   b

c   d

FIG. 4.4. For the lock striker plate to the left of (a) there are two different
    visible five-line feature groups that can be used to form recognition
    hypotheses by invariant indexing. These are highlighted in (b) and (c),
    and could each be used independently to recognize the object. However,
    a much better understanding of the scene would be achieved if the two
    hypotheses are combined into a single hypothesis describing the object
    (d).

tion that is tolerant to occlusion by building up a hierarchy of local and
semi-local measures. Extension should be compared directly to the work
on clique formation of Bolles and Cain (11) and the hierarchical object
descriptions of Ettinger (34). Both of these achieved extension, though not
in an invariant framework.

There are a number of different benefits realized through extension:

1. The first is that creating geometrical relationships between different
   invariant feature groups produces a more complete object description.
   Without extension the groups will each attempt to drive recognition
   independently. There should obviously be an interaction between the
   groups as they often share features. As will be shown below it is
   usually possible to derive more complete object descriptions using
   invariants rather than simply having the object composed of sets of

independent geometric features.

2. Combining individual measures provides better discrimination between objects. Certainly for the model base used in LEWIS1 we have found that a single feature group can index multiple objects. However, it is a very rare occurrence for two objects to share more than one invariant value unless significant proportions of their object boundaries are actually projectively equivalent. Consequently, through extension it is easy to find different descriptions for different objects.

3. This also leads to the fact that when two hypotheses index the same object in a single part of the scene, there is a significant increase in confidence that the match is correct. Thus the credibility of hypotheses can be ranked by the number of invariant feature groups that each contain.

4. Multiple hypotheses for an object give more matching model and image features than a single hypothesis. This is important for verification as it produces a better initial estimate of pose for the model (as with the hypothesize and test correspondence approach, the more initial feature correspondences provided by alignment the better the original estimate of object pose).

5. The verification process is very time consuming and should be called as little as possible. Obviously it is more efficient to validate two hypotheses simultaneously than to verify them separately and then combine into a single hypothesis.

The extension process forms joint hypotheses via the construction of an interpretation tree between the hypotheses resulting from indexing. A tree is constructed only for hypotheses that index the same model, and a separate tree is created for each indexed model. The procedure does not suffer from the problem common to the ITs discussed in (53), which have an exponential increase in the number of hypothesis combinations that have to be considered, because for each model we generally have a small number of high-order features (usually at most four or five invariant feature groups match any one object from the model base). This well-behaved property of the ITs is demonstrated later in Table 4.5 where it can be seen that the number of consistent nodes in the trees is comparable to the number of original hypotheses.

There is a second difference between the IT used in LEWIS and those described by Grimson in (53). This is that every node that represents a consistent hypothesis is verified, that is unless one of its descendents has been verified and found to represent a true recognition hypothesis first (the largest joint hypotheses are verified first). If this is the case, the node relating a smaller number hypotheses does not have to be verified as it must also represent a true (partial) recognition hypothesis. The reason that the winner-takes-all approach of (53), which terminates the search as soon as a single hypothesis is verified, is not used because it cannot account for either multiple object instances in a scene, or if it makes an incorrect judgement and returns a false positive, then false negatives are likely to result.

The constraints used to prune the tree take the form of *joint invariants*. These are invariants formed between features in potentially consistent hypotheses and take the form of binary constraints. For the algebraic invariant indexing system the constraints are given below in Section 4.2.5.1.

Testing for hypothesis consistency through the use of an interpretation tree constitutes a superior method to that used to date for combining hypotheses and should be compared to the process used by Wolfson (146) for joining pairs of hypotheses. Normally the extension process is done through voting where one accumulates support for the presence of an object by counting the number of invariants by which it is indexed (such as was done by Lamdan, *et al.* (68)). This method fails to discriminate between single and multiple object instances in a scene. Certainly one could subsequently use pose consistency to separate the different solutions, but the goal of extension is to join hypotheses in a frame invariant manner prior to verification. The extension process used in LEWIS does this. The interested reader should also refer to the work by Moons, *et al.* (87) that reports on when and how invariants can in general be formed between sets of features. This has particular relevance if the object is parametrized, or has articulations that effect the formation of the joint invariants.

4.2.5.1 *Hypothesis compatibility*

Two individual hypotheses (such as those for the five-line invariant shown in Figs 4.4b and 4.4c) can be combined if structures between them exist that are preserved under projection. In LEWIS1 the consistency of topology between the image and model invariant feature groups is exploited; for this to be achieved the groups must be *overlapping* (contrast with the overlapping and non-overlapping subpart strategy in (34)).

For example, consider three algebraic feature groups in a scene that index the same model and create hypotheses H_i, $i \in \{a, b, c\}$ (see Fig. 4.5). In this case H_a corresponds to an invariant formed from a pair of conics, and H_b and H_c to one from a conic and line-pair. H_a and H_b are compatible as the correspondence of model-to-image features is unique and is given by $\{C_1 : c_1, C_2 : c_2, L_1 : l_1, L_2 : l_2\}$. However, H_b and H_c are incompatible as the two correspondences $\{L_1 : l_1, L_2 : l_2\}$ and $\{L_5 : l_1, L_1 : l_2\}$ cannot be satisfied simultaneously.

This form of extension can be used to demonstrate the merging of the two hypotheses in Fig. 4.4 into a single joint hypothesis. Another example is given in Fig. 4.6 where the different lines and conics on the two objects form two distinct joint hypotheses each containing three individual hypotheses.

This form of extension has been used successfully in LEWIS1, however, one might investigate how to extend and improve the process. For example,

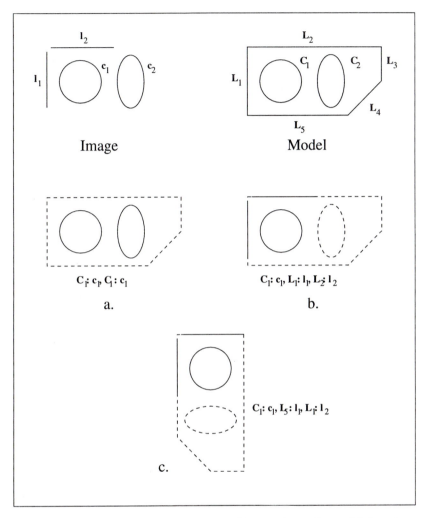

FIG. 4.5. A single view of an object yields two lines (l_1 and l_2) and two conics (c_1 and c_2). The two different hypotheses in (a) and (b) are consistent as in both cases the correspondence $C_1 : c_1$ is made and all the other correspondences are independent. However, hypotheses (b) and (c) are not consistent with each other as there is the contradiction $\{L_1 : l_1, L_2 : l_2\} \wedge \{L_5 : l_1, L_1 : l_2\}$.

one shortcoming of this method occurs when either the model or image feature groups are not overlapping. Should this happen the topologies of the different feature groups become independent and so there is no possibility of a contradiction occurring. Immediately we see that this can be overcome through a further use of projective invariants, and in fact in a way that will

a   b

FIG. 4.6. Two objects are indexed using the features in (b) which form
three individual hypotheses for each object. After extension single joint
hypotheses are created for each object.

usually provide a much stronger test of the compatibility of the hypotheses
than that achieved through topology. Rather than just measuring algebraic
invariants measured within single feature groups, one can also compute
other algebraic invariants between pairs of groups after indexing.

This more general form of extension is demonstrated in Fig. 4.7. Feature groups **a** and **b** in a scene are found through indexing to correspond
to model groups **A** and **B** (from the same model). Note that the correspon-
dence is not just **a** : **A** and **b** : **B**, but is $\mathbf{a}_i : \mathbf{A}_i$ and $\mathbf{b}_i : \mathbf{B}_i$, $i \in \{1, \dots, 5\}$
(indexing provides a correspondence between the individual features as well
as between the groups). If **a** and **b** come from the same object in the scene
rather than from different instances of the same model, there are other tests
of geometric consistency that can be applied. For example any projective
invariant for the features $\{\mathbf{a}_1, \mathbf{a}_2, \mathbf{a}_3, \mathbf{a}_4, \mathbf{b}_1\}$ should match (modulo noise)
that on the model for $\{\mathbf{A}_1, \mathbf{A}_2, \mathbf{A}_3, \mathbf{A}_4, \mathbf{B}_1\}$.

Therefore, in practice the consistency of two individual hypotheses
would be tested by computing invariants between any of the combinations
of the features in **a** and **b** and comparing them to invariants computed for
A and **B** (the model invariant values can be pre-computed and stored in a
look-up table). This form of compatibility test is used in LEWIS2.

Note that for the example in Fig. 4.7 one can form only twelve independent projective invariants from a set of ten points (using the counting
argument in Forsyth (41)), and so the comparisons must be done over such
an independent set. Sometimes there is no gain in using algebraic joint
invariants over topology due to it being impossible to form further independent invariants after indexing. The following example highlights this
case.

Example 4.2 Suppose we have a set of six points formed into two overlapping five-point configurations. For each set of five points measure two

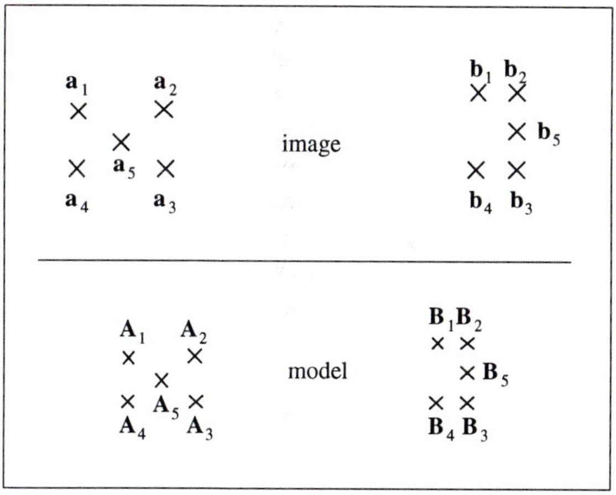

FIG. 4.7. Two feature groups index the same model and form im-age-to-model correspondences $a : A$ and $b : B$. One could test for compatibility between the groups a and b by checking for consistency of algebraic invariants with the model groups A and B. Details are in the text.

projective invariants (the maximum possible) and index to give model hypotheses; thus a total of four independent invariants have been used for indexing. Now, compute invariants for the joint configuration of the six points; using the counting argument four independent invariants can be measured. However, these must be functionally dependent on the four invariants used for indexing, and so nothing can be gained in using these for extension. As a result, in this case the only constraint useful for extension is topology.

In practice forming independent invariants for overlapping hypotheses such as are found frequently in LEWIS1 is often not possible. This is because neighbouring hypotheses may be different by only a single feature. Therefore, there is often little to gain through the use of algebraic joint invariants and so topology is the only constraint used in LEWIS1.

However, the above procedure suggests a general strategy for testing the compatibility of a pair of image hypotheses derived from invariant features within a single model. The method relies simply on the exchange of features from one feature group to the other, and then comparison of the newly computed invariants with those for the same configuration on the model. This has worked well for LEWIS2, and one can see how applications can be made to other object classes as well (113). As a result of forming invariants between different feature types one can conjecture that the entire geometry of objects can be described in a coherent projective manner.

4.2.6   *Verification*

Verification is the process that takes a putative recognition hypothesis (in LEWIS1 produced as a result of invariant indexing and extension), and applies a series of more rigorous tests to determine whether the hypothesized object could have feasibly created the observed image data. In many recognition systems the verification process performs correspondence as an initial step to object identification, or in fact as the only step (for example RAF, Grimson and Lozano-Pérez (50)). Ultimately, verification should output a list of object identities (and possibly poses) with associated certainties depending on the confidence that the system has in each hypothesis. Ideally all confidence levels should be unity or zero depending on whether the object is or is not present in the scene. However, current systems working with occlusion and clutter tend to fall well below this capability.

One might ask why verification is needed at all for a system such as LEWIS1 that has already used scene measurements to hypothesize the presence of an object. The answer is simply that the bounds on the local shape descriptions used for indexing are not sufficiently tight to discriminate between different objects. This principally arises due to:

1. Similarity in sets of features used to form the invariants (although not exact projective equivalence) means that under image noise an invariant can index incorrect models as well as the right one.

2. Non-completeness of the invariant measures (see Chapter 3) can cause a set of features to index a set of model features to which they are not projectively equivalent. This is generally not too serious a problem in LEWIS1 as care has been taken to use invariants with reasonable completeness properties.

3. Different objects share the same local shape descriptions and so cannot be distinguished without more global measures.

Trying to rule out these cases as they stand assumes that verification is designed to analyse only the correspondence between features used to form the invariants and the indexed model features. This is not the case. In fact, verification is used to gain further support for an object hypothesis using both model and image features not used during indexing. Verification can therefore be framed as a search in the image for data that supports or rejects the recognition hypothesis.

There appear to be three mainstream ways in which to do verification:

1. test for consistency of pose;

2. exploit a hypothesize and test procedure;

3. backproject the model into the image and accept the hypothesis purely by how much image data supports it.

The first of these uses voting in pose space; for LEWIS1 it would use an eight degree of freedom projective space as the pose space. The procedure is identical to that used for pose clustering that was reviewed briefly in Section 2.1.3. Given sets of matching image and model features the map taking one to the other is computed and votes accumulated within pose space. Pose space can either be quantized in a rectangular grid or one could use Cass' algorithm (23) to account for the expected errors more thoroughly. Either way, the problem with this approach (as noted in (53)) is that a large number of model features (twenty or thirty) must be matched to suppress incorrect voting by noise. The models used within LEWIS1 do not have this number of distinct geometric features and so the method is not suitable.

The second possibility is to implement a hypothesize and test routine. Indexing and extension produce a correspondence list between a small number of matched model and image features. Except for invariants that are formed by exploiting an isotropy (which is not true for any of the invariants in LEWIS1), the correspondence list will be large enough to determine the transformation that maps the model into the image uniquely. This mapping (or projection) can be used to replace an alignment process prior to using hypothesize and test to search for more matching features and so increase model support. This is a well-principled approach because the model-to-image map can be refined as more features are included.

One drawback is that a consistent strategy is required to compute the model-to-image map for all types of feature that are to be encountered in the image. How this is done for lines and conics is given in Appendix B; though for more general plane curves the computation is harder. A second problem is that the pose refinement process is not guaranteed to converge to a stable or even the correct solution. Certainly for images with the complexity of some of the images investigated (such as the aerial surveillance image in Fig. 6.7) the process fails as the projected model can very quickly become distracted by the multitude of lines that lie in the image. Furthermore, the iterative refinement process requires detailed knowledge of the error distributions that are to be expected in an image. As shown in Section 4.3.1 this is hard to obtain to any degree of accuracy. Because of these problems a more straightforward approach to verification is used in LEWIS, called backprojection; it is still unclear whether hypothesize and test would perform better.

4.2.6.1 *Backprojection* Backprojection is a strategy that was used by Mundy and Heller (91) in their vertex-pair matcher. It is a one-step procedure that projects the model into the image and determines the extent to which the image data accounts for the projected model data. The process works identically for three-dimensional or two-dimensional models. Verification proceeds for the planar case by:

1. Computing the projectivity mapping the indexed model algebraic features to their corresponding image features.

2. Checking that the projected model features actually coincide with the image features (this accounts both for image error and non-completeness).

3. Projecting the entire model into the image and searching for image support; this is similar to the verification procedures given in (12, 91). This stage is expensive as it involves the projection of a large number of model points. It should therefore be performed only when absolutely necessary.

For all of the plane algebraic invariants used in the system, the image features used to produce the model index and their corresponding model features provide a sufficient number of constraints to compute the projective transformation linking the model and image. For example a five-line invariant provides ten constraints on the map, two from each line, and the model-to-image projectivity has only eight degrees of freedom. Details of how the transformation is computed in general are given in Appendix B. Note that because invariants were used to hypothesize the initial match the computation of the projectivity is always overconstrained. Consequently, one can check that the image features used to compute the index are in fact projectively equivalent to the model. If not, the hypothesis can be rejected. As the algebraic features used within LEWIS1 are lines and conics, two simple sets of rules are applied to confirm algebraic consistency:

1. The model lines must project to within 15 degrees of the image lines. Although more precise distance measures could be used this simple test has proved satisfactory for the pruning the relevant cases.

2. The projected model conics must project to ellipses, and they must have similar circumferences and areas to the image conics. Due to fitting problems encountered in the fitting of hyperbolas they are never used as model descriptors (see Section 6.1.1.3 for details of conic fitting). Under the normal imaging conditions provided by a camera with a finite field of view, an ellipse will always project to an ellipse. Therefore, the projections of the model conics must be ellipses.

All of the thresholds used during verification (for instance the 15 degree constraint angle for lines) were determined empirically and set so that false negatives would be eliminated.

The reason for preventing false negatives is that it is hard to recover from their presence at a later stage during processing, whereas this is not true for false positives. Unfortunately, many recognition systems exploit a winner-takes-all strategy to make them run quickly. However, if such systems are to prevent false negatives they require backtracking to reinstate rejected hypotheses once it has been realized that the current search will fail to find an object. Knowing that backtracking is necessary implies

FIG. 4.8. The bracket in Fig. 4.2 is verified by projecting the model into the
image. The projected model is shown in white. 59.3% of the model edges
lie close to image edgels of the right orientation, and so the hypothesis
is accepted.

prior knowledge of the scene (that is that a certain number of objects are
present), which is not a generic condition.

The process of computing the model-to-image map and then projecting
the model algebraic features to the image is not time consuming as few
algebraic manipulation are necessary. This step is beneficial to the system
running time as it eliminates some hypotheses at little cost; full statistics
of the verification phase are given later in Section 4.4.

The final step that maps the entire model to the image is far less efficient. Using the computed projectivity, model edge data (from an acquisition scene, see Section 4.3) are projected into the image. If the projected
edge data lie close to image edge data of the same orientations (within 5
pixels and 15 degrees), it is assumed that the object caused the edge data
in the image, and thus counts as support for the object actually being visible. Note that this is similar to a one-stage hypothesis and test without
subsequent refining of the hypothesis. If more than a certain proportion
of the projected model data are supported (the threshold used is 50%),
assume that there is sufficient support for the model, and the recognition
hypothesis is confirmed. This part of the process is very expensive as for
most models $O(10^3)$ edgels have to be mapped into the image and so it
forms one of the slowest parts of the entire recognition process.

Figure 4.8 shows the bracket in Fig. 4.2 being verified after indexing
hypothesized its presence in the scene. Due to occlusion only 59.3% of the
projected model edge data is found to match during verification. This is
above the 50% and so the hypothesis is accepted.

A reasonable complaint to the above approach is that the errors observed by the misalignment of the model are caused by errors in three-
dimensional space, rather than in the image. Therefore, one should project
the image data onto the model and compute the Euclidean distance in that

frame. There are two replies to this observation: the first is that Euclidean models are not used in LEWIS and so the frame in which to do the comparison is unknown. This is a feature of the implementation and could be overcome through a different (Euclidean) model acquisition process. The second is more important and is that measuring the error in the image is more efficient than in the Euclidean frame. Generally the sacrifice in accuracy (which is marginal) is paid for by the improved speed performance; an image such as Fig. 4.2 contains in excess of 10^4 edgels, all of which would have to be projected to the model frame. Running the process the other way round requires that an order of magnitude fewer edgels have to be projected.

One immediate problem encountered with computing the Euclidean distance from a projected model point in the image to the nearest edge location is that the process is expensive. Instead, an approximation to the distance can be computed using the 3–4 distance transform of Borgefors (14). The distance transform is found by passing Chamfer masks over the image, which can be done during the image pre-processing. An example of the 3–4 distance transform output for a simple image is shown in Fig. 4.9.

During the process of increasing hypothesis confidence, the assumed orientation of image edgels are that of the Canny output, whereas that of projected features depends on the feature type:

1. For an edgel on a straight line in the model project the straight line into the image and use its orientation as the orientation of the edgel.

2. If the edgel lies on a conic, project both the edgel and the conic to the image. As the edgel lies close to the conic, its polar approximates the tangent to the conic, which directly gives its orientation in the image.[19]

3. If the edgel lies on a higher order curve the orientation provided by the edge detector output during model acquisition must be used, and that projected to the image. This is not as simple as the processes for straight lines or conics because it involves determining the tangent on the model, and then projecting the tangent line to the image. Furthermore, the edge detector provides weaker constraints on the edge orientation than the fitted lines and conics. This is because the fitting processes tend to integrate out error. Therefore the 15 degrees threshold is too low, and 30 degrees is used instead.

Verification is hard for occluded scenes because an incorrect match may have as much image support as a heavily occluded correct match; that is, for scenes where there is dense edge data it is quite likely that a large number of edges may be close to, and have the same orientation as, the projected

---

[19]For a point $\mathbf{x}$ and a conic C, the polar $\mathbf{l}$ of the point with respect to the conic is $\mathbf{l} = \mathsf{C}\mathbf{x}$.

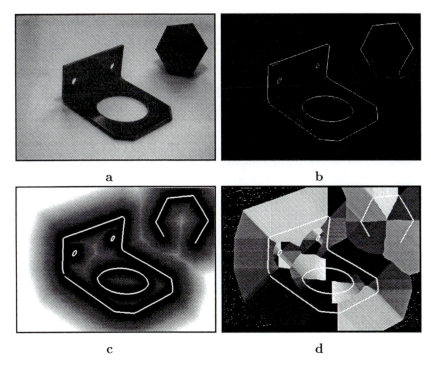

FIG. 4.9. (a) shows a simple scene with two objects in it. The output of
the Canny edge detector is shown in (b). The 3-4 distance transform
is computed for all edges over a certain strength and is displayed in
(c); distance from the nearest edge (white) is coded by intensity, with
zero being black. (d) shows, coded by intensity, the orientation of the
nearest edge to the pixel.

model edges. As industrial scenes are very structured, maybe only one or
two erroneous straight lines of the right orientation will be sufficient to give
over 50% support for a model and so render a false match. Obviously, any
object which is over 50% occluded will not be found by the recognizer, and
so there is a certain trade-off required when setting the support threshold.
As the threshold is lowered, an occluded object is more likely to be found,
but there will also be more false positives.

The verification strategy generally performs quite well. Unless there is
heavy occlusion the probability of a false negative is low; however false positives are frequently reported. If more than one invariant forms a hypothesis
that passes verification, the level of confidence in the result becomes significantly higher, though many hypotheses still result from single invariant
measurements. It is the author's belief that a significant amount of work
remains to be done so that increased confidence can be gained through
verification for *all* of the recognition results. Some possible extensions to

the verification procedure are discussed after Section 4.4 where a number of recognition examples are given. Prior to this, the model acquisition procedure for LEWIS1 is given.

4.3   Model acquisition and library formation

Model acquisition is achieved entirely from images and the process follows a very similar path to that just described for recognition. The reason why everything can be done from images is because the shape descriptors used (the invariants) are projective and are thus independent of the frame being used. Using projective shape descriptors has been of great benefit for the portability of LEWIS1 as the system has no requirement for camera calibration. Furthermore, the use of projective models has rapidly increasing in interest in the computer vision literature, spurred on by the three-dimensional projective work of Faugeras (36) and Hartley, *et al.* (54).

Doing acquisition from images makes model learning both easy and rapid. However, it is not the belief of the author that the process should be entirely automatic. It can be done off-line, and due to the concern that no errors should be introduced into the models, there appears to be no good argument for perfecting an automatic acquisition process.

An overview of the acquisition is as follows:

1. Take a number of images of an unoccluded object from a variety of 'standard' viewpoints (for algebraic invariants two images are used). Ensure that there is no clutter in the scenes so that all of the observed edge data must come from the object. A standard viewpoint is a view that would be observed during a recognition trial. Note that one such view could be from a fronto-parallel position; this provides what is called a *natural view* of the object.

2. Compute all of the invariants for each scene.

3. Compare the invariants between the scenes. The useful invariant shape descriptors remain approximately constant under a change in viewpoint. Therefore, record the invariants that remain constant in the model base. Any measures that are not constant are due to features that do not form correct invariant configurations (for example lines that are not coplanar), or are caused by unstable features.

4. Store edge data from one of the scenes for use during the final phase of verification. These are the points that are projected into the scene to test the validity of a hypothesis. For most of the objects in the model base there are $O(10^3)$ edgels observable in an acquisition view. For the same scene also store the lines and conics associated with the stable invariants.

A correspondence problem must be solved so that the invariants can be compared between different images. An ordered feature vector of the measured algebraic invariants is created for each view of the algebraic object. The vector is ordered according to the sequence of features in the edge chains (this is provided by the feature grouping routine), and the sequence is assumed to be closed. For example, for an object boundary with six line segments, there are six library entries representing the vector of five-line invariants which can be generated, starting at each line in the sequence. These sequences can be reversed if the objects may be seen from the opposite side, but here it is assumed that this reversal does not occur. The ordering in the vector is invariant to the viewpoint except for a cyclic permutation of the elements. Therefore one has to check only that components of the two vectors of image measures correspond cyclically, with the option of there being null or bad values within the vectors produced by variable segmentation or non-coplanar structures entering the boundary edge chains.

If the elements of the vectors are genuine invariants they will remain constant (modulo error) between viewpoints and so corresponding measures in both vectors should be found (constrained by the cyclic permutation). If such matching values are found, such that they match within 3% of each other, then the mean value is entered into the model library. The motivation for using this threshold is given in Section 4.3.1 below.

The observation that the measures remain constant between viewpoints does not necessarily mean that they correspond to invariant feature configurations, but if the viewpoints are generic then this will be the case. One example of a non-generic change in viewpoint is when the camera is rotated around its optical centre; in this case all projective measures taken between sets of features will remain constant. During acquisition we ensure that all camera movements are generic.

All the reliable feature measures are stored in the model library. The edge data forming all the coplanar feature groups for an object are also stored for use in the hypothesis verification stage. Therefore, a model consists of the following information:

- A name.
- A set of edge data from an acquisition view of the object.
- The lines and conics fitted to that edge data. In other index-based recognition systems these will be replaced by other features that form the invariants.
- The expected invariant values for the reliable configurations, and which algebraic features they correspond to.

Eighteen of the objects from the model base are shown in Figs 4.10 and 4.11; in these figures the models are represented by their edge data. Each library is segmented into different sublibraries, one for each type of invariant. Each sublibrary then has a list of each of the invariant values tagged with an object name, and is structured as a hash table.

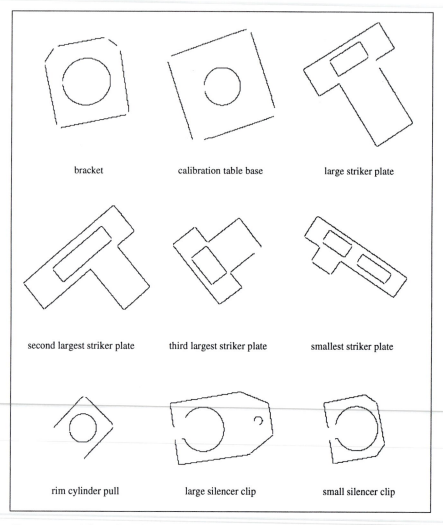

bracket   calibration table base   large striker plate

second largest striker plate   third largest striker plate   smallest striker plate

rim cylinder pull   large silencer clip   small silencer clip

FIG. 4.10. The edge data extracted from acquisition images for the first
nine models in the model base. More models are shown in Fig. 4.11.

An example of acquisition for two views of a right-angled bracket is
shown in Fig. 4.12. From each image (using the fitted forms as shown
in Fig. 4.13) all possible invariants are measured. The five-line invariants
are formed by taking all possible sequences of five lines around the line
chains, and the conic and three-line invariant are formed from the conic
fit to the central hole in the bracket and all triples of consecutive lines
in the chain. The measured invariants are shown in Tables 4.1 and 4.2.
All invariants that match to within 3% are entered into the model library.

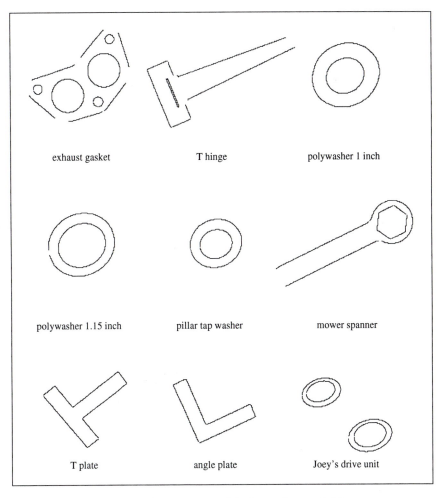

Fig. 4.11. Nine more models from the model base.

Some measured invariant values for each image are different because they share feature 'A' shown in Fig. 4.12. This feature is not coplanar with the other features used to define the invariant and thus the measured value changes with viewpoint. The measurements associated with feature 'A' are eliminated from the model description.

4.3.1 *Errors in the invariant measurement*

Knowledge of the error behaviour of the invariants under imaging conditions is very important with regard to the construction of the model libraries. Here we show how one can estimate the error performances for algebraic invariants: principally the process is empirical with expected error bounds on the invariant measurements gained from real images; but

FIG. 4.12. (a) shows one of the acquisition scenes for a right-angled bracket. A different view of the bracket is shown in (b). Feature 'A' produces an extra line in the edge chain, and so the measured invariants are different from (a). One is still able to find two pairs of matching five-line invariants as well as four conic three-line invariants between the two images. All invariants that stay approximately constant are entered into the feature vector for the object.

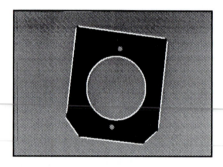

FIG. 4.13. The lines and conic fitted to the bracket for Fig. 4.12a. Note that the endpoints of the lines are not connected. This is because the corners perturb the fitting, and are therefore not used in the fitting procedure. However, the corners are used to define connectivity between the lines.

comparisons to analytic manipulations are also made. For example, one can obtain a rough guide to the size of expected errors under *ideal* imaging conditions by differentiating the invariant expressions given in Chapter 3 and assuming an isotropic noise distribution; such analysis was done by Forsyth, *et al.* (42) and Sinclair, *et al.* (119), and is also given at the end of this section.

The shortcomings of this type of formulation become apparent when real images are observed. Furthermore, it provides only a local understanding of the errors. The only way to understand the errors that may be encountered

Table 4.1 *The five-line invariants extracted from the two calibration images. Each image column shows the invariant feature vector for the corresponding image. The object feature vector is given by comparison of these two columns. The feature vectors for each image differ because of the difference in the apparent outline of the object in the two images. The % deviation between matching invariants is shown in the last columns of each table.*

Image	1	2	deviation ($\pm$)
1	(0.553,2.118)	—	—
2	(0.679,3.572)	—	—
3	—	(0.527,-41.855)	—
4	—	(1.013,0.984)	—
5	—	(0.539,3.477)	—
6	(0.844,1.229)	(0.839,1.239)	(0.3,0.4)
7	(0.451,5.200)	(0.458,5.040)	(0.8,1.6)
8	(0.837,1.412)	—	—
9	(0.684,1.880)	—	—
10	—	(0.896,1.245)	—
11	—	(0.658,1.513)	—

Table 4.2 *The conic and line invariants extracted from the calibration images. The invariants are ordered around the extracted edge chain which helps match the invariants from different scenes. Only the invariants with small deviations (less than 3%) are written to the model base.*

Image	1	2	deviation ($\pm$)
1	(2.489,2.455,5.644)	(2.466,1.383,3.142)	(0.5,27.9,28.5)
2	(2.455,1.339,2.885)	—	—
3	—	(1.383,1.196,2.435)	—
4	—	(1.196,1.343,1.493)	—
5	(1.339,1.313,2.638)	(1.343,1.303,2.619)	(0.1,0.4,0.4)
6	(1.313,1.308,1.899)	(1.303,1.297,1.871)	(0.4,0.4,0.7)
7	(1.308,1.354,2.653)	(1.297,1.325,2.530)	(0.4,1.1,2.4)
8	(1.354,2.489,2.946)	(1.325,2.466,2.959)	(1.1,0.5,0.2)

within a system is to study real images. All theoretical analysis has to assume some error model in image measurements; frequently this is founded upon a Gaussian error in the locations of individual edge locations due to what is often called *image noise*. The results given below demonstrate that *errors* occur due to serious shortcomings in the nature of the edge detectors used, and cannot be attributed to *noise*.

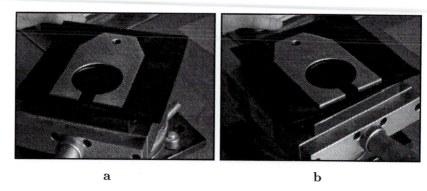

a   b

FIG. 4.14. The first and twenty-eighth image in the fifty-image sequence
used to test the reliability of the invariants. The rest of the sequence
was produced by rotating the calibration table by 2 degrees between
images. Three five-line invariants can be computed for this object using
the seven longest lines (shown in Fig. 4.15). The twenty-eighth image
demonstrates when line 3 becomes vertical, the finite thickness of the
object is observed, and hence the location of the edge boundary becomes
ill defined.

4.3.1.1 *Empirical investigation*   The first and twenty-eighth images from
the sequence used to do the tests is shown in Fig. 4.14. The object used has
a boundary made up of lines, seven of which can be segmented reliably and
used to form five-line invariants. The rest of the sequence of fifty images
were constructed by rotating the object at 2 degree increments on the
calibration table beneath the object. The lines fitted to the edge data of
Fig. 4.14a, with the seven lines used to compute the invariants, are shown
in Fig. 4.15. The direction of rotation used to form the sequence is also
marked. Three different five-line invariants were computed for each image
of the object. Note that the object is slightly specular, and is on a black
background of a similar nature. The images therefore do not represent
ideal imaging conditions though the edge detection would be expected to
be fairly reliable.

The mean invariant values for the image set are shown in Table 4.3.
These results show that the invariants are in fact very stable, with standard
deviations less than 1.5% of the mean values. From these results the error
measurements that are used during recognition and acquisition are chosen.
For the former the aim is to eliminate as many false negatives as possible
and so the error bound is high (that is 5%, which is well above the 3σ
mark), but during acquisition one should be more cautious so that only
stable invariants are used (and so 3% is used, roughly equal to 2σ).

The results are more revealing when they are studied in greater detail,
with the invariants plotted with an enlarged scale in Fig. 4.16. The second
invariant of I_2 is plotted for lines 2 through 6, though the shape of the

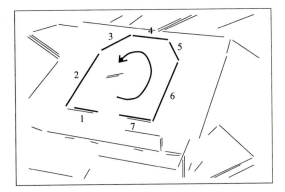

FIG. 4.15. The lines fitted to Canny edge data from Fig. 4.14a. The seven
lines used to compute the invariants and the direction of rotation are
marked.

Table 4.3 *The mean values for the three invariants measured from the image sequence based on the images in Fig.
4.14. The standard deviation σ is computed both as an absolute value, and as a percentage of the mean. Note that
the 3σ mark is well within 5% of the mean, and so such a
bound could be used during recognition. During acquisition
more caution is desired and a 3% bound used.*

	I_1	I_2	I_3
mean	(0.707,2.252)	(0.752,1.492)	(0.524,3.043)
σ	(0.0031,0.0170)	(0.0032,0.0086)	(0.0052,0.0433)
σ (%)	(0.44,0.76)	(0.43,0.58)	(0.99,1.42)

graph is characteristic of all of the invariants. The graph can be split into
three distinct regions:

1. **Region A:** All of the lines are located reasonably well by the Canny
   edge detector, and so the measured invariants remain constant.

2. **Region B:** When the object has been rotated so that line 2 becomes
   vertical in the image, the edge on the lower surface parallel to it to
   becomes visible. The edge detector does not find a pronounced second
   edge in this orientation, though because of its presence the intensity
   values no longer form a step edge at the correct feature, but instead a
   slope. The Canny output locates a position somewhere along the slope
   and not at the discontinuity. The fitted line is therefore incorrect and
   causes the invariant value to be measured erroneously. Notice that
   as the object is rotated more, the invariant value tends to decrease
   (though noisily); this is because the slope causes the fitted line to
   move further and further away from the correct edge.

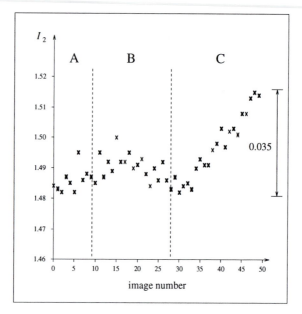

FIG. 4.16. When the invariants (in this case the second value of the second invariant) are plotted in greater detail a systematic error becomes apparent in their measurement. This is due to the edge detector becoming distracted onto incorrect image features, and is not due to image noise.

3. **Region C:** In this region the effect is more pronounced as edge 3 moves through the vertical. As the fitted line drifts off the edge there is a definite systematic error in the invariant measurement.

As can be seen from the graph the systematic errors produced by the edge detector due to distraction far outweigh any (Gaussian) noise observed in the points. One can even question whether Gaussian noise is present at all, or whether all the other observation errors are due to different noise models. Note that the errors will become larger as the thickness of the object increases, or when shadows and other distractors are present.

4.3.1.2 *Analytic investigation* The gross effects of the systematic error can be estimated by perturbing the algebraic expressions for the invariants. Given the expression used in the implementation for the second invariant:

$$I_2 = \frac{|M_{421}||M_{532}|}{|M_{432}||M_{521}|},$$

the aim is to determine the effect of, say, the third line on I_2. If the lines used to evaluate the expression are of the form $\mathbf{l}_i = (a_i, b_i, 1)^T$, $i \in \{1, \ldots, 5\}$, then:

$$\frac{\partial I_2}{\partial a_3} = I_2 \, \frac{|M_{245}|}{|M_{532}|.|M_{432}|} \, (b_2 - b_3),$$

$$\frac{\partial I_2}{\partial b_3} = I_2 \, \frac{|M_{245}|}{|M_{532}|.|M_{432}|} \, (a_3 - a_2). \tag{4.3.1}$$

The model for the error observed in the measurement of the fitted lines is a translation parallel to the line normal by δ. If the gradient of the line is $\tan \theta$, by letting $\alpha = \delta / \cos \theta$ the equation of the perturbed line is:

$$\frac{a_3}{1 - \alpha b_3} x + \frac{b_3}{1 - \alpha b_3} + 1 = 0.$$

This directly yields $(\partial a_3 / \partial \delta, \partial b_3 / \partial \delta)$, from which δ can be estimated given a known ΔI_2:

$$\delta = \frac{\Delta I_2}{\left| \left(\begin{array}{c} \frac{\partial I_2}{\partial a_3} \times \frac{\partial a_3}{\partial \delta} \\ \frac{\partial I_2}{\partial b_3} \times \frac{\partial b_3}{\partial \delta} \end{array} \right) \right|}.$$

From region C of Fig. 4.16 the value of ΔI_2 can be estimated as 0.035. This is assumed to be due entirely to the movement of l_3 and that all the other lines are measured correctly. Applying the analysis yields a value of $\delta = 2$ pixels for this ΔI_2; this certainly is of the right order of magnitude for the image sequence as can be seen by the error in the location of the fitted line l_3 in the image (though unfortunately not in the reproduction given here).

Obviously the other lines in the configuration will also be in error, but the analysis can easily be extended to account for all of their effects if they can be estimated. The important consideration is that the error is due to 3D world problems such as distraction (the finite thickness of the objects), shadow and clutter, and not predominately due to image-based noise.

In summary this section has demonstrated how invariant errors can be estimated and used in the construction of the index table. The emphasis has been on observing the error characteristics in images rather than assuming an error model and subsequently estimating the performance. The latter approach is likely to lead to an incorrect construction of the model base and hence reduced recognition performance.

4.4 Experimental results

This section reports on the testing of LEWIS1 over a large number of trials with a model library with over thirty objects. Generally the recognition performance is good, though certain key problem areas do exist which are highlighted in the discussion at the end of the chapter. The examples have

a   b

FIG. 4.17. (a) shows the bracket occluded in a scene by objects not in
    the library. In (b) the edge data from the first calibration scene (Fig.
    4.12a) are shown projected onto the test scene using the model-to-image
    transformation hypothesized by the match. The close match between
    the projected data (shown in white), and the scene edges shows that
    the recognition hypothesis is valid. Projected edge data from the model
    of a spanner are also shown projected into the scene as this was also
    recognized.

Table 4.4 *The invariants measured from Fig. 4.17 which are formed
by features actually corresponding to bracket features. The second column shows the library values and the third column scene values. In
the fourth column the deviations from the mean invariant values are
given; this shows that the five-line invariant is very stable under real
image conditions, and the conic and three-line invariant is reasonably
stable.*

invariant	library	scene	error %
five-line	(0.8415,1.2340)	(0.842,1.235)	(0.1,0.1)
conic-line	(1.3410,1.3080,2.6285)	(1.372,1.291,2.676)	(2.3,1.3,1.8)
conic-line	(1.3080,1.3025,1.8850)	(1.291,1.287,1.852)	(1.3,1.2,1.8)
conic-line	(1.3025,1.3395,2.5915)	(1.287,1.365,2.604)	(1.2,1.9,0.5)

been constructed with the system parameters set to return as few false negatives as possible, though some are observed due to specularity or shadow
disrupting object boundaries.

The first example of recognition is demonstrated using a bracket in a
scene with occlusion and clutter caused by other objects (Fig. 4.17). All
possible five-line invariants and invariants formed from sets of conics and
three-lines were measured and the matching values are given in Table 4.4.
From a scene such as this a large number of possible invariants can be
derived. It was found that two five-line invariants matched invariants of the
bracket, with the second (incorrect) one ruled out during verification. Three

conic and three-line invariants were measured in the scene that matched the invariants of the bracket, and all these constituted correct matches. All of the incorrect hypotheses were ruled out during the backprojection of the indexed models into the scene. For the bracket 74.5% of the projected edges match to within 5 pixels and 15 degrees of the image data. There is a second object from the model base, a spanner, also in the scene. This was correctly identified using three different five-line invariants. In this case an 84.5% projected edge match was achieved with the model data also shown in white in Fig. 4.17b.

Note from the values in Table 4.4 that the five-line invariant performs very well, with in this case only a 0.1% error. The conic and three-line invariant does not perform so well, and often a much larger error in its measurement is expected. This is due to the reduced *dynamic range* of the conic line-pair invariant. The larger error was the motivation for using three lines in the invariant rather than two so that discrimination between objects can be achieved consistently.

Figures 4.18 to 4.20 show LEWIS1 operating on a few test scenes with some of the match statistics shown. For Fig. 4.18, 1199 invariants were computed which indexed 38 hypotheses. These were converted into 83 joint hypotheses that had to be verified, of which 11 were rejected by first-stage verification (that is the projected model algebraic features did not match the index features) and 60 were discared by the second stage (full model backprojection). Eight of the remaining hypotheses were included in larger extended hypotheses that were accepted as suitable, and so they did not have to be verified. For Fig. 4.19, 806 invariants indexed 36 hypotheses, forming 44 joint hypotheses of which 13 were rejected by the first stage of verification, and 23 needed the second stage.

In Table 4.5 various match statistics are shown that have been taken from a very large number of scenes similar to that of Fig. 4.8. In each case, a single object was in the scene, and it was recognized correctly in all except one instance which was when verification broke down due to poor segmentation preventing a sufficient amount of edge support. The total number of indexes formed (an average of 1755.3) depends solely on the number of features in the scene and the way in which they are grouped. This number roughly equates to the number of hypotheses that would have to be verified per model for a hypothesize and test technique. After indexing these form only an average of 60.4 hypotheses, which constitutes a nearly thirty-fold reduction. Because of the redundancy in the shape representation multiple hypotheses are observed for a single model instance. Joint hypothesis formation processing yields an average of 72.7 joint hypotheses.

Verification is performed once the joint hypotheses have been constructed. On average 5.9 hypotheses do not have to be verified as their structures are subsumed by larger joint hypotheses. This means that only 66.8 joint hypotheses actually have to be verified, compared to 60.4 indi-

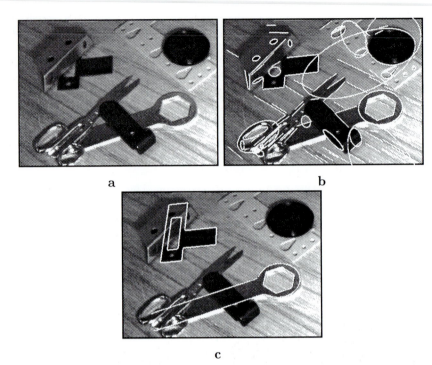

a   b

c

FIG. 4.18. (a) shows a scene containing two objects from the model base,
    with fitted lines (100 of them) and conics (27) superimposed in (b).
    Note that many lines are caused by texture, and that some of the conics
    correspond to edge data over only a small section. The lines form 70
    different line groups. (c) shows the two objects correctly recognized,
    the lock striker plate matched with a single invariant and 50.9% edge
    match, and the spanner with three invariants and 70.7% edge match.

vidual hypotheses. It is clear that hypothesis extension does not lead to
an exponential number of hypotheses being formed, and yet it provides
improved recognition.

Once the projectivity between the hypothesized models and the image
features has been computed a check is made that the projected and image
algebraic features are consistent. On average this removes 41.1 hypotheses,
6.4 due to line correspondences, 4.9 for conic and line configurations, and
29.8 for conic pair configurations. In the end only 23.7 hypotheses have to
be verified through full backprojection, compared with the 1755.3 original
indexes formed. In each case a single object should have been recognized.
The reason why 2.0 were observed in each scene was partly due to symmetry
of the objects causing incorrect verification for a wrong object pose (such
as in Fig. 4.21), and also due to the verification method allowing confusion
between projectively similar objects. There are a number of shortcomings

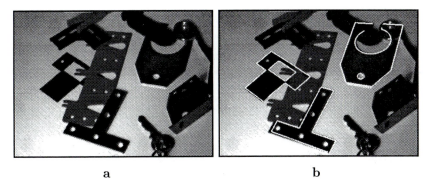

a   b

FIG. 4.19. Another typical scene containing three objects from the model
base. The recognized objects are outlined with 74.7% (2 invariants),
84.6% (1 invariant) and 69.9% (3 invariants) edge matches for the objects from left to right. 58 lines and 14 conics were found.

a   b

FIG. 4.20. Two objects from the model base are recognized correctly de-
spite strong perspective distortion.

of the current verification process and these are discussed at the end of the
chapter. A further recognition example is given in Fig. 4.22.

4.4.1 Complexity

Throughout this book the justification for using invariant indexing is that
it enables recognition to be achieved far more rapidly than for methods
that use a linear search through the library. In Section 2.3.1 it was predicted using general arguments that indexing could succeed in this; here
the predictions are confirmed by experiment.

The indexing technique computes a number of invariants that is entirely
dependent on the number of image features, though only a few of these will
be turned into hypotheses on indexing. Indexing dramatically reduces the
time taken for the entire recognition process. It was suggested in Section
2.3.1 that there should be a small linear growth in the number of hypotheses

FIG. 4.21. The spanner from Fig. 4.18 is recognized, but with the wrong orientation; due to texture in the image a 52.1% edge match is still found.

Table 4.5 *The average match statistics for LEWIS1 taken over a large number of images. See the text for an explanation.*

total number of indexes formed	1755.3
total number of individual hypotheses	60.4
total number of joint hypotheses	72.7
number not requiring any verification	5.9
number rejected by algebraic test	41.1
number rejected through full backprojection	23.7
number of hypotheses accepted	2.0
number of model instances	1.0

created as the size of the model base grows. However, as the time taken for the rest of the visual processing dominates compared to the indexing step (20 seconds for edge detection and segmentation compared to less than a second for indexing and joint hypothesis formation), the recognition process is essentially constant time (non-asymptotically) with respect to the number of models in the model base.

The linear growth is demonstrated in Fig. 4.23. The graph shows data collected over fifty evaluations of LEWIS1 in which a single model from the model base was placed in a scene and partially occluded by other objects that are not in the model base. The object used varied over the model base. Other non-library objects were also placed in the scene as clutter; Fig. 4.8 shows a typical scene. The average number of hypotheses computed as more objects were added to the library is plotted. The first model added to the library always corresponded to the actual model in the scene. Although 15.8% of the hypotheses were for the correct model (with a total of 33 objects in the library), as predicted by the theory, the shape of the graph is predominately linear.

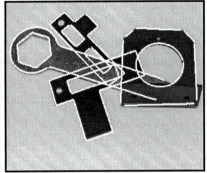

a   b

FIG. 4.22. Four objects are recognized correctly. Although the recognizer concluded that two more object instances were present, they can be ruled out as they were hypothesized by a single invariant and had less than 52% matches. The worst of the four correct identifications had two invariants and 60.3% match. More intelligent verification would mark the last two interpretations as unlikely because they share features with much better identifications.

The real benefit of indexing becomes apparent when one considers how many hypotheses would be produced if an alignment technique were used (maintaining the same grouping methods). On average, over 2000 feature groups existed for each image, and so 2000 hypotheses would be produced for each model feature group in the library (generally there are four or five feature groups per object and so the situation would be far worse). This would result in about 7×10^4 hypotheses for the entire model base compared to less than the 60 produced when indexing is used. As these all have to be verified it is clear that indexing produces a dramatic improvement in the system efficiency.

4.5   Conclusions

In this chapter we have defined the relationships between image features, invariants and index functions. Emphasis has been placed on the fact that invariants and indexing functions are not the same objects; for recognition we need indexes to gain fast access to model libraries, and indexes are computed most efficiently from invariants. An example recognition system LEWIS1 using plane algebraic invariants was then described in detail.

LEWIS1 has been tested over a large number of trials using different complexities of images. In general, very good recognition results have been achieved. Most importantly, Section 4.4.1 demonstrated that indexing produces a far more efficient route to recognition than a naive linear search through the model base. In fact the indexing and hypothesis confirmation

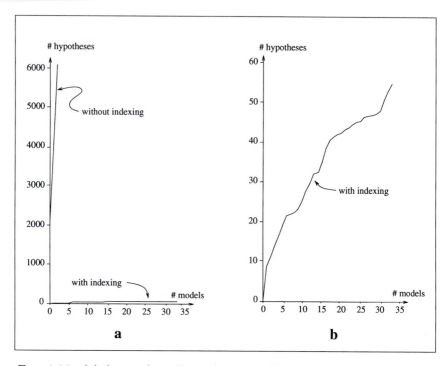

FIG. 4.23. (a) the number of hypotheses that have to be verified varies with
the number of models in the model base. The results show an average
over fifty scenes containing only one object in the model base, but with
other clutter and occlusion present. Over 2000 indexes are created for
the scene, which corresponds to the number of hypotheses that would
have to be verified **per model feature group** if an alignment paradigm
were used. Therefore, there is a rapid linear growth in the number of
hypotheses created as the model base is expanded. However, the number
of hypotheses created through indexing remains substantially lower;
the detail depicted in (b) which shows (a) scaled along the vertical
axis, demonstrates that approximately a low constant of proportionality
linear growth is observed. This ties in with the theoretical prediction of
Section 2.3.1.

stages are the least significant with respect to time consumed in recognition. The rate-determining steps are edge detection, segmentation and
fitting.

The following paragraphs highlight some of the lessons learned in building LEWIS1; comments are made both on the good and bad features of
the system.

4.5.1 *The architecture*

There are a number of benefits to using a simple pipeline architecture for recognition (Fig. 4.1). Principally it is easy to understand the flow of data structures through the complete recognition cycle, and also acquisition can exploit the same modules that are used for recognition. In fact, the architecture is very similar to many of the correspondence systems reviewed in (53), the difference really is only in the presence of the indexing and hypothesis merging modules.

However, observing the performance of the system makes it clear that there are certain limitations of the approach (for example too many false positives). The main problem is that there is not enough interaction between the modules; the flow of information is always unidirectional. In (150) an improved architecture, MORSE, is suggested that allows feedback between different phases. For instance, segmentation and grouping can be refined using knowledge of putative recognition hypotheses, also different invariants can be given varying confidences (or used at different times) depending on the current understanding of the scene. It appears that this form of architecture employing more dynamic interactions between the modules is the way to attack recognition. Current research is focused at testing out this approach within the invariant indexing paradigm.

LEWIS1 has also been built only with a single type of shape descriptor in mind (plane algebraic invariants). Chapter 5 demonstrates that the architecture is equally successful for smooth plane curves within the LEWIS2 system, and the same framework has been used to derive the invariant results given in Chapter 8. However, most objects in the world do not fit neatly into a single class (plane algebraic, smooth plane curve, polyhedral, etc.), and so any more general system must allow interactions not only between the different phases of the recognition process, but also between different types of invariant.

4.5.2 *Efficiency in grouping*

LEWIS1 uses a very simple grouping heuristic: all lines in a single group must be connected though the Canny edgel chains, and conics are grouped by proximity. Excessive occlusion can prevent any useful groups being formed and so recognition would fail unless a more robust grouping process is substituted. What one must not allow is an $^{l}P_n$ grouping algorithm for choosing groups of n features from an image containing l features. Such an approach would be catastrophic for efficiency.

Nevertheless, invariant indexing approaches to recognition can make use of the same grouping heuristics used by more conventional recognition systems to prevent a combinatorial explosion of permutations (even the correspondence algorithms fail to work in reasonable times without grouping). Some of these are investigated in Chapter 6 for a class of images that fail to provide meaningful connectivity within the edge data (aerial

surveillance images). It is our belief that although invariant indexing systems have worse grouping prospects than conventional systems in a world
that genuinely contains no structure, computer vision is seldom applied to
that type of environment and so both types of system have equal grouping
opportunities.

4.5.3   *Extension*

Recognition can be driven entirely through the creation of index hypotheses
and their subsequent verification. However many benefits have been recovered from the hypothesis extension process that creates joint hypotheses.
The most immediate ones have come from the improved levels of confidence that may be associated with larger joint hypotheses and also the
enhanced efficiency of recognition as multiple hypotheses can be verified
simultaneously.

However, the full benefits of extension probably have not yet been realized; the process could be used to pull together different varieties of local
shape cues into single invariant global descriptions. This not only leads to
the more complete description of objects entirely composed of one type
of invariant (such as the plane algebraic invariants of LEWIS1), but also
between different classes of invariant in both two and three dimensions.
These notions of extension are still being developed and require a substantial amount of work in system testing and in deriving scene understanding (more details about the approach for different object classes are given
in (113)).

4.5.4   *Verification*

Verification certainly does not provide the level of filtering that is ultimately
desired in a recognition system; incorrect recognition hypotheses are still
able to pass through the backprojection and support search procedures.
There are a number of different approaches that verification can take, apart
from those described in Section 4.2.6. However, the following discussion
concentrates on details directly relevant to the given method. It is true,
however, that most verification algorithms are prone to the same sorts of
errors observed in LEWIS1, and so the similar observations are applicable
to them.

As shown in Table 4.5 a significant number of false positive are observed
in each scene. These tend to take two different forms: the first is demonstrated in Fig. 4.21 in which an object with a realistic pose is located in
the image; the second type occurs where objects with extremely unlikely
poses are recognized due to sufficient levels of image support. Examples of
this latter class are shown in Figs 4.24 and 4.25. There are a number of
possible approaches that could be used to rule out these two cases:

- **Full scene understanding**: the most obvious way to rule out false
  positives is to assign every feature measured in a scene to an object

a   b

FIG. 4.24. An object from the model base which is superimposed in (b) can be recognized with over 50% edge support from the specularity on the pair of scissors in (a). Note the model-to-image map used in the backprojection represents a bizarre projectivity, though it is hard to differentiate strictly between sensible projectivities that are normally encountered and others by looking at the T matrices alone.

identity.[20] Then, if there is a conflict the most probable interpretation can be assumed, and the other rejected. Subsequently, all other hypotheses are adjusted to account for the scene data that has been explained by the accepted hypothesis. This approach certainly would not be guaranteed to work using the current verification capabilities because the most likely hypothesis can occasionally be incorrect itself. Therefore, although there is reason in the approach other improvements to verification must be introduced first.

- **Physics-based vision**: so far recognition has been driven entirely from geometric information about the objects. Although it is unlikely that properties such as shading, texture, contrast or colour are useful in the early stages of recognition, they would be useful for confirming or rejecting the existence of an object. For example, texture cues on the surfaces of an object or perhaps the correct signs and locations of contrast changes could be used to enhance model hypothesis support.

- **Pose computation:** LEWIS does not compute pose (except for the projective position of the object in the image). There are two benefits of computing pose: first, one can determine if an object is in an unlikely position (too far from the camera, beneath an opaque surface, etc.); secondly one can determine whether features that should be visible are in fact observed in the scene, rather then being occluded by other objects. Up till now only *positive* information has

[20] A number of systems actually try and assign individual image features to single objects. The objection to this approach is that an incorrect assignment is likely to lead to the creation of recognition false negatives.

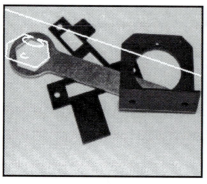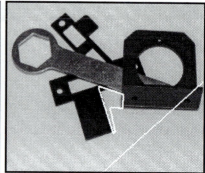

a   b

FIG. 4.25. The objects from Fig. 4.22a were recognized incorrectly. Unlike
the matches shown in Fig. 4.22b these two objects were hypothesized
by only a single invariant, and had less than 52% image support. In
both cases image support is provided by features that have already
been used to verify the hypotheses shown in Fig. 4.22b. The straight
line across each image is the projection of the line at infinity from the
acquisition images. Details are given later in the text for their presence.
Their closeness to the image centre indicates unlikely object poses.

been used (the presence of a feature), whereas with pose the lack
of observed data which is *negative* information can be exploited as
used in 3DPO (12) (up to the limitations of the feature detector).
Again, one could also arbitrate between objects by insisting that no
two objects occupy the same position in space. Unfortunately, this
also may result in the occurrence of false conclusions if an incorrect
interpretation is accepted prior to verifying a correct one.

The use of pose is probably the most likely approach to succeed. Pose
computation is relatively straightforward as is clear from the wealth of
literature on the subject. Recent work reported by Forsyth, *et al.* (46) has
highlighted how pose can be used to test for global scene consistency when
Euclidean models are available. Global consistency means that objects must
occupy different regions in space and also that certain constraints can be
tested between pose hypotheses (such as coplanarity, or the opaqueness of
objects preventing visibility if the line of sight to an object is blocked by
another object). Unfortunately, in this case complete Euclidean models of
the objects are not available because model acquisition is performed from
actual images.

Projective knowledge of the models can still be exploited in some cases
due to certain restrictions placed on the object poses allowable during acquisition. In practice the acquisition images are often taken from views
that contain at most affine distortions, and even from fronto-parallel posi-

tions. (It is suggested in Chapter 5 that the model should be learned from a fronto-parallel view which provides an equiform view, that is a scaled Euclidean view of the object. This provides what is called a *natural view*.) Using restricted acquisition views can help verification:

- If the projected model is too small in the scene during verification the three-dimensional object hypothesizing the image features must have been so far away that it would not be observed reliably. Therefore it can be rejected out of hand. An upper bound on the size of the projected model can be computed by bounding the model by a box and projecting that to the image prior to full verification; if it is too small, then the hypothesized object must be too small and so can be rejected. Using the bounding box reduces the computation time required for complex models. The convex hull could be used, though in practice the bounding box is the perimeter of the acquisition image used to obtain the model description.

- If the hypothesized object must take an extreme pose to account for the image features (for instance if it must have a very high slant or else it might have to lie well outside the field of view of the camera), the projection of the shape of the model in the image would be excessively distorted. One extreme could be that the projected object passes through the ideal line of the image. Such an event certainly cannot happen for the object that actually projected to the image features as it would have to pass through the plane containing the camera focal point that lies parallel to the image plane (compare with Fig. 3.14 in Chapter 3). This scenario occurred in Fig. 4.24, where all the model edgel points that projected into the image are shown in (b); a number of points were mapped to regions of the image plane near the ideal line, and continuous model line segments actually intersected it. This observation builds on the work of Sparr (122) for pose computation.

- Alternatively, if the hypothesized object has a very high slant in the world the projection of the model ideal line will lie close to the centre of the image (this line is just the horizon line[21]). Although the horizon line is a familiar entity in images, it is normally only observed for large objects, for example the world ground plane. Generally, for smaller objects it is observed only for extreme views for which one would encounter feature extraction problems. Therefore, a contradiction occurs if one can both form invariant feature groups and observe the object; thus the recognition hypothesis must be incorrect. The projection of the model ideal lines for two incorrect hypotheses are shown in Fig. 4.25, and the observation of these in the image is a clear sign that the hypotheses are false.

---

[21] Note that if an affine or equiform acquisition view was used, the model ideal line corresponds exactly to the Euclidean model ideal line.

In fact, preliminary experiments suggest that up to 25% of the incorrectly confirmed hypotheses can be ruled out using these tests. Additionally, such tests can be performed prior to full backprojection as they involve only a few of the model features (which are either a bounding box, line segments, or the line at infinity), and so not only are the verification results more trustworthy, but they are also produced more efficiently.

4.5.5   *Observed errors*

Section 4.3.1 produced a very important result, that is, errors can be observed in images which would not have been predicted by the generally accepted noise models. It is always important to take any theoretic result and determine whether it is really applicable to a situation; likewise it is beneficial to use any empirical observation to promote the derivation and correction of error models. Most of the understanding of the error characteristics in LEWIS1 has been done through experimental observation, though a full understanding of the problems that can occur in the three-dimensional world could assist in the analytic determination of the noise models.

5

PROJECTIVE INVARIANTS OF SMOOTH PLANE CURVES: LEWIS2

Invariants can also be computed for planar objects that contain more general plane curves than lines and conics. The subsequent discussion develops a process for forming invariant signatures for a class of smooth plane curves. These signatures provide a projectively invariant shape description from which indexes can be computed. Consequently, the process can be used within the LEWIS invariant indexing architecture for recognizing planar objects with boundaries consisting of higher-degree curves than lines or conics. The actual recognition system discussed in this chapter is called LEWIS2, and although a different system from LEWIS1, it shares many common processes.

The feature class used in LEWIS2 is of non-convex smooth plane curves. As has been shown, there is a relatively simple process that can be used to derive shape descriptors based on invariant indexing functions for low-order algebraic curves such as lines and conics. However, as the order of the curves increases, it becomes more and more difficult to find robust representations that are local or semi-local and subsequently have an appreciable independence from occlusion. Even cubic fitting is hard for small noisy data sets, Keren, *et al.* (65) and Taubin, *et al.* (131). Better fits can consequently be obtained only through using a more global shape description. This, however, makes the representation intolerant to occlusion.

Instead of fitting curves that *approximate* the image data well one can aim to *represent* them using lower-order curves such as conics (39). So long as an algebraic representation of the image data is found in a projectively invariant manner the fitted curve becomes a stable representation of the data and can be used for recognition. Then, invariants for the fitted curves can be used for indexing. Forsyth, *et al.* (39) showed how affine conic representations can be derived for point sets, and Carlsson produced a full projective representation (20). However, such representation schemes usually require a global description of shape and are thus affected by occlusion or poor segmentation.

An alternative way of computing invariants for plane curves is to use *differential invariants*. These invariants have expressions involving the locations of points and local derivatives of the curve at these points. The simplest differential invariant, which applies under plane Euclidean actions, is curvature. This is computed using second-order and lower derivatives. Under the full plane projective group the simplest invariant is reported by Wilczynski in (144); this requires knowledge of seven curve derivatives at a single point. The invariant was brought to the notice of the vision community by Weiss (141). The drawback of this invariant is that seventh-order derivatives cannot be computed with any degree of accuracy from discrete and noisy image data. Differential invariants can be computed using lower-order derivatives when the number of points included in the expressions increases. These invariants are known as *semi-differential invariants* and have been investigated by Van Gool, *et al.* (136) and Barrett, *et al.* (5). Invariants are computed either as invariant signatures (essentially an extension of the algorithm of Turney, *et al.* (135) who computed a $\theta - s$ representation of curves invariant to plane Euclidean action), or as indexing functions themselves. Section 5.0.2 goes through the process required for the computation of a semi-differential projective signature using the methods of Van Gool, *et al.* (21).

The curve signatures developed in this chapter are computed without using any curve derivatives of a degree higher than those required to determine curve tangencies. Using point locations and their first derivatives along the curve allows curves to be mapped to a canonical frame:

Definition 5.1 *A canonical frame for a curve is a projective representation of the curve that is by construction independent of viewpoint. The representation is complete and is unique for all curves.*

The construction employed to derive the invariants is just one example of the application of a *canonical frame*, Marr (78), and can be compared to the procedure used in Section 3.4.2 to derive the projective invariants for a set of five coplanar points. Although in this chapter the projective representation is realized primarily though the locations of tangencies, the method extends easily to curves possessing specific features with any order of C^n discontinuity or incidence.

It will be shown that invariants can be measured directly in the canonical frame. The curve in the canonical frame is called the *curve signature* and the canonical frame is reached by a *projective normalization* process.

5.0.1 *Plane curve normalization*

The goal of the normalization process is to reach a frame that is independent of the original viewpoint, but maintains the projective shape of the original curve. Fundamentally, all projectively equivalent curves will be mapped to the same frame. Under Euclidean transformations normalization is achieved by mapping the centre of area of a curve to the origin of the canonical frame and aligning the principal axes along the x and y coordinate axes. Note that the curve must be closed for it to have a well-defined area; if not, one could represent the curve by its convex hull or some other suitable measure.

By way of example, the result of applying the Euclidean normalization process to an ellipse would be an ellipse of the same area and aspect ratio as the original, but centred on the origin with the major axis aligned along the x axis of the canonical frame and the minor axis along the y axis. Extension to similarity (equiform) normalization involves isotropically scaling the curve so that it has unit area; therefore for the ellipse under normalization the aspect ratio would be preserved but not the area.

Generally, due to the requirement to compute the area enclosed by the curve (or more generally a set of arbitrary order moments), the entire curve has to be considered whilst determining the canonical frame. Consequently the above normalization procedure only provides a representation that is global. For instance, it is hard to see immediately how one would normalize a short curve segment that is continuous with a larger curve independently of any effect of the larger feature. However, if smaller curve segments can be extracted from the entire curve (without any prior knowledge of the curve), the algorithm can be made local. Such a segmentation process relies on the location of distinguished points; these are points that are covariant, or preserved, by the imaging process. The following example demonstrates the use of distinguished points for the computation of an invariant signature as used by Van Gool, *et al.* (21).

5.0.2   *Semi-differential invariant signatures*

Here we provide an example of the computation of a semi-differential description derived from a local curve segment. The description yields a projectively invariant signature for the curve. The original mathematics as well as results from real images are presented by Van Gool, *et al.* (21). The signature in this example is computed for the curve in Fig. 5.1a; this is the plane curve $y = x^4/4 - x^2/2 + 1/4$.

The signature is computed using only the curve segment between the points $\mathbf{b}_1$ and $\mathbf{b}_2$. Again we wish to use only local object descriptions to ensure tolerance to occlusion. The points $\mathbf{b}_1$ and $\mathbf{b}_2$ define the line bitangent to the curve near to the origin. A third point used in the construction is the point $\mathbf{c}$; this is located at the intersection of the two inflection lines to the curve between $\mathbf{b}_1$ and $\mathbf{b}_2$; $\mathbf{c}$ lies at $(0, 1/3)$. The curve signature is also computed using the location of the point marked as $\mathbf{h}$. This point is defined using a (semi-differential) projectively invariant parametrization of the curve $\mathbf{x}$ that is expressed as an integral of determinants of matrices:

$$s(\mathbf{p}) = k \int_{t_1}^{t_p} \mathrm{abs}\left(\frac{|\mathbf{x} - \mathbf{c} \quad \mathbf{x}'|}{|\mathbf{x} - \mathbf{b}_1 \quad \mathbf{x} - \mathbf{b}_2|^2}\right) dt,$$

where t is an arbitrary parametrization of the curve that takes the value t_1

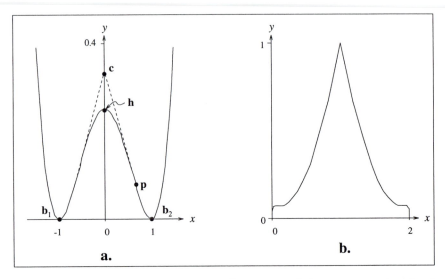

FIG. 5.1. *Invariant signatures can be computed for curves using local semi-differential descriptions. (b) shows the projective signature of (a).*

at b_1, and t_p at p. The parametrization t does not have to be projectively invariant and so it could be arc-length, or even in this specific example the x coordinate of the curve. x' is the derivative the curve with respect to t, and the value of k is set so that $s(b_1) = 0$ and $s(b_2) = 1$. The point h is defined such that $s(h) = 0.5$. Note that the denominator of the expression can tend to zero for certain positions on the curve. This can cause problems as noted by Van Gool, *et al.* (21). In this example h is located at $(0, 1/4)$ due to symmetry.

The four points $\{b_1, b_2, c, h\}$ are distinguished under projective transformations. Once they have all been located two invariant parameters are computed:

$$I_x(\mathbf{p}) = k_x \int_{t_1}^{t_p} f(\mathbf{x})\ dt,$$

$$\text{where} \quad f(\mathbf{x}) = \begin{cases} \mathrm{abs}\left(\dfrac{|\mathbf{x}-\mathbf{b}_2 \quad \mathbf{x}'|}{|\mathbf{x}-\mathbf{b}_2 \quad \mathbf{x}-\mathbf{c}|^2} \right) & \text{if } s(\mathbf{x}) \leq 0.5, \\[3mm] \mathrm{abs}\left(\dfrac{|\mathbf{x}-\mathbf{b}_1 \quad \mathbf{x}'|}{|\mathbf{x}-\mathbf{b}_1 \quad \mathbf{x}-\mathbf{c}|^2} \right) & \text{otherwise,} \end{cases}$$

$$I_y(\mathbf{p}) = \begin{cases} k_y \text{ abs}\left(\frac{|\mathbf{x}-\mathbf{c} \quad \mathbf{x}-\mathbf{b}_1|}{|\mathbf{x}-\mathbf{c} \quad \mathbf{x}-\mathbf{b}_2|}\right) & \text{if } s(\mathbf{p}) \leq 0.5, \\ \\ k_y \text{ abs}\left(\frac{|\mathbf{x}-\mathbf{c} \quad \mathbf{x}-\mathbf{b}_2|}{|\mathbf{x}-\mathbf{c} \quad \mathbf{x}-\mathbf{b}_1|}\right) & \text{otherwise.} \end{cases}$$

k_x and k_y are parameters set such that $I_x(\mathbf{h}) = 1$ and $I_y(\mathbf{h}) = 1$. The invariant signature is plotted as $(I_x(\mathbf{x}), I_y(\mathbf{x}))$ and is shown in Fig. 5.1b. This signature is invariant to any projective action on the original curve and is similar to the descriptions that are developed in the rest of this chapter.

The normalization process employed in LEWIS2 makes use of distinguished points, but does not require the evaluation of integrals. Although the distinguished points in the above example were selected by hand from the sample curve, the segmentation process can be automated. The method used is a direct extension to the work of Lamdan, et al. (68), who derived a semi-local normalization procedure for non-convex curves under affine imaging. Not only is the construction extended to projectivities, but also indexing functions are defined and actually used within a working recognition system. First, the construction is introduced and it is then shown how the normalized curves can be reduced to a set of indexes. After this, it is revealed how the construction fits into the recognition framework that was used in Chapter 4 for the description of algebraic curves.

5.1   The canonical frame construction

The construction maps distinguished features on an image curve to corresponding features in the canonical frame (as with the canonical frame construction described in Section 3.4.2 for the measurement of the invariants for five points). The algorithm is developed using points of tangency and bitangency as used in the initial implementation of (109). It will then be argued that such points actually provide the best solution. There are three important considerations that should be addressed before assessing the quality of the construction:

1. What is the best choice for the shape of the canonical frame? The distinguished points should be placed in the frame so that the process is stable, and allows an easy choice of discriminatory measures.

2. What distinguished features should be used? Points and lines of tangency are only one choice; inflection lines and points could also be used. The curves under consideration are smooth curves, and consequently points of incidence and tangency discontinuity are not considered. However, if such points were available, and if it is possible to extract them robustly, one would be equally able to use them within the canonical frame construction.

3. Which imaging model should be used? For a pinhole camera model projective transformations cover all the distortions that are present in the imaging process, but it is possible that one might be able to use an affine approximation with an equal degree of reliability. It is assumed that if radial distortion effects are present in the image then they can be removed using the techniques of Slama (121), though as yet the effects of radial distortion have made no significant difference to the result of the construction.

5.1.1 *The basic construction*

Lamdan, *et al.* used three points to define an affine canonical frame. For a projective representation four points in general position are required. The aim is to find four distinguished points (or lines) on a curve, and use these to define the projectivity T that can be used to take the whole curve to the canonical frame; the projective transformation is defined using the formulae in Section 3.1.3. The construction is identical to that which was used to form invariants for sets of five points in Section 3.4.2.

The method is shown in Fig. 5.2: for the given image curve, determine the location of the points of bitangency following the method given in Section 6.2. These are (A) and (D), and they segment the $\mathcal{M}$ curve from all other image data. Through these points find the *cast tangents* (lines tangent to the $\mathcal{M}$ curve that pass through the bitangency points) that make the largest angle with the bitangent line; the points of cast tangency are (B) and (C). Although there are potentially many cast tangents, these ones are used because there is no requirement for redundancy within such a local curve segment (more details about the choice of cast tangents are given in Chapter 6). This is an example of subsumption, Brady (15), because a single description is used to cover a larger number of other possible descriptors that would have resulted through the use of other cast tangents; subsumption is the process by which local shape cues are included within more general ones. The four points {A,B,C,D} are then mapped by a projectivity T to the corners of the unit square defining the canonical frame. The result of the projection of the $\mathcal{M}$ curve into the frame using T is the *curve signature*; it is a projective representation of the original object curve.

5.1.2 *Using the canonical frame for recognition*

If we want to use the curve signatures of smooth planar curves for recognition there are three important criteria that should be considered:

1. **Discrimination:** curves in the canonical frame belonging to different objects should differ.
2. **Semi-local description:** descriptors should not encompass entire objects; a number of different descriptions should be used for each object. The use of multiple shape measures for a single object is called *redundancy*.

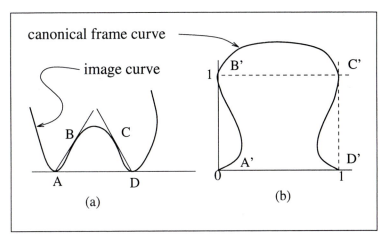

FIG. 5.2. (a) Construction of the four points necessary to define the canonical frame for an image curve. The first two points, (A) and (D), are points of bitangency that mark the entrance to the concavity. Two further distinguished points, (B) and (C), are obtained from rays cast from the bitangent contact points and tangent to the curve segment within the concavity. The curve segment ABCD is called an $\mathcal{M}$ curve. These four points are used to map the curve to the canonical frame. A projection is constructed that transforms the four points in (a) to the corners of the unit square. The same projection transforms the curve into this frame. (b) shows the curve in canonical frame; this is an *invariant signature*.

3. **Stability:** curves in the canonical frame for differing views of the same object should be similar.

The rôles that each of these criteria play in recognition are discussed more thoroughly in Chapter 7; the rest of this section shows that the basic construction goes some way towards their satisfaction.

5.1.2.1 *Discrimination* Examples of the canonical frame construction for single views of three different objects are given in Fig. 5.3. A single $\mathcal{M}$ curve for each spanner and the pair of scissors is marked in (a), (b) and (c), and these are projected into the same canonical frame in (d). All three signatures are different and so the construction provides discrimination between the objects. Although the spanner curves extracted from (a) and (b) are reasonably similar, they are sufficiently different for recognition purposes.

5.1.2.2 *Local description* Local descriptions must be used if objects are to be recognized under occlusion. Each local shape must satisfy a range of different shape criteria such as those suggested here, but there must also

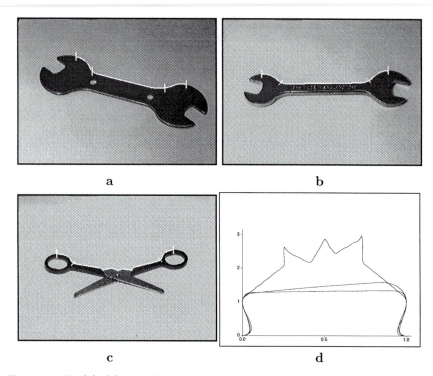

FIG. 5.3. In (a)–(c) a single $\mathcal{M}$ curve and the four distinguished points are marked on each object. The three curves are projected to the canonical frame and superimposed in (d). The scissor signature is obviously very different from each spanner, but in fact the two spanner signatures are sufficiently different for recognition purposes.

be a number of different descriptors on each object so that there is not an excessive requirement for a single object region to be visible; this is called redundancy. As can be seen in Fig. 6.10, single objects frequently possess large numbers of bitangents; this provides a high degree of redundancy as each bitangent can be used to form an $\mathcal{M}$ curve and its associated signature. However, such a degree of redundancy is not required for recognition and only a few bitangents are actually used for shape description (details of which ones are chosen are given in Section 6.2.1). For the spanner in Fig. 5.3a, four suitable bitangents exist and bound $\mathcal{M}$ curves. The four $\mathcal{M}$ curves are shown in Fig. 5.4. Note that in reality only the two largest of the four $\mathcal{M}$ curves yield stable signatures due to local effects near the bitangent points of the smaller ones; the stability of the construction can be computed automatically using the process given later in Section 5.4.2.

5.1.2.3 *Stability* The final criterion discussed in this section is stability: if the construction is to be useful, similar signatures must be obtained for

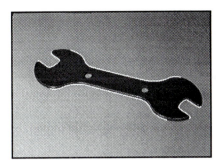

FIG. 5.4. Even for a simple object such as a spanner there is a sufficient
degree of redundancy when the canonical frame construction is used.
Here, four useful $\mathcal{M}$ curves are shown that essentially cover the entire
perimeter of the object, and yet each one is potentially a sufficient
recognition cue on its own.

different views of the same object curve. Even if the signatures are not
identical, they should be sufficiently similar so that discrimination between
objects is possible. This is the case for the canonical frame construction.
Three very different views of a spanner are given in Fig. 5.5 (they vary by a
full perspective distortion, and not just an affine one). The same $\mathcal{M}$ curve
is marked in each image, and these are mapped to the canonical frame in
(d). As can be seen the construction is stable even over a wide change in
viewpoint.

5.1.3 Refining the construction

Now that the basic form of the canonical frame construction has been introduced we can analyse carefully whether certain improvements can be
made that will either enhance the shape criteria just discussed or improve
efficiency. For example, one may consider the effects of using a different
canonical frame, the use of other distinguished features, or even the use
of an alternative imaging model instead of projection. The following discussions use a pair of experiments that are designed to provide information about the complete range of distortions to object curves that may be
encountered in practice. In each experiment an object is rotated on a calibration table under a typical viewing geometry. The objects are rotated
through a total of 180 degrees in increments of 5 degrees for each series and
so each experiment provides thirty-seven images for analysis. So that minimal emphasis can be placed on unmodelled aspects of the edge detector
(such as the effects of specularity, shadow, and the finite thickness of real
objects that caused the problems in the experiment of Section 4.3.1), the
first object was printed on paper using a laser printer. Its actual shape was
modelled on the fronto-parallel view of the second object, a spanner. Two
of the images in the sequence of the printed object (the first and twentieth)

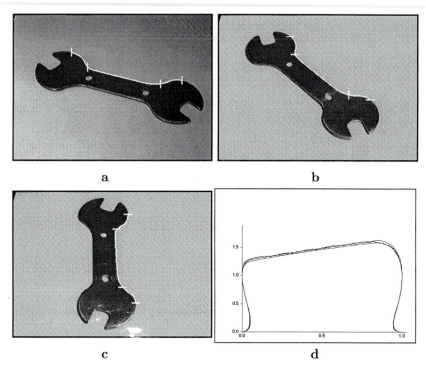

FIG. 5.5. (a)–(c) three views of a spanner with the extracted $\mathcal{M}$ curves and distinguished points marked. Note the very different appearance due to perspective effects. (d) shows the signatures for the three different views. The curves are almost identical, demonstrating the stability of the method. Of course, the same signature would result from a projective transformation between the object and canonical frame.

are shown in Fig. 5.6. The spanner is shown in Fig. 5.7; the $\mathcal{M}$ curve of interest is the left-most one in (a) and the distant one in (b).

The reason for studying the artificial case of the printed object is to test whether the assumptions used during the canonical frame construction are valid for real images: these are the preservation of tangencies and inflections under perspective imaging. Mathematically it is known that the construction is correct, one is simply testing whether image quantization effects and the segmentation process affect the utility of the construction. However, the main interest is in using the construction for real object recognition; this is the motivation for the second sequence. For the spanner the edge detector will fail to convey accurate geometric information about the scene due to distraction and other errors and so one is determining how much the construction is affected by the reduced performance of the early vision component of the processing.

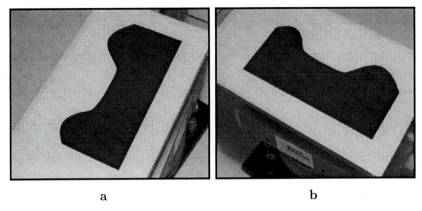

a   b

FIG. 5.6. The first and twentieth views of the object in the sequence are shown. An image was taken every 5 degrees over a total rotation angle of 180 degrees.

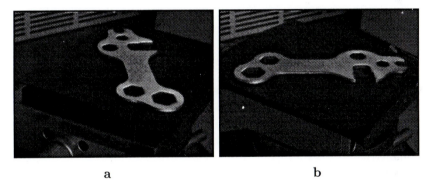

a   b

FIG. 5.7. The first and twentieth views of the spanner in the sequence are shown. The $\mathcal{M}$ curve of interest is the left-most one in (a), and the distant one in (b).

5.1.4   Choice of frame

The examples up to now have used a canonical frame with reference points at the corners of the unit square. One may question where it is best to place the distinguished points in the frame. Using different positions can have dramatic effects on the shape of the observed signatures. The main concern is that plane projectivities cause non-uniform magnifications in different portions of the plane and so noise effects for one part of a curve may be enhanced to such a level in one region that they dominate the signal in another. For example, consider the extreme case arising when a circle projects to a hyperbola: when viewed on a plane framed by a Cartesian coordinate system such as in an image, there are points infinitesimally close on the circle that can be projected to points that are infinitely far apart on the hyperbola. Consequently if noise is added to the circle its effects will be most noticeable towards the infinite parts of the hyperbola as this is where magnification is largest and it will certainly be larger than the signal content in the high-curvature segments of the curve.

In more generic cases, and within the bounds of the finite image, the non-uniformity is not so severe. We certainly do not intend to account for such extreme projectivities within a recognition system. However, the effect of errors being magnified can still be observed. Consequently, in the same way that image features become distorted, noise also projects in a non-uniform manner. More importantly error in the locations of the distinguished points can cause the non-uniform treatment of information. Essentially (approximately) isotropic image noise becomes non-isotropic in the canonical frame; it is desirable to have as uniform an error distribution as possible in the measurement frame.

The actual form of the projectivity is determined by the shape of the canonical frame and this subsequently determines the extent to which image measurements project non-uniformly. Therefore, using the wrong choice of frame will cause a bias in the measurement of any invariants. The effects of using a different frame are shown in Figs 5.8 and 5.9 in which the two image sequences have been mapped to the *natural frame* of the object as well as to one defined by the unit square. The natural frame is given by a similarity transformation of the original object curve. It is appealing that the natural frame should have better error performance as it will, over the complete range of viewpoints, represent the frame of minimal projective distortion of the image curves. Therefore it will also distort the noise distribution minimally.

The result of this experiment is that for a particular object, the natural frame gives rise to the best error suppression. Therefore it is used within LEWIS2 for the construction of invariant object signatures. However, one problem with defining a preferred frame is that it must be used for all objects (yet each object has its own intrinsic natural frame), and each object is likely to have a different performance in the single frame. It is clear that a single natural frame cannot exist for the entire model base. There are two ways to approximate to a single frame for the model base:

1. Pick a frame that is as close to the natural frame of all of the model curves as possible.

2. Use a range of frames and compute invariant signatures for each frame individually. Recognition can proceed so long as for a given $\mathcal{M}$ curve one of the frames provides a stable representation.

For the models used in the recognition system (which are given in Section 5.3) a single frame has been used. It is hard to choose automatically an optimal frame for all of the curves, but the current one performs well. Ultimately, a number of other frames should be used so that the second

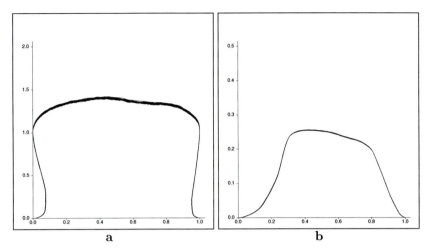

FIG. 5.8. (a) demonstrates the projection of the 37 $\mathcal{M}$ curves for the
printed object into the unit square canonical frame, and (b) the projection to the natural frame. Note that the scales for the two graphs are
different. Along the horizontal portions of the curve the original image
errors have been amplified more for the unit frame case rather than the
natural one; this shows that the former is a bad choice of frame.

criterion is satisfied (in practice use a set of descriptors that describe the
objects in parallel).

A final comment with regard to the use of the natural frame is in its use
during acquisition for the extraction of an object model. As was discussed
in Chapter 4, an object model consists of a series of edgels measured in a
view of the object. For the same reason that a canonical frame provides the
best performance for the canonical frame construction, an equiform view of
a object also provides the best vantage point from which to form an object
model.

5.1.5 Choice of distinguished features

The examples up to now have all used points of tangency and bitangency as
distinguished features. There are other features that can be used, namely
points and lines of inflection.[22] Any non-degenerate set of features could
be used to define the canonical frame; for example one could be computed
using a mixed set of points and lines (with the image-to-frame projectivity
computed using the method given in Appendix B). However, it should be
noted that finding an over-constrained map to the canonical frame will not
lead to a projectively invariant description unless the distinguished features
are projectively equivalent on all of the model curves. This situation is

---

[22]Inflection line and point detection is described in Section 6.2.3.

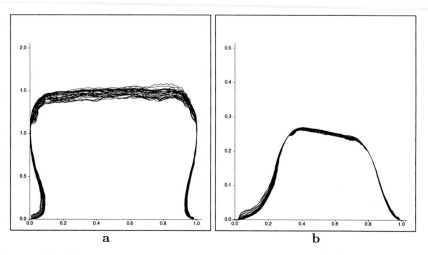

FIG. 5.9. The curve signatures in the unit and natural frames for the
spanner which is specular and has finite thickness. Again the image
error is suppressed more uniformly for the natural frame than for the
unit frame.

unlikely. For example, there is no reason for a pair of $\mathcal{M}$ curves to have
five distinguished features that are in *exact* projective correspondence and
so it would be impossible to choose five points in the canonical frame that
would produce consistent signatures for the two objects. Therefore minimal
sets of distinguished features must be used that only sufficiently define the
image-to-frame map.

An alternative frame could be defined by the line of bitangency and the
inflection points and lines (exactly fixing the normalization projectivity by
eight constraints). The results of using these features to define the map to
the natural frame for the two image sequences is shown in Fig. 5.10; these
should be compared to the results of Figs 5.8 and 5.9. In conclusion we see
that the original choice of distinguished features that exploit tangency are
the best to use. This has been confirmed not only through the use of this
test with the bitangent line and inflection line–point configuration, but also
against a number of other possible configurations.

The reason that the alternative construction fails is this case is that
(for this model class) it is hard to locate the inflection points accurately
using the current segmentation procedure. This results from the uncertainty
principle discussed in Section 6.2. The principle states that one may either
locate a bitangent line accurately or the associated bitangent points, but
not both (and likewise for inflections). Overall, the points of bitangency
and cast tangency have proved to give the best stability and accuracy
performance under imaging and so they are used within LEWIS2.

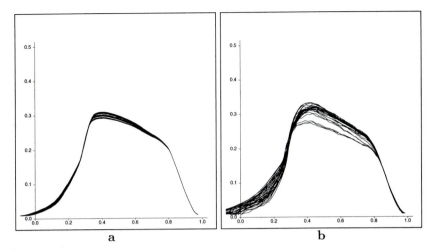

FIG. 5.10. The natural frame can be defined using the bitangent line and inflection lines and points rather than the points of tangency and bitangency used for the original construction. The results for the printed object are in (a) and for the spanner in (b). Note that this construction is not as stable as the original one shown in Figs 5.8 and 5.9.

5.1.6 *Choice of imaging model*

The final issue that motivates which canonical frame construction should be used is whether a full projective imaging model must be assumed (accurate except for non-linear distortions such as those caused through the use of a real lens rather than a pinhole camera), or rather if the frequently used affine approximation would suffice. The latter was used in the paper that motivated the use of the projective canonical frame construction discussed here (by Lamdan *et al.* (68)), and has been used for the construction of other canonical frames (for example by Åström (1)). Affine distortions apply only when the depth of the object under view is at least an order of magnitude less than the distance of the object from the camera and when the camera has a narrow field of view. Therefore the imaging model should not be used if the workspace is close to the camera, or frequently for aerial reconnaissance images.

Under affine distortions there is another invariant other than incidence[23] that can be exploited for the location of distinguished features: this is parallelism. Furthermore, three points only are required for an affine representation of the plane rather than the four for projectivities. Lamdan and his colleagues used tangency and parallelism to find three distinguished points:

---

[23]Tangencies and inflections are just special cases of incidence, the former represent locations of double contact with a line, and the latter triple contact.

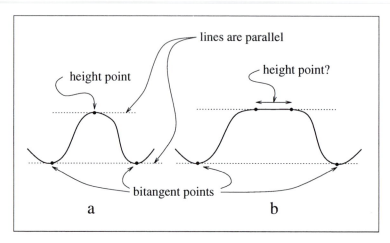

FIG. 5.11. (a) the construction used by Lamdan, *et al.* (68): first a bitangent line is found, then the height point is determined; this is the
point within the M curve most distant from the bitangent line. As
parallelism is preserved under affine transformations this point is distinguished. This process yields three distinguished points and hence a
canonical frame can be constructed. Unfortunately, many objects have
M curves similar to that in (b) where the parallel line most distant to
the bitangent line has a high multiplicity of intersections with the M
curve. In these cases the location of the height point is ambiguous, and
the construction fails.

1. Find the bitangent line across an M curve and use the points of
   bitangency.

2. Determine the line tangent to the M curve between the points of
   bitangency that is most distant to, and parallel to, the line of bitangency. Use the point tangent to this line as a reference point; this is
   known as the *height point* and is preserved under affine projection.

The weakness with this construction, as noted by Mukherjee, *et al.* in (90)
is that the line found by the second stage is frequently tangent to the M
curve at many points. This is apparent in Fig. 5.11. This is a re-occurrence
of the principle of uncertainty, and applies to many of the curves of the
model base of LEWIS2. Consequently the method of Lamdan, *et al.* cannot
be used reliably in this context to form an affine canonical frame.

An alternative affine frame that could be defined might use a different
set of distinguished features: the original bitangent line and a pair of inflection lines within the M curve would suffice. These three lines can be
used to define an image-to-canonical-frame affine map. However, as inflection lines cannot be located sufficiently accurately for the model base of
LEWIS2 this does not provide a stable frame (a result of Section 5.1.5).

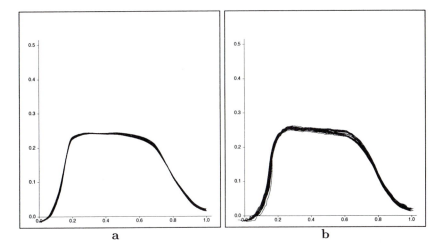

FIG. 5.12. A natural affine frame can be defined using a least squares formulation and the four points of tangency and bitangency. The printed
object signatures are in (a), and those for the real spanner in (b). In
comparison with Figs 5.8 and 5.9 it can be seen that the affine approximation is not the best choice of imaging model.

Instead, an affine map can be computed using the four original bitangency and cast tangency points with a least squares formulation.[24] Figure
5.12 demonstrates the use of these distinguished features for projecting image curves to their natural affine frames. There is a reasonable difference
between the affine curves and those from Figs 5.8 and 5.9, and certainly
enough to note that worse performance is expected when the affine imaging
model is being used. Ultimately, however, in the computation of the most
reliable affine frame a sufficient number of features have been extracted to
enable a projective frame to be produced and so its better performance
may as well be utilized.

The conclusions that can be drawn from this series of investigations
into the canonical frame construction are as follows:

- A natural frame should be used to provide the best error performance
  for the derivation of the signatures.

---

[24]Such a least squares formulation is permissible as the natural frame of the object is
known (the actual affine coordinates of all four points are known). In practice such an
affine frame could not be used for recognition as the positions of the four distinguished
points are likely to have different affine coordinates for different objects in the model
base. If one were to employ the affine frame in practice a set of features that may be
used would be the two bitangency points and the mid-point of the cast tangency points;
these three points are preserved under affine distortions.

- The use of points of bitangency and cast tangency as distinguished points provides the best localization and hence the greatest stability in the signatures.
- A full projective imaging model provides the most accurate representation of the imaging process and so should be used for the normalization process.

5.2   Index functions

Section 5.1 has introduced the canonical frame construction and demonstrated that stable projectively invariant curve signatures can be recovered from images of smooth curves. These curves are essentially projectively invariant *templates* for the shapes and so one may attempt to do signature recognition using traditional template matching techniques. However, as emphasized throughout this book such methods require a linear search through the model library and are therefore too slow. Indexing strategies must be used.

Here we demonstrate how different indexes can be extracted from the signatures and then used during hypothesis formation with the LEWIS system architecture. The whole signature is not used because it is not an efficient index; only enough information to discriminate between objects is needed. The signature information that is not used for indexing is not discarded once the indexes have been computed, but is used during the first stage of hypothesis verification.

As the construction is projective, any measure within the canonical frame will be projectively invariant. The aim is therefore to compute a function of a signature that uniquely identifies from which model $\mathcal{M}$ curve it may have come. A number of different index functions were considered during the system development:

- Using different orders of moments of the signatures as indexes. However, even the zeroth-order moment (arc-length) can be affected badly by noise if it is measured at the wrong scale. Some degree of smoothing must be applied to the signatures to reduce noise, but as the errors affecting the imaging process under all imaging conditions will not be known, the optimal size of the smoothing kernel cannot be determined. Furthermore, the effects of the non-isotropic magnification of noise increase the difficulties encountered in computing measures accurately.
- Different order moments for the area enclosed between the signature and the x axis can be used. The computation of area is itself noise smoothing, and so it should behave more reliably than curve-based methods. For the models considered, though, lower-order moments did not provide sufficient discrimination between the signatures, and higher-order moments were susceptible to noise.

- Data compression techniques can either be applied to the curve or to its enclosed area. These include Fourier techniques or other digital transforms such as the Walsh, Karhunen-Loève or discrete cosine. However, for the model base of curves in the library there is not sufficient data reduction for the transforms to provide suitable routes to indexing, that is, a large number of transform coefficients are required to discriminate between the signatures. Ideally a small number of indexes is required, of the order of tens rather than hundreds. Although the large number of transform coefficients do actually carry all of the indexing information, the computation of an efficient hashing function for such a high-dimensional index space is hard.

- Local fitting can be applied to the signatures, say spline fitting, and then the curves represented by the curve parameters. The drawback of this approach is that the shapes are frequently more general than those of low-order splines (see curve g in Fig. 5.19 which has local high-curvature regions). Although only a representation of the curve is required, the curve must be resampled at unit arc-length points to remove biasing of the imaging process, and this task is affected by image noise.

- As the arc-length in the canonical frame is invariant (modulo noise), distinguished points can be marked out at equi-arc-length positions around the signature, and these used as invariant indexes. As with splines, such a representation will not cope with higher-order components of the shape, though this time the cause is aliasing. The natural frame has enforced the quasi-uniform scaling of noise around the entire curve and so movement of the points should be limited. However, it was found that although movement of the points normal to the curve was very small, there was too much displacement in the tangential direction due to non-uniformity in arc-length for the indexes to provide sufficient discrimination between the signatures.

- Mark off equi-angle rays from a point (say $(\frac{1}{2}, 0)$) in the frame and use the intersection points of each ray with the signature as indexes. Although this approach is prone to a sampling error (aliasing), the number of rays (and their positions) can be adjusted to suit the model base and so provide the required discrimination between objects. This is the method of forming invariants that is used within the LEWIS2 and more complete details are given below. Note the similarity of the technique to the *footprints* of Lamdan, *et al.* (68), though points are used rather than areas.

The invariant indexes used are constructed using the geometry of Fig. 5.13. A set of rays at constant angle intervals are drawn from the point $(\frac{1}{2}, 0)$, which is in the centre of the frame, to the signature. The length of the ray from the central point to the signature is used as an index; for n rays an

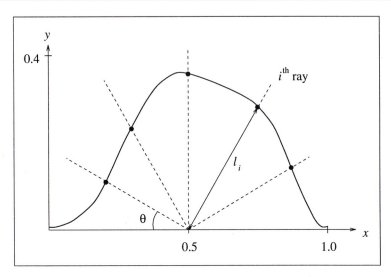

FIG. 5.13. A set of n rays are drawn from the point $(\frac{1}{2}, 0)$ so that they intersect the curve signature. The aim is to construct an n-dimensional index $\mathbf{M} = (l_1, \ldots, l_n)^T$, where l_i is the distance from the intersection point of the ith ray to the point $(\frac{1}{2}, 0)$. This distance is projectively invariant. In the implementation the angle between the rays is constant, though this need not be the case: $\theta = 180/(n+1)$.

n-dimensional index is formed. In the implementation $n = 9$. The drawback of this method for measuring invariants (in comparison to the one that uses arc-length in the canonical frame) is that the choice of which point to use can become ambiguous; this is shown in Fig. 5.14. If the curve doubles back to a sufficient extent one of the rays may cut it more than once, and so the index point is multiply defined. Although one could use a convention and always take the point producing minimum length this can become unstable in some situations under image noise (see the caption in Fig. 5.14). However, such an event does not occur for the model base discussed in this chapter.[25]

Due to the stability of the canonical frame construction the index formation process will also produce stable values (this approach does not suffer from the accumulation of noise as the arc-length-based methods). This is demonstrated in Fig. 5.15 for the image sequence used in Fig. 5.9: the value of the first invariant measured for each image is plotted as the spanner is rotated through 180 degrees. Note in (a) that the value of the invariant is stable, but again a systematic error is apparent when the graph is observed in more detail. This should be compared to the result for the five-line invariant given in Section 4.3.1.

[25]If it did occur the choice of angles of the rays could be changed to prevent any ambiguity.

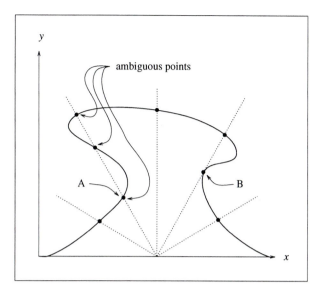

FIG. 5.14. If the signature doubles back, the choice of which index point to use becomes ambiguous. In such cases, one could always use the point producing minimal length, (A). However, under image noise it is not clear whether (B) will actually exist or not (depending on whether the ray has zero, one or two point contact with the signature), and so the construction is unstable.

Discrimination between signatures can be improved by increasing the number of rays used. It should be noted that different rays carry different amounts of information; the dimension of the information content is unlikely to be as high as the number of measurements. The dimension of the index can subsequently be reduced using a classifier. In LEWIS2 the Fisher linear discriminant (FLD) is used (details of the FLD are given in Duda and Hart (33)), which is an optimal linear classifier (a non-linear classifier could be used that would provide better discrimination, though as yet such a move has not been necessary). The FLD encodes information by minimizing the intra-class distribution, and maximizing the inter-class separation. It does so by transforming the data to a new (orthogonal) basis such that classification is maximized under projection onto some of the basis directions, and minimized onto others. Each direction is ranked by how much discrimination it yields. Then, enough of the maximally discriminating directions are chosen to provide the desired classification between the signatures. The actual number of basis dimensions used is seven.

The overall benefit of using the FLD is that the initial indexes (the nine-dimensional input) can be optimized over the model base off-line to provide maximum discrimination between the object signatures with only

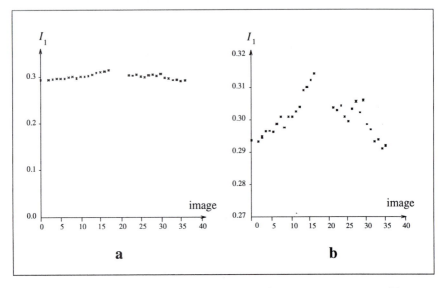

FIG. 5.15. The first invariant measured for the image sequence in Fig. 5.9 is plotted as the spanner is rotated by 5 degrees between images. Note again the presence of a systematic error which is more apparent in the detail depicted in (b).

a seven-dimensional index. The smaller index means that hash table construction and subsequently indexing can be performed more efficiently. Admittedly the FLD does not provide a proper treatment of errors in that the world error distributions are distorted under the projection from the nine-dimensional to the seven-dimensional space. However, as we do not as yet have a sufficiently good understanding of the original world errors such a distortion is acceptable.

A feature of using the classifier for model learning is that now an analytic understanding of the noise characteristics of the process is not required. Simply, a number of examples of a single object $\mathcal{M}$ curve are built up over a number of images, and the classifier adjusts its action to account for the variation within each imaged curve. This contrasts with the analysis applied in Section 4.3.1 for algebraic invariants. An example of a signature for one of the objects in the model library (shown later as curve g in Figs 5.18 and 5.19) is shown in Fig. 5.16. The signature was extracted from the image in Fig. 5.17a. The values of the nine-dimensional input to the FLD, that is each l_i, $i \in \{1, \ldots, 9\}$, and the projected index $\mathbf{M}$ are also given.

5.3 The model base

Now that we have seen how to derive a stable and discriminatory invariant signature and their related invariants indexes based on the use of local ob-

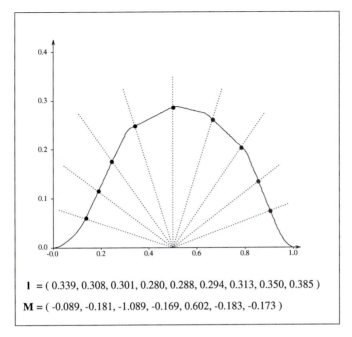

$$l = (0.339, 0.308, 0.301, 0.280, 0.288, 0.294, 0.313, 0.350, 0.385)$$

$$M = (-0.089, -0.181, -1.089, -0.169, 0.602, -0.183, -0.173)$$

FIG. 5.16. The signature of curve (g) from Fig. 5.17a with the index points marked. In the implementation, $n = 9$ provides sufficient discrimination between the different signatures. The invariant length vector l and the projective index vector M which is actually used to index into the hash table are given. M is related to l by a linear computation, $M = E\,l$, where E is provided by the classifier.

ject measures we can attempt to perform recognition for a class of objects that contain $\mathcal{M}$ curves. The rest of this chapter provides a brief summary of the recognition process and then describes the structures of the object model base of LEWIS2; the actual structure of the model base is subtlely different to that for LEWIS1 in that the use of subparts is made more explicit. After this, inclusion of the construction within the LEWIS architecture is given in detail along with examples of the system working on cluttered and occluded images.

5.3.1 *Overview of recognition*

Recognition using the canonical frame construction can be considered to have exactly the same flow of data as the LEWIS architecture of Chapter 4. However, it is also enlightening to consider each $\mathcal{M}$ curve to be a *focus feature* (as used by Bolles and Cain (11)) that is first identified and then used to index a model. Each of these local features is called a *class*. Although the basic features used to recognize an object are classes, a single class need not correspond to only one model. In fact, classes are very similar to the subparts described by Ettinger (34). Therefore, once a class has been recognized it is used to form a hypothesis for any of the possibly many objects in which it is contained.

More explicitly, the flow of recognition is:

1. Segment each $\mathcal{M}$ curve from the scene and compute its signature. From the signature measure an index vector and use this to index into the class model base. Every time a hit is scored hypothesize the presence of a class in the scene.

2. Treat each class hypothesis as a possible object presence in the scene and perform verification. However, the scope of the verification is restricted only to the domain of the original $\mathcal{M}$ curve and its signature.

3. Treat every verified class as an identified scene feature. Use them to index into the object model base to form object hypotheses for every object that is known to contain the class. Note that a single class hypothesis may result in multiple object hypotheses if the class is shared between objects.

4. Extend individual model hypotheses (as was done in LEWIS1) into joint hypothesis.

5. Verify model hypotheses by backprojection.

As a result of this process there is a requirement for two distinct model bases: one for classes and one for models. The latter is indexed using results from the former. The need for two different model bases emphasizes the fact that recognition should be achieved through the use of *hierarchical* object description. In fact, this two-layer hierarchy may be too restrictive in some circumstances and there is no reason why more layers should not be introduced if necessary.

5.3.2 *Acquisition and recognition of classes*

Three pieces of information are stored with every class in the class model base to assist in identification:

1. Data enabling the indexing of the class from $\mathcal{M}$ curves measured within a scene.

2. Information for the verification of class hypotheses.

3. A set of indexes to the models that contain the class.

The $\mathcal{M}$ curve indexes contain only sufficient information to provide efficient access to the library. The class model base contains a large number of examples of the measured indexes taken from a wide range of viewpoints of the same $\mathcal{M}$ curve (note again that acquisition is done directly from images). These sample indexes are used to train the linear classifier that is used for indexing. Employing a number of measurements taken from real images is an example of the use of statistics for error analysis, rather

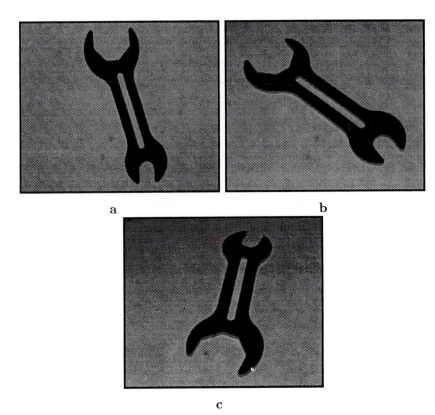

a   b

c

FIG. 5.17. The class curves are acquired from a number of views of the
    unoccluded object. Three views of model 3 are shown. For the labelling
    of Fig. 5.18 the extracted M curves map to the signatures in Fig. 5.19.
    The view in (a) is fronto-parallel: this is because it is best to use the
    natural frame of the object for acquisition as it reduces the distortion
    expected of noise over all other viewpoints.

than requiring the computation of analytic functions as was done for the
algebraic invariants used in Chapter 4. Three of the views used to build
the class models are shown in Fig. 5.17 for one of the objects in the data
base. Note that (a) is fronto-parallel, and so provides information about
the natural frame of the spanner and of each of its four M curves. The rest
of the model base (as well as the locations of the four M curves) is shown
in Fig. 5.18.

Classes are verified in the canonical frame. As has been seen in Section
5.2 the indexes do not provide a *complete* description of the class shape,
and so a typical class curve within the canonical frame is also stored (again
measured from a fronto-parallel view in an image). The final piece of data
stored is the list of objects and their particular M curves that are modelled

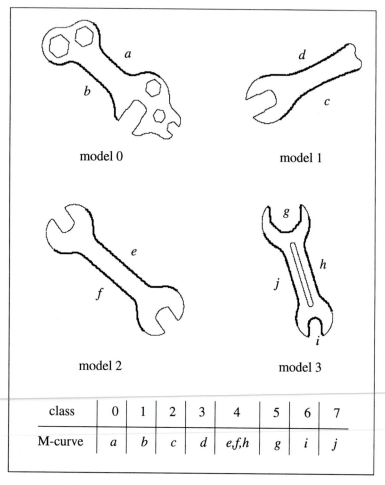

class	0	1	2	3	4	5	6	7
M-curve	a	b	c	d	e,f,h	g	i	j

FIG. 5.18. For the model base consisting of the four spanners there are ten useful $\mathcal{M}$ curves. These are shown by thick lines and labelled a to i. Due to the projective similarity of e, f and h, eight classes are sufficient to represent the local shapes of the spanners. The correspondence between the $\mathcal{M}$ curves and the classes is given in the table. The global shape of each spanner is also required for recognition; this includes the geometric constraints between each $\mathcal{M}$ curve within the spanner and also the entire set of edge locations and orientation data used for verification.

by the class.

For the model base in Fig. 5.18 there are ten $\mathcal{M}$ curves that satisfy the recognition criteria of discrimination, local description and stability. Stability over three different views of each $\mathcal{M}$ curve (comparable to those of Fig. 5.17) is demonstrated in Fig. 5.19 for each object. From the figure it is clear that the signatures change little with change in viewpoint. However, the projective similarity of $\mathcal{M}$ curves e, f and h is apparent. These are therefore recognized using the same class (class 4). This means that the class model base consists of eight classes that represent ten object $\mathcal{M}$ curves.

One question that has not been addressed sufficiently to date is how to choose the single canonical frame that should be used to describe a model base of more than one class. The frame used in Fig. 5.19 is the natural frame for curve a. As this is actually similar to the natural frames for all of the other $\mathcal{M}$ curves (except curves c and d), it provides a stable frame with uniform noise properties. However, excessive enhancement of noise can be observed for curves c and d which correspond to classes 2 and 3 in the class model base.

5.3.3 *Acquisition and recognition of objects*

After class hypotheses have been used to create putative object hypotheses two pieces of information are required to extend them into joint hypotheses:

1. Geometric information about the positions of the $\mathcal{M}$ curves within the objects. This is used both for hypothesis extension and for computing the projective relationship between the model and the image for verification.

2. Boundary data of the object for the second phase of verification (back-projection).

Knowledge of the location of each $\mathcal{M}$ curve within a model can be used to compute the relative locations of classes in an object and hence a joint invariant for hypothesis extension. A similar extension procedure to that used in LEWIS1 has been developed for the canonical frame route to invariant formation, and details are given in Section 5.4.3. The absolute locations of the classes enables the computation of the plane-to-plane projectivity that maps the model into image. Subsequently the model can be constrained sufficiently for verification and the model outline projected into the image. Again the outline consists of a set of edgel locations (position and orientation) which represent the object boundary. The model data is stored for a fronto-parallel viewpoint.

5.4 Model-based recognition

So far this chapter has demonstrated how projectively invariant indexes can be computed for smooth plane curves. These should be compared to the algebraic invariants in Chapter 3. Each class curve can be recognized using a mechanism very similar to that given in Chapter 4, and class hypotheses merged together to form object hypotheses just as in Section 4.2.5. The rest of this chapter details how the canonical frame construction can be

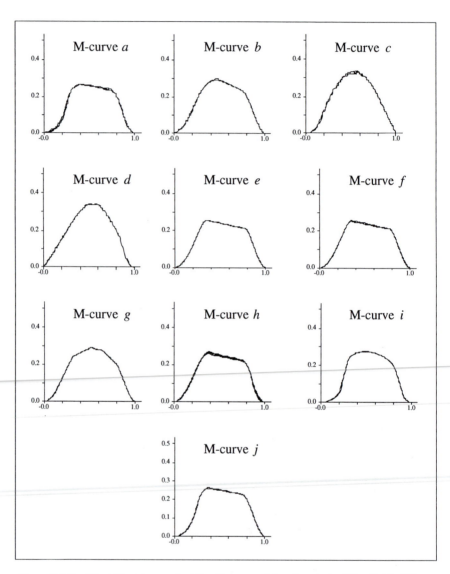

FIG. 5.19. The signatures for the four models shown in Fig. 5.18. Three images of each object were used and the curves superimposed; the very close match between each signature highlights the stability of the construction. Note the similarities between curves *e*, *f* and *h*; these are essentially the same and are therefore represented by the same class. All the other curves are in their own class.

used within the recognition framework of LEWIS; most of the details are given in Chapter 4, the differences only are highlighted.

5.4.1 *Segmentation*

The details of the segmentation algorithm are given in Chapter 6. Segmentation output is sets of points of bitangency and cast tangency located to subpixel accuracy. As all of the class information is contained within a single connected edgel set, grouping is trivial (linear in the number of $\mathcal{M}$ curves in the scene).

5.4.2 *Stability*

The linear classifier provides an understanding of the noise characteristics of each class as part of the model base. However, it is useful to have a direct confidence measure for the stability of each signature as it is extracted from the image. This can be done as follows:

1. Compute the Jacobian of the measured index with respect to movements in the distinguished points.

2. Consider the worst-case displacements of the distinguished points; these maximize the change in the index vector. Compute the corresponding vector.

3. Measure the infinity norm of the index vector; if this exceeds a threshold, the signature is marked as unstable.

The reason for using the infinity norm is that too large an error in any one of the index dimensions can prevent the index from selecting the correct model. The infinity norm highlights the largest error in any dimension and so represents a worst case. In practice the Jacobian computation draws attention to $\mathcal{M}$ curves that have the distinguished points too close together. These intuitively represent bad cases as image error will represent a significant proportion of the separation, and will subsequently be enlarged on mapping to the canonical frame.

The stability measure is used at two different times. The first is during acquisition when a decision is made whether a measured signature is sufficiently stable to be considered a worthwhile shape cue. For example only the two largest of the four $\mathcal{M}$ curves in Fig. 5.4 are stable enough to enhance recognition performance. Secondly, the measure is used during recognition when the confidence associated with a class hypothesis can be related to stability. In the longer term we will be able to make use of stability measures to form priorities of interest for measured shape cues; it is expected that initially one will have to expend effort only for the most stable shape cues, and only if these fail to produce conclusive recognition hypotheses will weaker measures have to be considered.

5.4.3 *Hypothesis merging*

Again benefits can be realized by joining together index hypotheses for single objects prior to verification. The case is made in Fig. 5.21d where a single $\mathcal{M}$ curve is used to compute the model-to-image map; there is an accurate alignment of the model in the vicinity of the $\mathcal{M}$ curve, but the correspondence is less good over the rest of the object. Often we find that the backprojection process behaves well near to the index features but extrapolates poorly away from them. However, if two $\mathcal{M}$ curves are used as in Fig. 5.21c the model registration is more precise and a much better understanding of the scene is achieved. Another example is shown in Fig. 5.26 where a pair of $\mathcal{M}$ curves are joined into an extended hypothesis prior to verification.

Within the current model base the $\mathcal{M}$ curves are distinct; as each curve corresponds to a subpart, the subparts are non-overlapping. It is conceivable that this will not be the case for some objects, and so the hypothesis extension strategy accounts for both overlapping and non-overlapping subparts (hence topology is not used as in LEWIS1). The strategy is exactly the same as in Section 4.2.5, except that for smooth curves hypothesis compatibility is redefined.

The method used to test compatibility emphasizes the simplicity with which the coordinate frames of pairs of $\mathcal{M}$ curves can be related when geometric invariance is exploited; this process is called *frame propagation*, Brady (15). In our case, if a joint invariant between a pair of hypothesized classes matches the joint invariant measured on the model for the same classes, then it is likely that the pair of image classes are compatible. The actual invariants used are algebraic invariants between the distinguished points on each $\mathcal{M}$ curve (formed as suggested in Fig. 4.7 in Chapter 4). Class frame propagation is demonstrated in Fig. 5.20 for a pair of classes: initially one might hypothesize the presence of two classes, (a) and (b), in an image. If these classes come from different subparts of the same model, compatibility is tested as follows:

1. Locate the central point of each class using the four distinguished points.

2. Compute the five-point invariants between the central point of one class and the reference points of the other class, and vice versa. As the distinguished points are ordered around the image curve there is no permutation action. Furthermore, as there is an assumed correspondence between the image and model classes the ordering of the invariants is known. Form a four-vector of the measured invariants.

3. Compare the measured invariants with those for the model (stored in a look-up table). If the difference is small (using the cost function defined below), the class hypotheses are taken to be compatible.

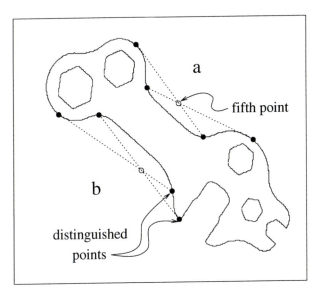

FIG. 5.20. For a pair of $\mathcal{M}$ curves there are 8 distinguished points which could be used to form $2 \times 8 - 8 = 8$ different five-point invariants. Rather than computing so many, which is unnecessary, invariants are computed between the four distinguished points of each $\mathcal{M}$ curve, and the central point of the other. This yields four invariants, and does so using a symmetric construction. These invariants are sufficient to hypothesize compatibility.

The simplest cost function that could be defined is the Euclidean distance between the image and model invariant vectors. However, as the expected errors in the measured invariants are roughly proportional to their values, the errors should be normalized (see Section 4.3.1). This leads to an error function of the form:

$$e = \sum_{i=1}^{4} \left| \frac{M_i - m_i}{M_i} \right|,$$

with $\mathbf{M}$ and $\mathbf{m}$ the model and image invariant vectors and M_i and m_i their i^{th} components.

5.4.4 Verification

As in LEWIS1 verification proceeds in two stages, though the distinction between them can be made more clearly through the use of the different class and object libraries. Essentially hypothesized classes are verified in the first phase and object hypotheses in the second:

1. Check that the measured class (hypothesized through indexing) is similar to the model signatures in the canonical frame. This is analogous to testing that a good projectivity can be computed between sets of matching algebraic data (Section 4.2.6).

2. Search the image for model support from other model features. This is backprojection and is the same as the second stage of verification in LEWIS1.

5.4.4.1 *Class verification*   The indexing process hypothesizes matches between the class database and the image. Although each class within the database will access a number of possible models, at this stage no link is made between the image $\mathcal{M}$ curves and specific models.

The invariant index is not complete due to the data compression needed to perform indexing and so aliasing problems are possible. However, so long as indexing does not incorrectly hypothesize too many classes, erroneous hypotheses can be ruled out efficiently by a match in the canonical frame. Simply, the difference in areas between the image class signature and the model class is computed (using a rectangular quantization in the canonical frame); if the difference is sufficiently small, the hypothesis is assumed to be correct and the class match is entered into the hypothesis extension process.

The efficiency of the indexing process can be demonstrated empirically: from a series of typical images such are those in Figs 5.22–5.27 an average of 56 $\mathcal{M}$ curves were observed; 27.8% of these produced class hypotheses on indexing; and 23.9% of the original 56 were verified as classes. Note that although a large number of classes were hypothesized in the scene, only 14.0% of the indexed hypotheses were later found to be incorrect. Therefore, indexing does not produce an excessive number of false positives

5.4.4.2 *Object verification*   This proceeds along very similar lines to the mechanism in Section 4.2.6. First, the model-to-image map is computed, then there is a search for image support for the model. For each individual matching class there are four points which can be used to compute the projectivity. However, matching using these tends to produce a transformation that performs well in the locality of the $\mathcal{M}$ curve but extrapolates poorly to distant parts of the object (see Fig. 5.21d). The hypothesis extension stage improves this by providing extra matching points and hence a least squares formulation for the computation of the model-to-image transformation and hence superior model registration (Fig. 5.21c).

In the image frame the projected model points are matched to image data as before, testing for distance to an image edgel and the difference in orientation. However, as there are now no algebraic features on the model that can be used to constrain the orientation, the edge direction of each model point is always that of the Canny output. As the Canny filter can reliably only measure the edgel direction to within ±15 degrees, the orientation error threshold is increased to ±30 degrees.

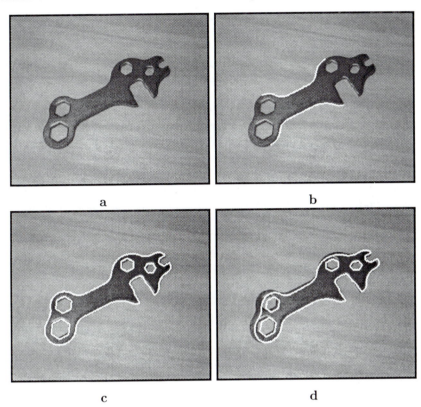

a   b

c   d

FIG. 5.21. (a) shows an unoccluded view of model 0. The class recognition algorithm correctly locates classes 0 and 1 in (b). These form an extended hypothesis for model 0 which is verified by backprojection and finds 92.8% image support. This is the only model match found with a reasonable pose (that is, the object is not too small). A very good registration of the object is achieved in (c); this is when both $\mathcal{M}$ curves are used to compute the model-to-image transformation. Sometimes, as in (d), if only the lower $\mathcal{M}$ curve is used the registration is good in the region of the curve but extrapolates poorly over the rest of the object. Consequently, a worse geometric understanding of the scene is realized than when two $\mathcal{M}$ curves hypothesize the presence of the object. In this case, a single $\mathcal{M}$ curve is sufficient for recognition as a 68.9% projected edge match was still found.

5.5   Experimental results

The first example shown in Fig. 5.21 shows a simple unoccluded view of model 0. This object can be recognized using up to two $\mathcal{M}$ curves indexing classes. First, the class recognition algorithm locates classes 0 and 1 as marked in 5.21b, and uses these to form a single joint hypothesis by the procedure of Section 5.4.3. The joint hypothesis is verified through back-projection in which 92.8% of the model outline is matched to image data. A 100% confidence is not found (as would be expected for an unoccluded object) because the Canny edge detector fails to extract and localize all of the object edges correctly. This results mainly from specularity on the object. The same effect can be observed in all of the images in this section because the objects are metallic. Another effect that results from the edge detector failing is due to the finite thickness of the objects. Frequently, an edge extracted from the image can swap between portions of the outline on the upper and lower surfaces of an object. As the canonical construction is local this does not present a major problem, though its effects are occasionally noticeable.

In Fig. 5.22 the recognition system is tested on a more complex scene where there is clutter and occlusion. A single class is found for model 3 (class 5), which is then localized correctly in the image to give 55.5% edge support. Although a total of 16 class hypotheses were formed, yielding 22 joint hypotheses, only the correct hypothesis was given sufficient confidence by backprojection (over a 50% projected edge).

The canonical frame construction works very well under significant perspective distortion. This is demonstrated in Fig. 5.23. For this relatively simple scene three classes are hypothesized, and only one produces a hypothesis that passes through the object verification procedure. This gives an 83.6% edge match. As may be seen from Fig. 5.18, under image noise model 2 (which is the one identified in Fig. 5.23) is projectively rotationally symmetric.[26] This means that the spanner will always be projected into the image in two different poses differing by the equivalent of a 180 degree rotation and still match correctly.

Figures 5.24 to 5.27 show further recognition examples in which the correct objects are always recognized. No false positives were found in any of the images, though this is not always the case. Although some hypotheses had sufficient edge support the hypothesized sizes of the objects were so small that the objects would have to be too far away and so can be ruled out (for example model 0 was identified as shown in Fig. 5.25). Full details of the recognition process are given in Table 5.1.

---

[26]If an object is projectively rotationally symmetric, there is a projective view of the object for which it has rotational symmetry.

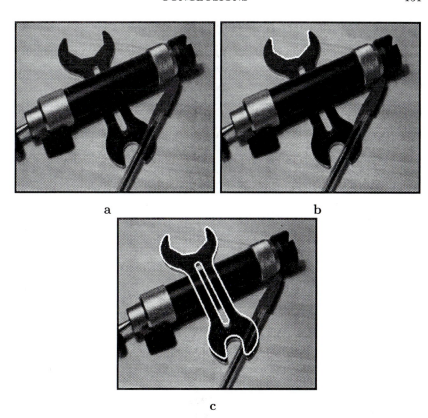

FIG. 5.22. For the occluded and cluttered view of the spanner (a), a total of 16 potential class matches were found. However, the one that correctly identifies model 3, marked in (b), was the only one that produced a sufficiently high verification score (55.5%) to be accepted.

5.6   Conclusions

This chapter has introduced a projective extension to the work of Lamdan *et al.* (68) and has demonstrated how invariant signatures can be computed for smooth plane curves that allow rapid access to a model library. Although the signatures cannot be used immediately for indexing, a straightforward process exists for the computation of indexes from them. The signatures are found through the accurate and reliable location of points of bitangency and cast tangency followed by a map to a canonical frame. Not only have a variety of different distinguished features been investigated, but also the best shape of canonical frame has been estimated (the natural frame) and a comparison made to the poorer affine imaging model.

The natural frame is a very important concept for the suppression of noise. We have seen how the signature representation can be made less sus-

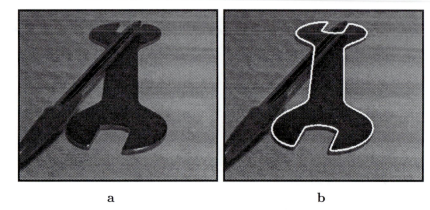

a   b

FIG. 5.23. Even under severe perspective distortion the recognition system
performs well and finds model 2 with 83.6% confidence using a single
$\mathcal{M}$ curve.

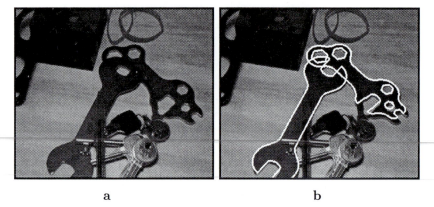

a   b

FIG. 5.24. Single classes are sufficient to recognize the two model instances
shown in (b). The redundancy of the canonical frame representation
gives much better tolerance to occlusion than global shape methods.
The left-hand object gained 67.1% boundary support, and the right
object 81.6%.

ceptible to image errors through its use, though many questions still remain
unanswered with regard to the optimization of the frame over the entire
class model base. Furthermore, the natural frame can be used to provide
more stable model representations for entire objects. Not only does it ensure a more uniform treatment of noise around the entire object boundary,
but as suggested in the conclusions to Chapter 4 knowledge of the equiform
frame of an object allows the use of pose measures within verification.

   The actual segmentation methods used for the formation of the canonical frame are described in detail in Chapter 6. Again they allow signatures

FIG. 5.25. In Fig. 5.24 incorrect objects were identified, but these occupy such a small region of the image that they can be rejected (the object pose would mean that the object is too distant). Here, model 0 receives a 77.9% edge match, but has a total projected object width of 24.7 pixels which is so small that reliable segmentation could not be expected. Consequently the hypothesis is rejected.

Table 5.1 *The matching statistics for Figs 5.24 to 5.27. The number of $\mathcal{M}$ curves extracted from the images and how many class hypotheses result from indexing are shown. The class hypotheses are used to form joint hypotheses that are verified or rejected by the following tests: if a larger subsuming joint hypothesis has already been accepted then no verification is required; if a good model-to-image projectivity cannot be computed; if backprojection results in an impossible pose as was discussed in Chapter 4.*

Figure	$\mathcal{M}$ curves	classes	jh	no verif.	poor proj.	poor pose
5.24	42	13	18	0	1	5
5.26	79	18	23	2	0	3
5.27	99	24	39	4	1	2

to be computed efficiently. However, the grouping problems experienced for the algebraic invariants used in Chapter 4 do not exist for the $\mathcal{M}$ curve detection algorithm as the measures are sufficiently local that connectivity is guaranteed (ideally we expect the entire semi-local feature to be extracted within a single edgel chain from the image; the signature cannot even be computed if this is not possible). This means that grouping is not actually necessary at the lowest level in LEWIS2 and the number of indexing actions made is equal to the number of $\mathcal{M}$ curves observed. Grouping need only be applied at the level of hypothesis extension when we have only a small number of well-defined features.

It has also been demonstrated how invariant indexes can be extracted from the signatures so that the formation of object hypotheses can be

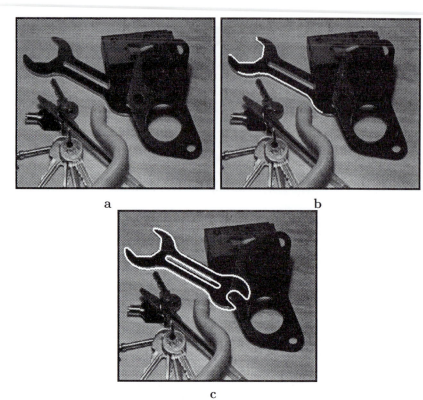

a b

c

FIG. 5.26. Two classes are recognized (b) and are joined into a single extended hypothesis to recognize model 3 with 68.0% edge support (c).

made efficient using the LEWIS architecture. The ability of LEWIS to work with different invariants and feature types is a real benefit for enhancing its scope. In practice, the LEWIS2 system uses a two-stage indexing process with hypothesis extension to make full use of the invariant indexing paradigm. Although the invariant measures are local, thus providing tolerance to occlusion, they provide very strong global constraints on object identities. Overall the use of non-global shape descriptions with their associated redundancy have provided a very stable representation of shape.

The extension process itself makes use of the algebraic invariants discussed in Chapter 3 (specifically the five-point invariant), and through the use of distinguished features extension can be generalized very easily to account for a variety of different feature types (whether algebraic or not). For example, the interchange of features between the invariant feature groups for the formation of joint invariants can be extended to any class of invariant. Generally, the same features used to form an invariant index can also be used to form joint hypotheses between indexed feature groups. Thus

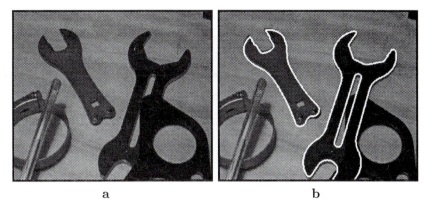

a   b

FIG. 5.27. Both models 1 (91.4% support) and 3 (75.7%) are correctly recognized and projected into the image as shown in (b).

many more examples of extension readily become available such as for the semi-differential invariants of Barrett, *et al.* (5) or Van Gool, *et al.* (136).

LEWIS2 has been tested over a number of images and has a similar recognition performance to LEWIS1. Principally indexing provides a dramatic reduction in the number of hypotheses that have to be created and verified. Although only one example of a canonical frame has been demonstrated there are a number of extensions available. Objects are frequently complicated combinations of continuous but not necessarily smooth curves and so a number of methods must be used to provide reliable descriptions. Wherever distinguished points or lines can be located there is an opportunity to produce a canonical frame construction: such points are C^n discontinuities and locations of arbitrary order incidence.

Finally, we have described a simple process that computes stability measures for each index and thus also their associated hypotheses. Within simple scenes we require only an indication of stability, but in more complicated environments subsequent use will have to be made out of feature confidences measured at a very early stage of processing. This will prevent the system being overloaded with decisions about which hypotheses require further examination. In the proposed MORSE system (150) much tighter control between the recognition modules will be used that, for example, will mean that one will have to consider more rigorously whether a single $\mathcal{M}$ curve really might provide a stable measure of a object. If not, more fruitful collections of features should be examined first. Through the two examples of the LEWIS architecture shown so far in this book, we have realized that considering recognition to be composed of three distinct selection–indexing–correspondence phases is not optimal; in reality the flow of data between the different processes must be more dynamic.

6

SEGMENTATION AND GROUPING

Segmentation is important because it provides the features required for shape description; these have to be localized and then represented in a suitable manner. This chapter describes the segmentation and grouping algorithms that are used by the two planar recognition systems described in the previous chapters that use the LEWIS architecture. All of the algorithms that will be described can be substituted directly into the architecture.

If the object descriptions are to be based on algebraic invariants both *lines* and *conics* must be extracted efficiently and accurately from images. The features are actually measured from the underlying edge data which they represent rather than attempting to fit them directly to the intensity data. This chapter describes how such algebraic forms are segmented and fitted to edge data. For descriptions that use the canonical frame construction, sets of $\mathcal{M}$ curves have to be extracted from image edgel curves; one of the segmentation tasks is to locate pairs of bitangency points that bound the $\mathcal{M}$ curves. Other features of interest are cast tangents and points or lines of inflection. The extraction of all of these features is covered in this chapter.

Grouping (or selection) is important because it isolates features from single objects prior to shape description and so cuts down the amount of search required in finding model-to-image correspondences. It also tends to cut down the number of hypotheses that have to be considered after an indexing step. The overall result is that recognition is made more efficient. The grouping method used in LEWIS1 is described in Section 6.1.2; in short it is achieved through the connectivity associated with the Canny edgel chains. Extensions to the approach are also discussed due to its shortcomings. At the end of the chapter the degree of grouping required is contrasted with that required for the canonical frame description; essentially grouping is trivial withing the LEWIS2 system.

Generally, within recognition grouping is not performed as well as it could be and so the discussion at the end of the chapter indicates current directions of research that are being considered to improve the situation. Certainly, it is hard to perform grouping for global object descriptions under occlusion and noise with any real degree of robustness. This is why we are trying to exploit local and semi-local measures rather than using global descriptions.

6.0.1 Overview

The invariant descriptors used within LEWIS1 and LEWIS2 require the extraction of features from images. The first step in this process is edge detection. Both of the systems use the Canny (22) edge filter as the first process applied to a grey-level image. This provides, through *non-maximal suppression* and *hysteresis*, connected edgel chains located to subpixel accuracy. The next process is segmentation. This can be broken down into three phases:

1. the extraction of discrete edgel chains from the image;

2. the location of breaks between features, and more generally the detection of boundaries between each feature and other data;

3. the accurate representation of image features.

The first step is common for both the algebraic and smooth curve invariants. Single edge curves are extracted from the edge image using a following routine. The non-maximal suppression step within the Canny filter produces edges with subpixel accuracy which provides better localization of the edge locations. This yields invariant values with marginally smaller variances (about 10% better) than those computed from integer edgel locations; the reason why there is not such a marked difference in accuracy as one might expect is because the representation processes smooth out image quantization.

Even with hysteresis in the Canny single pixel breaks can occur in the edge chains. Such events will defeat a crude edge following algorithm that produces edgel chains by following paths of eight-way connected neighbours. These breaks can be overcome using directional look-ahead to predict where an edgel should be found if a gap has been encountered. The local implementation of the Canny filter used in LEWIS never produces three-way connected corners (because of excessive smoothing), and so the edge data can be stored as single ordered lists. If the edge detector does produce actual junctions in the edgel chains the algorithm used to find the features of Fig. 6.7 must be used. This treats each edge chain between a pair of junctions (or trivially endings) individually, then features between different edge chains are *merged* if they appear to come from the same underlying structure. Overall this merging process requires a more sophisticated grouping method which is described later. However, in general the quality of the edge data encountered within the images of interest for LEWIS is quite good and the basic following routine with single edgel look-ahead works well. However, more sophisticated paradigms are available that make use of methods used within the tracking literature; see Sha'ashua and Ullman (116) or Cox, *et al.* (27) for details.

The details of the other two stages of the segmentation process depend on the type of invariant that is to be formed; algebraic feature fitting and

$\mathcal{M}$ curve detection are discussed separately. The other theme of this chapter is the rôle of grouping: grouping is essential if a recognition system is to be efficient, and is important whichever indexing and correspondence algorithms are used.

6.1   Line and conic extraction

Both lines and conics must be extracted accurately from the edgel data sets for the algebraic invariants used in LEWIS1. Points are not used because they can be found only with sufficient accuracy by intersecting higher-order algebraic features (such as lines). As these higher forms are themselves used to form the invariants, any invariant using points will be functionally dependent on them; lines are therefore used directly.

The actual segmentation routine relies on a pair of incremental fitting techniques. The fitting methods perform very well, and have the potential advantage that they scale easily; the algorithm for locating conic sections is almost identical to that for straight lines and the concepts scale further to any order of curve (though it is questionable whether one would want to use high-order algebraic curves to represent objects when more robust descriptions can be achieved through methods such as the canonical frame).

Neither of the fitting methods exploit frame invariant fitting techniques such as those discussed by Carlsson (20), or Forsyth, *et al.* (39). By non-frame-invariant we mean that the fitting process does not necessarily commute with the imaging process.[27] The application of the two methods used in the LEWIS1 systems have frequently been criticized due to their non-frame-invariant properties. However, little benefit has been realized through the use of the more costly frame invariant techniques. This is because the data requiring approximation (rather than representation) really comes from either lines or conics and so we can use very tight fitting thresholds to reduce the effects of non-invariant fitting. Briefly, an *approximation* of data by a feature means that the data and the feature must have the same visual appearance. Alternatively, a *representation* and its data set may have a totally different appearance, but if the representation is frame invariant it can still be useful. As an example, an approximation to a set of data points lying on a square could be four straight lines, but a reasonable representation could be a circle if the circle were recovered using a frame invariant technique.

Frame invariant fitting techniques were actually tested during the development of LEWIS1. For example the original conic fitter used was based on the method given by Forsyth, *et al.* in (39). However, when its results were compared to those of the current algorithm used (an extension of the Bookstein (13) algorithm), is was seen that generally the latter algorithm

---

[27]If the fitting process is frame invariant the projection of a fit to a data set is equal to the fit to the projection of the data.

performed as well for large data sets and better for small ones. In conjunction with this the latter method renders a far more efficient implementation and so the frame invariant fitting properties were sacrificed.

6.1.1 *Segmentation*

Frequently conics and straight lines are terminated by tangency or curvature discontinuities. Consequently image edge data can be assigned to the different algebraic features by finding peaks in different derivatives of the edgel chain slopes. Tangency discontinuities can be segmented by finding peaks in the first derivative of the slope; curvature discontinuities using peaks in its second derivative. However, noise and errors in the image often mean that false peaks are registered in the derivatives and so scale space filtering must be applied to track the peaks to finer scales and so improve localization (Witkin (145)). A detailed analysis of such a segmentation algorithm is given by Asada and Brady in (2). Briefly, scale space is used to track events measured at a coarse scale with a large smoothing kernel (but that have poor localization) to scales with lesser degrees of smoothing where they have better localization. The noisier and less robust features tend not to appear at the coarse scales and so they fail to produce tracks and are subsequently not registered.

As demonstrated by the TINA system (101), looking for slope derivatives is a very effective way to locate corners in an image but due to noise effects the same process tends to locate curvature discontinuities poorly. Other segmentation algorithms, such as the use of *worms* and *split and merge* algorithms, also fail to segment such curves correctly. Details of such algorithms are deliberately omitted and the interested reader should examine the book by Pavlidis (99). The algorithm used in LEWIS1 for finding discontinuities is more successful. It uses a model-based approach and is tailored specifically for the extraction of features that are visually similar to lines and conics.

The method makes use of efficient incremental fitting routines within a *merge* strategy (8, 99) to detect when it is likely that a data point belongs to a specific category of feature. These algorithms can be made to run very fast and have shown good performance. Using a single *seed* region forces the algorithm to be serial. However, as it can be used as a pipe directly reading the output from the hysteresis or following processes, this does not affect the overall efficiency. This approach should be compared to that used by Cox, *et al.* (27) in which segmentation is driven by predicting the locations of edge data to be included and checking that observed data actually falls within a validation region.

6.1.1.1 *Straight line fitting: overview* The incremental fitting algorithm starts off with the use of a *seed region*. This is a small, locally connected set of edgels that are assumed to approximate well to a straight line. The

aim is to grow the seed region until it encompasses all the edgels that also
lie on the line. Edgels neighbouring the seed region are selected and tested
for membership of the region, the criterion for selection being whether they
also lie on the same line. When a point is found that does not, the search
is terminated and a new seed region is generated and grown. The location
of the new seed is found directly adjacent to the last set of edgels under
consideration.

The algorithm must address the following issues:

- how one determines whether a seed region actually corresponds to a
  straight line;
- how to grow the region efficiently;
- how to determine when a test point does not lie on the line, that is
  how to realize when the growing process should be terminated;
- whether a shrinking process should be used which incorporates outlier
  rejection to account for false positives in the assignment of edgels to
  line segments;
- whether the process depends on the initial choice of seed region, that
  is, whether it is stable under permutation of the points and any effects
  of the imaging process.

It will be seen that the process is not vulnerable to the last problem as the
aim is to approximate only data that was formed by straight lines rather
than to represent all of the image data. The thresholds on the fitting process
are so tight that effectively the same fitted lines result under any meaningful
transformation on the points.

Lines are fitted using orthogonal regression which minimizes the Euclidean distance from the data points to the straight line. A cost is returned by the algorithm which is simply the root mean square distance of
the points from the fitted line (the details of the algorithm, as well as the
update rules, are given in Appendix C.1).

Testing whether the seed region approximates well to a straight line,
and determining the time at which fitting to a specific line should be terminated, comes under the control of the threshold used to limit the maximum allowable fitting cost. One would expect the choice of such a threshold
to affect the scale at which the algorithm works, though in fact the same
thresholds are used for images as different as those shown in Figs 6.1 and
6.7.

The efficient extension of the seed region comes in two parts: the first is
that variables storing all of the information for the current growing region
can be created and then updated by simple additions for new points without
having to recompute the values derived for the entire data set again each
time. The set of variables is called the *fitting parameter vector* and contains
the following summations: $\sum_n x_i$, $\sum_n y_i$, $\sum_n x_i^2$, $\sum_n x_i y_i$ and $\sum_n y_i^2$ for a
data set of n points. The fit can be computed solely from these variables.

Secondly, the use of a predicted upper bound that includes the cost of fitting to the current data set, and to all other individual edgel points which are assumed to lie on the same line, can be used. The data set can be extended and the upper bound cost recomputed without the need for refitting. Fitting to all the new data points needs to be done only when the fitting threshold has been exceeded.

Finally, outlier rejection can be implemented in precisely the same manner in which new points are accepted within the fits. If an edgel within the fitted data set lies too far from the fitted line (by some threshold), its effect on the fit can be eliminated efficiently by deleting the point and refitting.[28] Generally we find that points towards the ends of the fitted line segments make the largest contribution to the fitting cost as they are often affected by smoothing effects at corners, etc. (which mark the ends of line segments). Therefore, the outliers are frequently located towards the limits of the fitted lines. The rejection process is principally useful for polishing the fits after the process has terminated.

6.1.1.2 *Control of line fitting*

The control of the line fitting algorithm is given more precisely as follows:

1. Select the first *min_fit* points from the edge chains. This is the seed region, and is set to 20 edgels.

2. Fit a straight line using the method in Appendix C.1.

3. Observe the mean fitting cost. If it is sufficiently low (default of 0.2 pixels) the fit is accepted. Otherwise the fit is rejected and if there are still more data points, remove the first point of the fitting set using the incremental algorithm, add the next unused point, and refit. Generally the quality of the images causes the bulk of the data on a straight line to fit well below this threshold, and it is only the termination points that do not.

4. If the fit from (3) has been accepted and there are more data points, estimate the cost of adding another point by combining the current cost with the distance of the new point to the current line. This cost will be an upper bound and if low enough, we see that including the extra point must produce a valid fit. Do not refit, but include the point in the vector of fitting parameters. If the fitting cost for n points is e_n, and the distance of the $(n+1)^{\text{th}}$ point to the line is d_{n+1}, the upper bound cost is $e_{est} = \sqrt{(ne_n^2 + d_{n+1}^2)/(n+1)}$.

5. If no more points can be added accept the current fit and create a new seed region using the next *min_fit* adjacent points.

---

[28] Admittedly, this chooses the best point to reject on the evidence of the current fit, rather than the best depending on the fit without the rejected point (cf. Shapiro and Brady (118)). As yet it is unclear whether the second strategy will provide a significant improvement in performance for the relatively structured image data used by LEWIS.

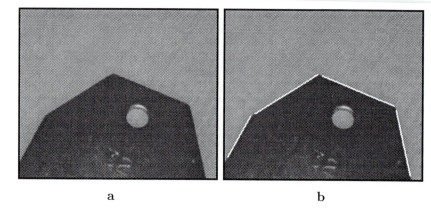

a   b

FIG. 6.1. The line fitting algorithm locates straight lines very accurately.
These can then be used to locate the positions of corners if desired.

6. Otherwise, continue adding points until the estimated cost is just
   below the fitting threshold, and then refit. After refitting continue to
   add more points using (4) if possible.

7. Terminate either when there are no more points, or when there are
   not a sufficient number to create a new seed region.

This algorithm will successfully fit straight lines to edge curves, and it
marks out line endpoints with reasonable accuracy. However, the process
tends to overrun by one or two edgels at corners as it takes a while for
the fitting cost to exceed the threshold (the contribution made by small
numbers of outliers is outweighed by the large number of good points). The
fitted lines are therefore slightly displaced from their correct positions. This
is remedied by removing *end_tol* data points (3 edgels) from either end of
the data set using the incremental formulation, and refitting. The resulting
lines are then a very good approximation to the actual image data, and
tend to have total error costs of a small fraction of the upper bound on the
fit. Note that the main concern is not to determine which edgels correspond
to the lines, but rather to represent the underlying data; therefore removing
too many points does not cause problems so long as the appearance of the
fit is not affected. Examples are given in Figs 6.1 and 6.2.

An alternative way of improving the localization of the fits is to apply
outlier rejection to the fitted line data sets. This may be done simply by
removing all points that are greater than a threshold distance from the line
and then refitting. The threshold may be the same as the original fitting
threshold, or different. Iterations are repeated until the desired quality of
fit has been attained. Although such a method will scale much better than
just removing a set number of points from the ends of each line segment,
it has been found in practice that the qualities of the fits do not improve
sufficiently compared to the time expended searching for the erroneous data

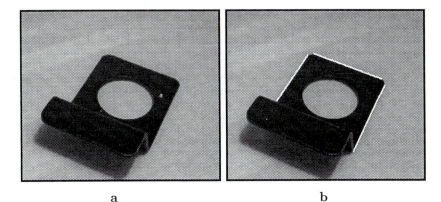

FIG. 6.2. Even for smooth corners the lines are fitted well. The edge data from the corners are ignored in the fit.

points. Therefore, this form of outlier rejection is not used.

6.1.1.3 *Conic fitting: overview* Conic fitting has exactly the same flow as straight line fitting. A small data set is selected, and points are incrementally added or deleted as required. As well as having a maximum permissible fitting cost, ellipses of only a modest eccentricity are accepted because it is unusual to observe long thin ellipses in an image. As fitting can be unstable to noisy data a reasonable proportion of a conic segment must be visible for the fit to be accurate. Since only a small portion of a hyperbola can be visible, fits to such curves are rejected.

The basis of the algorithm used for conic fitting is that given by Bookstein in (13) and also reviewed in Appendix C.2. Note that there are two significant problems with the standard Bookstein algorithm:

1. The fit is biased because using algebraic distance as a cost function gives extra weighting to points lying near flat regions of the conic. Therefore, systematic noise on the low-curvature parts of a conic section will cause the fit to deviate more than noise in the higher-curvature regions. See the paper on conic fitting by Sampson for details (114).

2. The algorithm is numerically ill-conditioned for short data sets.

One way to overcome the first problem is not to use algebraic distance as the error measure, but rather Euclidean distance (or an approximation). An iterative scheme that starts with a Bookstein fit and then fits according to an approximation to Euclidean distance has been suggested by Sampson (114), and has been extended for more general curves by Taubin (132). Sampson's algorithm was tested within LEWIS1, but because the data that is to be approximated corresponds very closely to real conics there was no significant improvement over the basic algorithm. It is this observation that illuminates the fact that for the data under consideration, the biasing effects are minimal. The numerical ill-conditioning causes a more severe problem.

6.1.1.4 *Pre-conditioning the Bookstein algorithm*

An understanding of the Bookstein algorithm (given in Appendix C.2) is required to see why pre-conditioning is necessary. Unfortunately, the fact that it is hard to fit properly to small low-curvature data has been misinterpreted to mean that one cannot fit at all to such data; the truth of the matter is that the familiar algorithms have been formed incorrectly and that fitting is possible. The cause of the error is that the algorithms themselves are numerically ill-conditioned.

Part of the computation of the conic fit requires the formation of a *scatter matrix*, S, which contains polynomial terms in the image x and y coordinates. These terms are of the form $x^a y^b$, where a and b are integers such that $(a + b) \leq 4$ and $a, b \geq 0$. Since (x, y) are image edgel locations the individual terms become as high as $O(512^4 n)$ and as low as n for a 512×512 image and n data points: hence S can be ill-conditioned. For small data sets this effect tends to be exaggerated and often the scatter matrix S ceases to be positive definite (when implemented on a machine with finite numerical accuracy). This suggests that a fit with a negative algebraic distance can be obtained because the distance is proportional to the smallest eigenvalue of S (shown in Appendix C.2). A negative algebraic distance subsequently yields a negative fitting cost which is unreasonable and shows up a weakness in the algorithm.

Pre-conditioning the matrix overcomes this: essentially one wants to reduce a measure of the condition number by scaling the elements of S so that they are all of the same order of magnitude.[29] One way to do this is by renormalizing the data. This is done in the following way:

1. Translate the data set to its centre of mass.

2. Rotate the data so that its principal axes are parallel to the coordinate frame axes: $\sum_n x_i y_i = 0$.

3. Scale the points so that the variance of the data sets is unity along the two frame directions: $\sum_n x_i^2 = \sum_n y_i^2 = 1$.

4. Fit a conic using the Bookstein algorithm.

---

[29] One can compare the effectiveness of the pre-conditioning algorithm by looking at the eigenvalues of S formed for the original and the pre-conditioned algorithms. Note that the correct fit should be achieved at a low cost that is proportional to the smallest eigenvalue of S. As the cost and hence the smallest eigenvalues for both S matrices is ideally zero for a noise-free data set, one cannot compare the matrices using a condition number, but must rather form a comparison between the largest eigenvalues. In practice a difference of $O(10^5)$ can be observed in the ratio between the largest non-conditioned scatter matrix eigenvalue and the largest from the pre-conditioned matrix.

5. Transform the fitted conic to remove the effects of the coordinate frame change: scale, rotate, and translate.

As a number of the terms in the scatter matrix are zero after the normalization the eigenvalue computation can be done without the need for any matrix inversion (unlike in the Bookstein algorithm given in Appendix C.2); this both further reduces numerical error and improves efficiency.

The effects of the normalization are demonstrated in Fig. 6.3. The flat region of an ellipse has been sampled uniformly along the x axis, and the locations of the sample points are computed to machine accuracy without any added noise. Then, conics are fitted using the traditional Bookstein algorithm and the new algorithm. Seven of the data points considered for the fits are marked on the figure. When the central five points of this set are used to compute the fit there is a dramatic difference in quality of the new and the Bookstein algorithms. The new algorithm yields a conic close to the actual conic, and the Bookstein algorithm provides one of very high aspect ratio which is far too small. For seven or more points there is no distinguishable difference between the actual fit and the fit recovered by the new algorithm. The Bookstein algorithm performs very poorly though; for seven points a hyperbola is actually fitted, and it is not until many more points are used that the fit approximates the actual conic (15 points in this case).

Unfortunately the new algorithm suffers from two drawbacks compared to the Bookstein algorithm, though these are negligible in comparison to the benefits of the pre-conditioning. The first is that the Bookstein algorithm produces a fit invariant to similarity transformations but the new algorithm does not. However, it has already been noted that frame invariant fitting is not an issue.

The second effect is more important: the new algorithm is not truly incremental. Although the parameters needed to normalize the data can be adapted incrementally (these are $\sum_n x_i$, $\sum_n y_i$, $\sum_n x_i^2$, $\sum_n x_i y_i$ and $\sum_n y_i^2$), the scatter matrix cannot be computed until the points have all been normalized. This is essentially because a different normalization is used for each incremented data set. However, as with the line fitting algorithm, the fit is not recomputed as each point is added but rather when the fitting threshold has been exceeded. This therefore makes the algorithm as fast as possible.

Generally, under image noise the fits produced by any conic fitting algorithm will not be good enough to form precise invariant measurements unless a reasonable portion of the conic is visible (often a third, or so). However, the importance of being able to produce stable fits to small data sets should not be underestimated. For the correct functioning of the incremental segmentation approach the existence of such an algorithm is essential so that the growth of the seed region can be achieved stably.

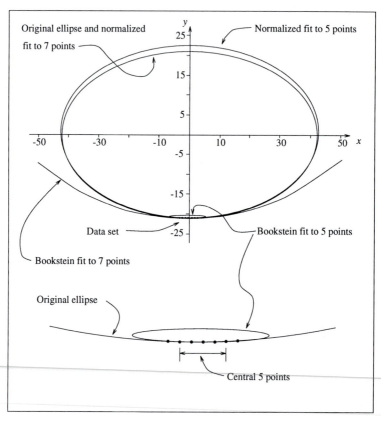

FIG. 6.3. The upper figure demonstrates the differing qualities of the fits produced by the Bookstein and normalized fitting algorithms. For the central five points of the data set ellipses are fitted using the two algorithms; the minimum number of points that can be used for a general conic fit is five. The lower figure is an enlarged version of the upper figure that demonstrates the poor quality of the Bookstein fit. The normalized fit performs substantially better. For seven or more points the normalized fit produces results indistinguishable from the original conic, whereas this is not true for the Bookstein algorithm until many more points are used. In fact, for seven points it incorrectly fits a hyperbola rather than an ellipse. Note that the only errors effective during the fitting process are due to the finite numerical accuracy of the machine; this therefore represents a best case compared to attempts to fit to real image data.

6.1.1.5 *Combined conic and line fitting* Both lines and conics have to be used simultaneously to describe the edge data within LEWIS1. Consequently the order in which lines and conics are fitted is important. To avoid curves being represented by polygonal approximations conic fitting is applied prior to straight line fitting. Furthermore, it is often the case that noise or surface irregularities can cause excess segmentation and so consecutive lines or conics are compared as they are fitted to determine whether they are likely to be part of the same geometric structure:

- For lines it is determined whether the endpoints of each line segment lie close to the other fitted *algebraic* line. Essentially the test determines whether the four endpoints of a pair of line segments are (approximately) collinear.
- For conics the test exploits the equivalence of the geometric structures of a pair of fitted conics. Briefly, this is done using the conic pair invariants I_1 and I_2 given in Section 3.5.2; for identical conics both invariants should equal 3. Therefore, a cost function is computed between two conics c_1 and c_2 with the form:

$$e = [I_1(c_1^{-1}, c_2) - 3]^2 + [I_2(c_2^{-1}, c_1) - 3]^2.$$

If a pair of lines or conics are estimated to be equivalent a fit is performed using edge data from both structures, and if satisfactory, the original structures are replaced by their union.

Examples of the fitting process are given in Figs 6.4 to 6.6. The segmentation is generally good, though as with all algorithms the quality of the fitted data is impaired by specularity and shadow. For such cases the extracted data cannot be relied upon and is thus discarded. Other points to note from the examples are the accurate location of tangency discontinuities by deletion of edgels towards the end of straight line fits, and also the precise location of curvature discontinuities where the curve tangents are continuous. For example, note that in Fig. 6.5e no constraints have been used to constrain the fits between the lines and the conic, and yet the lines are visually tangent to the conic. Using incidence and tangency constraints would provide a useful improvement to the segmentation algorithm and so further enhance fitting. See also that the conic has been fitted to the upper surface of the object and is not distracted from the upper to the lower edge data as is the edge detector which simply follows the high-contrast object boundary; this is because the edge chain is composed of two smoothly joined conic sections which together do not approximate to a single conic section (the furthest one from the upper surface, and the nearer from the lower).

Generally the fitting paradigms provide good segmentation over a range of image types and image sizes, and frequently without any requirement to change the thresholds. This property is of benefit to a general recognition

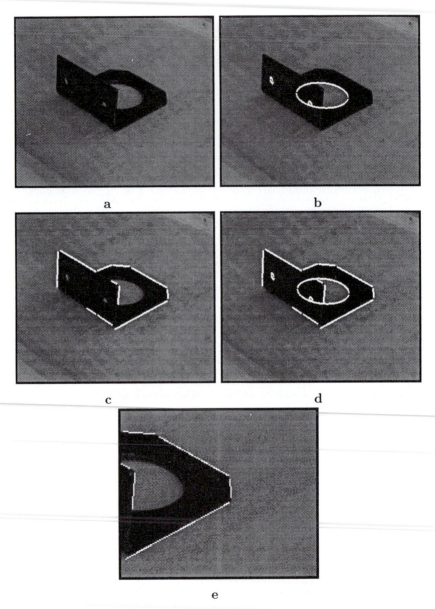

FIG. 6.4. (a) shows a simple unoccluded view of a bracket. (b) and (c) show the conics and lines fitted using the incremental procedures. They are superimposed in (d). Note that shadow on the lower left of the object causes a poor-quality edge to be observed, and so the fit to edgels in this region is discarded. (e) shows detail of lines fitted to the scene that emphasizes the removal of the influence of edgels at corners: the ends of the lines do not coincide, but their intersection locates the corner accurately.

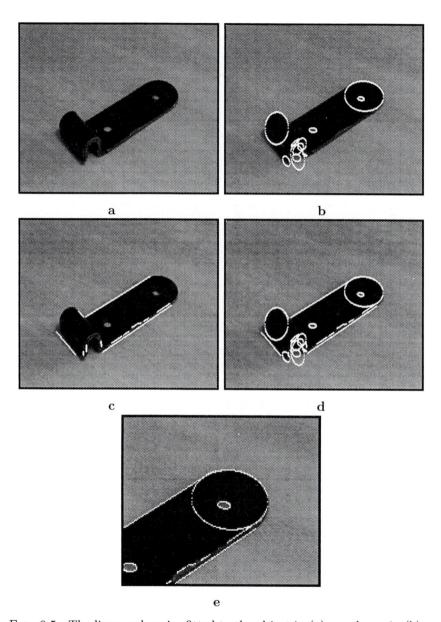

FIG. 6.5. The lines and conics fitted to the object in (a) are shown in (b), (c), and (d). Curvature discontinuities are frequently hard to locate with accuracy. The success of the segmentation algorithm is demonstrated in (e) which shows how well the straight lines and conics are fitted to the outline of the object.

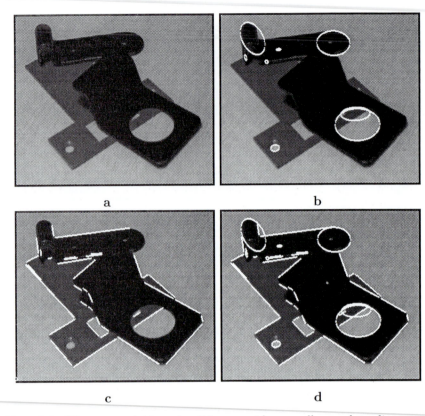

a   b

c   d

FIG. 6.6. The segmentation algorithm provides equally good quality sets of lines and conics for more complicated scenes. Other examples are given in Fig. 6.7 and Chapter 4.

system. For example Fig. 6.7 shows segmentation of an image with large amounts of texture and noise.

6.1.2   Grouping

Since image segmentation is often unreliable and fragmented, feature grouping cost increases exponentially with the number of features required to detect model consistency. There is therefore a strong motivation to use minimal feature groups. The key advantage of using a specific model hypothesis to guide recognition is that the number of image features required to detect the inconsistency of the hypothesis is quite small. Since consistency is frequently computed using pose, all that is required are enough model and image feature correspondences to map the hypothesized object into the image frame. Generally the number of features required to do this is fewer than that needed to compute invariants.[30]

For example, in the alignment approach of Huttenlocher (57) in which an affine imaging model is used, a model hypothesis can be tested from only three vertex assignments. This is because under the affine transformation assumption, the model pose can be determined from three point correspondences. Once three points have been selected the rest of the model can then be projected onto the image frame and the remaining features checked for consistency. In contrast, four points are generically needed to form an affine invariant which could be used to index into the model base. Therefore, without exploiting prior scene knowledge, the task of choosing enough features to form an invariant is harder than that for choosing features to be used in alignment.

For the projective case five lines are needed for an invariant description. This, in its naive form for l features will produce an $^lP_5 = O(l^5)$ grouping cost compared with the more favourable $^lP_4 = O(l^4)$ for a projective alignment technique. This ignores the model indexing effects, but for large numbers of features the difference in the exponent will be significant even with indexing present.

Exploiting structure in the scene for grouping can make both the invariant and alignment approaches have equal complexities with respect to the number of image features. Such a technique is used in LEWIS1. The approach used exploits the connectivity (topology) provided by the edge chains: if points were to be used, one would use points that are adjacent on an edge curve as well as making use of the ordering provided by the curve (hence removing permutation actions). Using such grouping complies with common sense; features that are close together are more likely to come from the same object than features that are distant. The algebraic invariants are constructed from lines rather than points, but again the segmentation algorithm has provided both connectivity and an ordering on the lines. Therefore, invariants are formed from sets of consecutive lines within single edge chains at a cost that is linear in the number of lines in the scene (that is $O(l)$). This precise type of grouping was also exploited by Huttenlocher in (58) who was again able to achieve a linear grouping cost.

The downfall of such a linear grouping algorithm becomes apparent when the connectivity within the edge chains breaks down. This will occur as a result of poor segmentation or excessive occlusion. In these situations any recognition algorithm will be affected but those that index using invariants will tend to suffer more due to their larger group sizes. An immediate way to overcome this problem is to use local measures and their associated redundancy as these tend to reduce the scale at which the correspondence search must be performed.

---

[30]This is true in all cases in which an isotropy does not exist.

Some efforts have been made by other researchers to provide grouping that does not depend only on connectivity, but also searches for other local invariants. One such invariant is parallelism. This approach was taken by Binford (9) using the *in the absence of other evidence, assume...* constraint, and later by Lowe (72) and Dickson (32). However, proximity in itself provides a very strong constraint for grouping which has been exploited below.

Aerial reconnaissance images represent a class of situations for which segmentation is frequently very poor. Large regions of texture and low resolution makes edge detection unreliable and connectivity useless. Figure 6.7 is an example of one such image. The approach for this type of image is to fit lines (and if desired conics), and then ignore all the given connectivity. Wherever a junction is produced by the edge detector it should be broken and fitting applied to the fragmented edge chains. Then, any pair of lines which appear to represent the same line segment should be merged together and a refit performed. Subsequently lines are grouped by proximity of endpoints into graphs of lines instead of the chains provided by the original algorithm. The graphs have exactly the same appearance (and topology) as the sets of connected image lines; the edges of the graphs represent the lines and the vertices connectivity. Forming the graph in this way preserves the notion that lines are connected at their endpoints rather than at any arbitrary point along their length. This latter type of incidence generally results from occlusion and hence not physical 3-space connectivity.

This grouping process will, of course, be scale dependent. For Fig. 6.7 lines within 5 pixels of each other are marked as being connected. Ordered sets of five lines can then be extracted from the graph by performing a graph traversal and noting the order in which the edges are passed. So that an allowance is made for extra erroneous lines that have been included in the structure, all different choices of ordered lines are taken from the traversed path. This gives an $^nC_5$ complexity algorithm where $n \ll l$, n being the number of lines in a path and l the number of lines in the image. As yet it is unclear how well this approach will work; current research is testing its viability. However, in a series of tests on 256×256 tiles from reconnaissance images a significant reduction (an order of magnitude) was found in the number of lines in a group compared to the total number in an image. On average, 130.0 lines were found per image; after grouping, 4.8 groups large enough to form invariants were output, each containing an average of 11.3 lines. Even then, 11.3^5 invariant groups do not have to be computed but normally less than 20% of this number due to the ordering imposed on the lines within the graphs.

A final benefit of representing the world through algebraic objects is the reduction in the number of features that require description. The actual lines and conics provide unary constraints and are also far less numerous than the original number of edge data that was extracted from the scene.

a

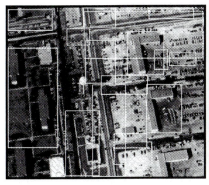
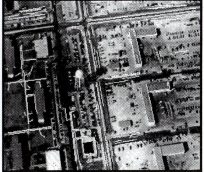

b   c

FIG. 6.7. For aerial reconnaissance images, such as the one shown in (a),
the edge detector produces very little useful connectivity. A typical task
for a recognition system would be to locate the positions of the large
buildings. The edge detector fails due to the vast number of small edges
produced by texture and small features such as vehicles and shadows.
However, some useful grouping can be done: (b) shows bounding boxes
around groups of lines that are considered to lie sufficiently close to
each other to come from single edge groups. The actual lines are shown
in (c). Proximity grouping produces graphs of lines from which one can
recover the connectivity necessary to compute invariants efficiently.

Subsequently they reduce the combinatorial cost of grouping. In the case
of the invariant formed by a conic and three lines the cost of grouping is
$O(cl^3)$, where c is the number of conics and l the number of lines. This is
for a case when no image structure is assumed, if connectivity is reliable
the cost reduces to $O(cl)$. The grouping cost for the joint conic invariants
is only $O(c^2)$. For the images under consideration l is in the order of a
hundred, and c a few tens.

6.2   The canonical frame: detecting $\mathcal{M}$ curves

The canonical frame construction described earlier in Chapter 5 and used in LEWIS2 requires both the accurate location of curve bitangents and other points tangent to a curve whose tangents pass through a given point. For the latter points the given point is generally located at a bitangency, and the tangent line called a *cast tangent*. The other features that are projectively distinguished are points and lines of inflection. This section reviews the methods used to detect bitangencies, tangencies and inflections.

Note that image curves are discrete, and yet terms such as tangency and inflection only apply correctly to continuous curves. The given context makes clear the meaning of such terms.

6.2.1   *Bitangent location*

Image bitangents are located using the following four-stage algorithm:

- Eliminate points that lie on approximately straight portions of curve. These cannot correspond to actual points of bitangency and so should be ignored.
- Find points on the same edge curve that have approximately common tangents.
- Check that such pairs of points do in fact correspond to bitangents.
- Improve the localization of the bitangent points using quadratic interpolation.

Straight portions of curve are found by fitting a straight line to short segments of the curve using the method given at the beginning of this chapter and testing the value of the fitting residual (21 points are used for the fit). Approximately straight portions have a low residual.

The next step is to map the curve into its tangent dual space and look for self-intersections of the dual curve. Bitangents correspond to self-intersections; this is shown in Fig. 6.8. The location of the point in dual space corresponding to an image edgel is found from the line fitted by the process used to remove linear sections of curve. The fitted line will be locally tangent. The tangent space is parametrized by the slope, θ, of the local tangent and the perpendicular distance of the tangent to the centre of the image; this yields a uniform parametrization in that all image line orientations are treated equally.

The tangent space is quantized into discrete cells. As the image curve is discrete at points of high curvature the distance between adjacent points in the tangent space can become large. This is overcome by linearly interpolating between consecutive points in the dual space. Self-intersections, and hence bitangents, are found using a voting scheme in the dual space. Two image points voting in the same cell in the tangent dual space represent a self-intersection. Due to noise these events frequently give rise to false bitangents, therefore a filter is used after the initial bitangent detection:

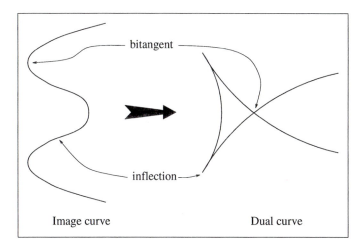

Image curve   Dual curve

FIG. 6.8. The canonical frame construction manipulates $\mathcal{M}$ curves such
as the one shown on the left. For continuous curves bitangents in the
image correspond to self-intersections in the tangent space. Likewise
inflections correspond to cusps.

locally, for regions of image curve in the proximity of bitangent points, the
bitangent corresponds to part of the boundary of the convex hull of the
data set (see Fig. 6.9). Due to noise the hull points and tangency points
may not correspond exactly, but so long as the hull points are not on the
limits of the local region it is clear that a genuine bitangency exists. The local regions used are those 5 edgels either side of the hypothesized bitangent
points.

The hull construction provides the location of the bitangencies for discrete image curves. A significant improvement in performance can be obtained by interpolating the bitangent locations between the actual measured edgel locations. Locally fitting quadratics provides location of the
bitangent points to subpixel accuracy. This is done by rotating the image
data so that the initial estimate of the bitangent line is horizontal and fitting quadratics of the form $y = ax^2 + bx + c$ to data sets either side of the
two bitangent points. The cost used is a least squares error in the y direction and is done by a simple 3×3 matrix computation. The interpolated
bitangent is the line simultaneously tangent to both parabolas.

In the implementation the number of points used for each quadratic fit
is 13 (6 either side of the hypothesized bitangent point). The data sets are
centrally weighted using a Gaussian. The weighting was set empirically by
observing how the quality of canonical frame construction changed as the
number of points was altered. The type of experiment performed is similar
to that described in Section 6.2.2 and Fig. 6.11 with the fitting parameters
adjusted by observing their effects on a large number of views of a typical

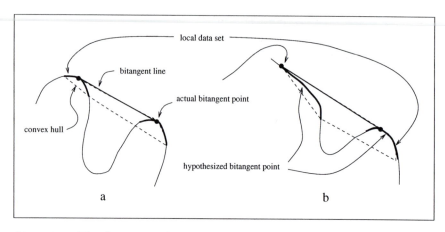

FIG. 6.9. The bitangent line lies on the convex hull of local data sets around the bitangency points. This is shown in (a). The hypothesized bitangent points may map to the same points in the tangent dual space, but in fact do not correspond to a real bitangent. These will be eliminated using the construction described in the text as the convex hull passes through the limits of the local region (b).

object. The results demonstrate that a locally fitting parabola is a good choice of curve. Note that this sort of fitting is not projectively invariant and in fact the shape of the parabolas fitted around the tangency points varies quite dramatically with the number of points used in the fit. However, the location of the actual bitangent point moves very little. The effectiveness of the technique in improving the quality of the canonical frame construction demonstrates its value.

The bitangent detection scheme finds many bitangents along single image curves. This is demonstrated in Fig. 6.10. Due to excessive redundancy in the shape representation (that is there are many $\mathcal{M}$ curves that could be used to describe the object), many of the bitangents can be eliminated from consideration and preferably those that are not sufficiently stable:

- Eliminate any bitangents that have their endpoints too close together.

- Remove bitangents whose associated $\mathcal{M}$ curves are not very deep (only a few pixels).

- For all of the remaining $\mathcal{M}$ curves compute the stabilities of their corresponding signatures using the measure given in Section 5.4.2 (based on the Jacobian of the signature index). If the measure is too high eliminate the $\mathcal{M}$ curve.

- Do not use tangents that cross the $\mathcal{M}$ curves. These will be stable, but are removed simply to reduce redundancy as excessive representation reduces efficiency.

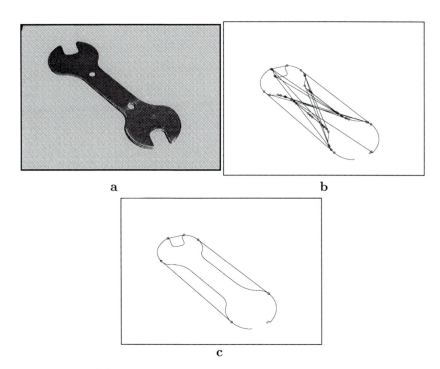

FIG. 6.10. In (b) it is shown that there are a large number of bitangents that can be found even for a simple object such as the spanner in (a). Each one enables the construction of a canonical frame curve, though only curves that do not cross their own bitangents are used. This reduces the level of redundancy. Bitangents that will not produce a stable construction are also deleted; this leaves the three bitangents shown in (c).

6.2.2   Cast tangents

Cast tangents are distinguished tangents to image $\mathcal{M}$ curves between bitangent points. The points of tangency to the cast tangents are required to map $\mathcal{M}$ curves into the canonical frame for the construction of the invariant signature. The cast tangents are distinguished because they are lines that pass through the points of bitangency and are tangent to the $\mathcal{M}$ curve. Many such points may exist, but only two are required; the two that make the largest angle with the bitangent line are used. These ones usually provide the largest spread of the distinguished points in image and thus yield a more robust signature. These tangents will actually lie on the convex hull of the $\mathcal{M}$ curve. The construction is projectively invariant for a real camera as a result of the ordering constraint introduced in Section 3.3.1. The cast tangents are found by:

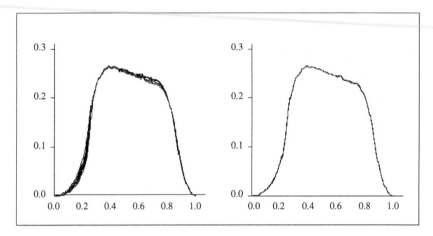

FIG. 6.11. The left-hand plot shows a series of 10 curves mapped to the canonical frame using the discrete locations of the tangency points. When the localization is improved using quadratic fitting the projected curves become indistinguishable. This is shown on the right.

1. extracting the $\mathcal{M}$ curve;

2. computing the convex hull of the $\mathcal{M}$ curve;

3. finding the vertices of the convex hull that lie on the same edge of the hull as the actual bitangent points.

Again, the location of the cast tangents is improved by quadratic fitting. This proceeds in a manner similar to that for the bitangent point interpolation: rotate the data set so that the tangent line is parallel to the x axis; fit a parabola; determine the line tangent to the parabola that passes through the rotated bitangent point; map the tangent point back to the image frame.

The effectiveness of the quadratic fitting process is demonstrated in Fig. 6.11. The experiment used was similar in nature to that of Section 5.1, though the actual details are slightly different: an object was placed on a calibration table to effect a full perspective distortion and the object was rotated by 5 degrees at a time; an image was processed for each location. Results for ten images are shown. So that only the discrete imaging effects are measured the object was a curve constructed by printing a black figure on white paper (though the curve corresponded to an actual object curve). This means that localization errors in the edgel points should be minimized as there is no possibility of the existence of nearby edges distracting the edge detector (say due to the finite thickness of the object). Notice that there is essentially no difference in the curve signatures for the curves on the right in which fitting was done.

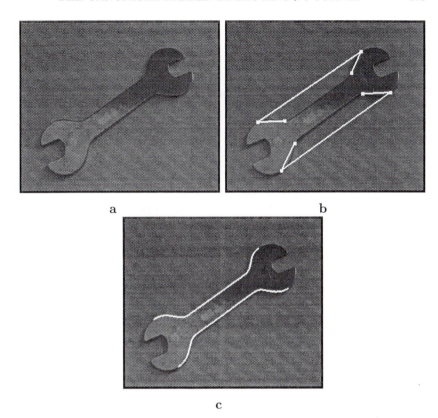

FIG. 6.12. For a simple object such as the spanner shown in (a) there
are two reliable concavities that can be constructed. The bitangent and
cast tangent points and lines are shown superimposed in (b). These
are located to subpixel accuracy using the quadratic fitting method
described in this section. The $\mathcal{M}$ curves bounded by their bitangent
points are shown in (c). The concavities at the ends of the spanner are
not used because their canonical frames cannot be determined stably;
stability is computed automatically for each $\mathcal{M}$ curve using the process
in Section 5.4.2.

A sample segmentation for a simple view of a spanner is given in Fig.
6.12 in which the bitangent and cast tangent points and lines are superimposed onto the object. The bitangent points bound the $\mathcal{M}$ curves that are
shown in (c).

6.2.3 Inflection points and lines

Although inflection points and lines are not used in LEWIS2, their location
was required for choosing the best form of distinguished feature to use
for the canonical frame construction. The assumption is that a pair of

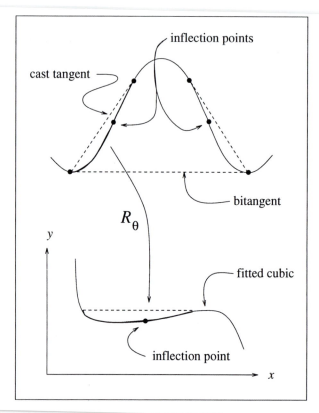

FIG. 6.13. Typical $\mathcal{M}$ curves have a single inflection point between each
bitangent point and cast tangent. The inflection points and lines can
be localized accurately by taking the edge data between each bitangent
and cast tangent point, and rotating it so that the cast tangent line is
parallel to the x axis. Then, a cubic of the form $y = ax^3 + bx^2 + cx + d$
is fitted (having just a single inflection point), and the inflection point
and line of the cubic used as an approximation to those of the actual
image data.

inflections generically exist within each $\mathcal{M}$ curve, and that each one is
located between the bitangent points and their cast tangents (see Fig. 6.13).
The procedure to find them is:

1. Rotate the curve between each bitangent point and cast tangent point
   so that the cast tangent becomes parallel to the x axis.

2. Fit a cubic of the form $y = ax^3 + bx^2 + cx + d$ to the points between
   the bitangent and cast tangent points using a least squares cost over
   the error in the y direction. The reason that a cubic of such a simple
   form is used is because it can possess only a single inflection, and

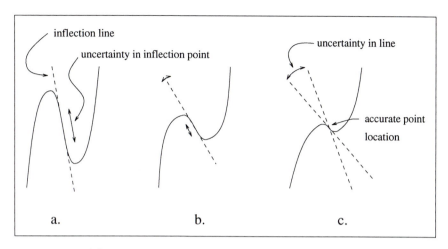

FIG. 6.14. (a) demonstrates a case in which the inflection line can be located with a high accuracy, but the inflection point poorly. The converse is shown in (c). Compromise situations arise for the uncertainty principle as in (b).

    generally such a curve approximates closely to the curve.

3. Determine the inflection line and location of the inflection point for the fitted curve.

4. Transform the line and inflection point back to the image frame.

This process produces inflection points and lines that are visually localized with high accuracy.

    A final issue concerning the location of tangencies and inflections is that there is an uncertainty principle involving a trade-off in the localization of a feature point and its corresponding line. One can either locate the line well and the point poorly, or vice versa. Compromise situations do arise in which both can be located reasonably well. Figure 6.14 demonstrates the principle for inflections.

    An example of inflection point and line detection and localization for the view of Fig. 6.12 is shown in Fig. 6.15. In accordance with the uncertainty principle, for this class of object the inflection lines are located well but the inflection points poorly.

6.2.4 *Grouping*

The canonical frame construction has a linear grouping cost and computes the same number of signatures as $\mathcal{M}$ curves in the image (after those $\mathcal{M}$ curves that are unlikely to be robust are eliminated). This is because all of the features used to form the frame are ordered around single image curves and is also a benefit of using a semi-local object description. This result

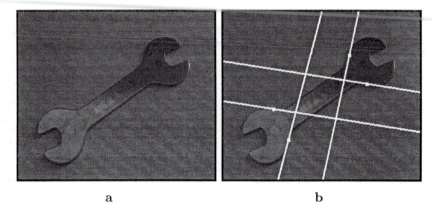

a b

FIG. 6.15. In a similar manner to that used to locate bitangents and cast tangents in Fig. 6.12, points and lines of inflection can be estimated using a locally fitted cubic.

is identical to that used by Huttenlocher (58), and means that recognition using the construction is very efficient.

6.3   Conclusions

This chapter has reviewed the segmentation and grouping algorithms used in the two LEWIS recognition systems. The line and conic detection algorithms that provide features for invariant formation in LEWIS1 are efficient due to the incremental fitting formulations, and also provide both accurate localization and repeatable results. In practice the same algorithms provide equal qualities of performance over a range of different imagery and the incremental framework allows for efficient outlier rejection. Even though neither fitting process makes use of projectively invariant fitting techniques there has been no reduction in segmentation performance due to the tight constraints used to control the feature fits.

In fact, the reliability of the fitting process has been enhanced through the creation of a superior conic fitting algorithm derived from the conventional Bookstein method; the motivation for producing the new algorithm came from the realization that numerical ill-conditioning frequently makes the Bookstein method perform badly. A significant improvement in performance has been achieved for small flat data sets for which conventional conic fitting algorithms fail. Being able to fit reliably to short data sets is essential within the incremental region growing algorithm.

The grouping process used in LEWIS1 which relies on the use of edgel chain connectivity has also been discussed. Under controlled imaging conditions the process is linear and yields reliable recognition results. However, the method is not sufficiently flexible to be effective over images where either occlusion is significant or image quality poor. Although the use of semi-local shape descriptions provides some tolerance to occlusion (by increasing the probability that a single edge chain remains connected), other grouping heuristics have had to be employed for more varied image types. For example, proximity has so far proved an effective replacement for connectivity in the formation of likely object feature groups. Other cues such as those discussed by Binford (9) or Lowe (71) may yield further benefits.

Another avenue that is currently being investigated (113) is the use of either *quasi-invariants* as described by Binford and Levitt (10), or invariants of lesser imaging deformations such as affine invariants. These could be used to recognize feature groups using the invariant indexing paradigm, though because the imaging model assumed for their formation is only an approximation to the actual deformation more error (and hence less discrimination) would have to be accounted for in the index table. However, these invariants require fewer features for their derivation and so the grouping cost would be better than for forming full projective invariants. Then, after indexing the hypothesis extension process given in Chapter 4 could be used to combine these feature groups of approximate invariants together into more discriminatory projectively invariant feature groups that can be used to index again into the model base. Such a hierarchical approach to recognition may possibly provide the most efficient method for the overcoming of the problems presented by grouping.

Finally, the method used to extract $\mathcal{M}$ curves for the canonical frame invariant construction used in Chapter 5 was introduced. Within the implementation of the canonical frame system LEWIS2, the $\mathcal{M}$ curves are described through the accurate location of points of bitangency and cast tangency using quadratic interpolation between image edgels. Although points or lines of inflection could be used as alternative features for the formation of a canonical frame it has been found that tangencies provide far more robust feature locations (for more details see the discussion in Section 5.1.5). Grouping has been shown to be trivial for the canonical frame construction due to the local exploitation of connectivity. Principally, using connected local measures vastly simplifies the complexity of the grouping task.

7

CRITERIA FOR REPRESENTATION OF SHAPE

During the development of the LEWIS systems it became apparent that there are a number of basic properties that a shape descriptor should possess for recognition. In this chapter these have been converted into criteria that should be appreciated whenever a new object description is developed; the criteria are therefore reported in light of the work in building the systems of the earlier chapters in this book. The descriptors of interest are always invariant indexes as these are essential for fast recognition: however, as each criterion is reviewed there will occasionally be comparison with other cues to highlight why indexes must be formed from invariants. Similar criteria have previously been suggested by other researchers as being important for other approaches to object recognition; the most notable of these are by Marr (78) and Brady (15).

The criteria will be considered in order of importance, though the ordering is not necessarily to be taken strictly as some of the properties should be ranked together and considered as essential, while others may be desirable or even unimportant. Perhaps the two most important are discrimination and scope; descriptors are useless without them. Subsequently local description, extension and uniqueness feature as other important properties.

7.1 Discrimination

A shape descriptor contributes nothing to recognition unless it takes different values for different objects. All non-trivial invariants satisfy this. In fact, maximum discrimination between objects is desired irrespective of whether an invariant descriptor is used. For invariant cues one might believe that discrimination can be improved between sets of models by exaggerating the change in value of a measure with respect to changes in the object parameters. However, this will also emphasize changes in the invariant value due to noise (this is stability and is discussed in Section 7.6). It is important to see that the effects of noise and discrimination are inextricably linked; if the noise in the measurement of the invariants belonging to two objects is so large that the invariant ranges overlap, then there will be no formulation of the invariants that prevents the conflict.

The conflict between discrimination and noise can be seen by considering the case shown in Fig. 7.1. In the figure a one-dimensional situation is considered where there is a single independent invariant function $I(x)$. As

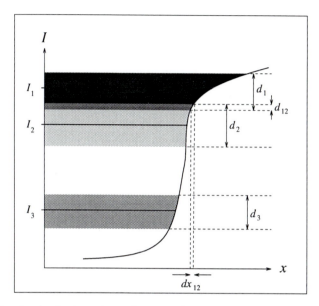

FIG. 7.1. A single invariant I is used to describe three objects; the noise-free values of the invariants are I_i, $i \in \{1, \ldots, 3\}$. Due to noise the values of I_i will never be measured exactly in an image, and they can be computed only within the ranges d_i as shown. As these ranges overlap for objects 1 and 2 (within dx_{12}), it will be impossible to discriminate between the two objects should such an invariant value within d_{12} be measured. Note that this is only for the given invariant function I; one may wish to use a different invariant function to try and improve discrimination. However, without using any more information no other independent invariants can be formed for the three objects; all that can measured is a dependent invariant $f(I)$. It is obvious that no choice of f will ever cause d_{12} to become separated and so in this case discrimination is always impossible.

shown in the graph, the ideal situation in which the invariant is complete (see Section 7.7) arises as $I(x)$ is strictly monotonic. Note that the choice of $I(x)$ as the invariant function is completely arbitrary and in fact any measure $f(I(x))$ could be used just as well as the invariant.

The error-free invariant values are $I_i, i \in \{1, \ldots, 3\}$, but because of image effects the invariants can be measured only within the ranges given by d_i. From the graph the observation that any invariant value in the range of d_{12} results in the ambiguous interpretation of either object 1 or object 2 being present can be made. Irrespective of any map f that may be used to change the error characteristic dI/dx, it is clear that the conflict between objects 1 and 2 cannot be resolved within the range $f(I(dx_{12}))$.

It is generally assumed that one cannot cater efficiently for both system noise and discrimination between objects as they are conflicting requirements (see Marr (78)). The suggested way to overcome this problem is to choose the measures so that they discriminate, and then understand the associated noise model so that caution can be applied to ambiguous results. This way shape estimates can always be traced back to the correct objects. There will necessarily be circumstances when shapes cannot be distinguished under noisy imaging as pairs of shapes can intersect in the shape space (even if the invariant space is complete). No transformation of this space will ever dislocate the intersected region into two parts.

7.2   Scope

The scope of a cue is a measure of both the size of the class of objects that it can describe and of the set of circumstances (transformations) under which it applies. Most shape cues have limited scope in its first sense as each is designed so that a specific class of objects can be recognized: a descriptor developed for the recognition of sets of coplanar points would be useless for a smooth 3D surface. It would be foolish to pretend that a single measure could ever distinguish between all objects; the real concern is whether a class of descriptors can be designed to recognize all objects of interest. Put succinctly, within the LEWIS approach to recognition we must determine whether invariants can be used to describe the world completely, or if other shape cues are needed as well.

The lack of scope of a measure can be overcome by integrating many cues into a single system; that is the extraction of each type of shape from an image should be done in parallel. If this is done a wider class of objects can be recognized. This was demonstrated for plane algebraic invariants within LEWIS1 where three different shape measures were used. In fact, LEWIS1, LEWIS2, and a system using the 3D invariant shape descriptors that will be discussed in Chapter 8 can all be employed as separate modules in a much larger recognition system. One should compare such an approach to the parallel architecture head of Murray, et al. (74, 96) which requires arbitration between a wide range of different visual processes before an understanding of the environment can be achieved. In fact, one of the goals of current research is an attempt to integrate the different descriptors into a single recognition system (through using MORSE, an improved recognition architecture described in (150)).

Many of the shape cues used in successful recognition systems to date have very limited scope in its second sense. For example the descriptors used by Grimson in (53) work only under a plane Euclidean imaging model. Invariants can be designed to have arbitrary scope, though the choice may not always be optimal.[31] Projective invariants have been used in LEWIS as these model most imaging situations accurately (the pinhole camera projection model with an uncalibrated camera, though they fail if radial distortion is not corrected (121)). Should recognition be required within restricted environments then lesser imaging models and their associated invariants can be used. One such set of measures would be an affine model and its invariants. However, we have not discussed the use of such measures in any detail in this book. Although their utility is noted, affine invariants have a more limited scope than projective invariants and do not apply in all of the environments that have been considered.

7.3   Local versus global

Global shape descriptions such as the Fourier measures of Walker and Chatwin (137), or the moment invariants of Taubin and Cooper (130), have little or no stability under occlusion. Although in some environments it can be guaranteed that objects of interest will not be occluded there is a requirement for descriptors that do not collapse under occlusion. Furthermore, poor segmentation is frequently indistinguishable from local occlusion events and so tolerance to occlusion is always desirable. One way to provide immunity to occlusion is to use local or semi-local measures. Local measures are defined at a point, semi-local refers to measures taken over a small number of proximal points. A sufficient number of these non-global descriptors must be used so that recognition is still possible when any (small) number are hidden from view. Using more than a single descriptor is known as redundancy. Generally, invariants can be found that are either local or semi-local. However, when choosing a non-global descriptor one must ensure that each cue on its own can be used for recognition.

Each non-global descriptor is commonly called a subpart. The decomposition itself does not have to be into just two layers (objects and subparts), but instead, as suggested by Ettinger (34), into many. Subparts defined for single objects that share features are termed overlapping, and those that do not non-overlapping. Both types are used in the LEWIS systems, overlapping in the algebraic object recognition framework and non-overlapping for more general plane curves.

A further issue if non-global measures are to be used is how they are to be tied together to form a coherent global description for an object. If this cannot be done the entire global versus local strategy is superfluous. This process is called extension, and is important also because local and semi-local descriptors are by nature weaker than global ones.

---

[31]Under general perspectivities for planar objects with 6 *dof.* (degrees of freedom), projective invariants (8 *dof.*) must be used as they form the smallest enveloping group. This means that the invariants account for two extra degrees of freedom in the transformation and so provide less discrimination between objects that would otherwise be possible.

7.4　Extension

Extension encompasses the joining together of local shape descriptors into a hierarchical description. This is important if objects are to be recognized in their entirety. The process can be done in a straightforward manner when the local shape descriptors account for overlapping rather than disjoint subparts (34). The method is demonstrated in Chapter 4 for algebraic objects. Extension for non-overlapping subparts is possible, and is shown for smooth plane curves in Chapter 5. In both cases the geometry of the object is exploited (through further use of invariants) to constrain the unification process. One of the significant results that came out of the building of the LEWIS systems was the requirement for extension.

Alternative approaches, such as that of Lamdan *et al.* (68), simply use voting schemes. These are bound to be weaker than using geometric constraints between the subparts, but can be made effective. However, they can never be used to derive a complete geometric understanding of the scene as through their use it is impossible to distinguish between a pair of consistent hypotheses for a single model or two hypotheses for distinct objects. The distinction can only be realized during verification which introduces an unnecessary delay in forming an interpretation compared to that which can be achieved through extension. The important principle is not to put too much emphasis on the use of an object-based coordinate frame within the extension process (that is one should not exploit propagation as defined by Brady (15)), but to use a more general invariant frame.

7.5　Uniqueness

If a shape cue is unique its value will be the same for all viewpoints of an object. Obviously the outline of an object is not a unique description under 3D imaging transformations due to perspective distortions and scaling, and so it would be a useless shape descriptor. It is the lack of uniqueness for most natural object descriptions that makes recognition so hard. Effective recognition can be performed only if the same object description can be extracted reliably from any expected viewpoint. If this is not the case, the match search space will be large even for a single object and subsequently recognition will be slow.

Uniqueness is trivially satisfied by invariants (by definition), and so the criterion is superfluous; it is only because other shape descriptors do not naturally possess the property that it has to be considered. Unique descriptions can be derived from images using other cues, but is usually done by a process that computes an object-centred description from the image (as shown by Marr (78)). Usually this means that a significant amount of extra work has to be done before indexing can even be attempted.

7.6   Stability

The stability of any shape cue can be computed as a measure of how much the shape value changes as its features are perturbed (due to error in their measurement). The local stability of an invariant **I** computed from a set of features **x** is given by $\nabla \mathbf{I}(\mathbf{x})$ for a one-dimensional index, and a Jacobian for higher dimensions; for simplicity, the notation for the 1D case will always be used. It is important to note that enforcing stability on an invariant descriptor does not mean that $\nabla \mathbf{I}(\mathbf{x})$ has to be small, but that it must be *known*. A measure for a set of features can lie within a large range, so long as that value does not infringe on the measure for any other feature set (or for that matter on noise). Infringing has been described in detail in Section 7.1 and Fig. 7.1. Generally there is a trade-off between stability and discrimination, though the latter tends to dominate the consideration.

There are two ways to study the cause of error: one is by computing an analytic expression for $\nabla \mathbf{I}(\mathbf{x})$ in terms of expected error in feature measurement and the other is to form a statistical model of the invariant value over a large number of trial measurements of the invariant (from images). Both of these methods have been employed in the LEWIS systems. However, noise behaviour can only be understood properly by studying real image data because it is frequently hard to make correct assumptions about noise models; for example one should question immediately whether errors arise out of noise in the image, or in three space, or from numerical error. Furthermore, many analytical evaluations are valid only locally; noise effects are frequently observed over extended domains.

7.7   Completeness

Completeness affects the amount of time spent performing verification after recognition hypothesis formation. One usually has little control over it with respect to a specific invariant type (Chapter 3 demonstrated cases in which the limited control can be used to good effect). A shape cue is complete if a specific value of it defines an object modulo the action of the imaging deformation; a formal definition was given in Section 3.3. For example, if the imaging process is one of plane Euclidean distortions, a suitable complete description of a model base of squares would be their area; for rectangles, area is not complete, but area and aspect ratio are. Completeness can be contrasted from uniqueness in the following way: if a descriptor is complete, it defines the object; if it is unique, the object defines the value of the shape descriptor.

Completeness of an invariant significantly affects the efficiency of recognition. If an invariant is not complete a given measure of the invariant does not absolutely define the geometric configuration of the object features that caused the measurement (modulo effects of the transform group). Subsequently, after indexing verification is required to discriminate between geometrically different model alternatives.

For a given algebraic configuration of features there is always a maximal set of independent invariants that can be measured (see the introduction of Mundy and Zisserman (92)). This will be the best set of invariants to employ as it allows the use of a minimal number of measures to describe any shape; note that this applies only to algebraic configurations, but in the limit the argument can be extended to other cases. If the invariants are not complete one way to ensure that an absolute description is obtained is to use more invariants (the extra invariants assist in the formation of a complete description). Doing so may in itself be inefficient and so there is a trade-off between the number of invariants that should be used and the degree of ambiguity tolerated in the description.

7.8   Accessibility

The accessibility of a shape cue is a measure of how efficiently it can be computed from image data. This property also covers whether such information can actually be extracted from an image due to limitations on resolution and accuracy of the early vision processes, but here the emphasis is on the efficiency of the computation. In practice, many invariant functions can be computed directly from image data and so accessibility is no more than an afterthought. In fact, even those that have to be computed in a different frame do not require a large amount of computation (relative to that required for early vision or verification). Thus the comparison of invariant measures with other shape descriptors should not be made too heavily; almost all *sensible* shape descriptors are in fact accessible.

Expense as a result of grouping costs should be considered as a more important aspect of accessibility. The desire to extract features from an image that come from single objects, without naively using brute force and grouping all possible features together, makes one of the most significant differences to the running time of recognition algorithms. Some simple and effective grouping algorithms were discussed in Chapter 6, but grouping cost affects all types of shape descriptor. These methods should be contrasted to those of Binford (9), Lowe (72), and others.

7.9   Conclusions

This chapter has outlined the criteria that should be considered for shape representation using knowledge gained from building working recognition systems. Although the literature contains lists of ideal properties for shape cues, very few really need consideration. Those that must be addressed are discrimination, scope, local description and extension. The others are applied later during the implementation stages of a system. All of the other criteria listed in this chapter follow naturally when invariant descriptors are used, for example *propagation* (Brady (15)) is covered automatically by extension when invariant coordinates are used.

The aim is not, however, to trivialize the theoretic aspects of choosing a shape descriptor. The main four criteria are important (discrimination, scope, local description and extension), and are all satisfied by the invariants used in the LEWIS systems. The dominating fact is that, as described in Chapter 2, invariant indexes are essential for fast recognition, and so the criteria should guide the choice of invariant rather than suggest the pros and cons of using them.

8

INVARIANTS FOR 3D OBJECTS

So far we have been able to demonstrate that index-based recognition systems can be built around invariant shape descriptors. The previous chapters have been dedicated to proving this. The LEWIS architecture has been used successfully to recognize two different object classes using either algebraic invariants or a canonical frame construction. In fact, as a result of building the systems we were able in the last chapter to formulate a list of criteria that all shape descriptors should possess. Nevertheless, it should be borne in mind that the object classes used in the systems so far are very limited; it has been demonstrated only that planar objects can be recognized reliably. There is a real concern that the scope of the available invariant descriptors should be broadened.

It is the author's belief that as yet no reliable system has been demonstrated that recognizes three-dimensional objects using indexes extracted from greyscale images in a general environment. This may be a concern considering the maturity of much of the previous work on recognition reviewed in Chapter 2, but more realistically it should be a pointer to where future work should be applied. Basically, the problem of recognizing 3D objects from single views is much harder than that for 2D objects. This is because planar objects are viewed by a non-singular transformation (which has been represented in the preceding text by a 3×3 matrix $\mathbf{T}$), whereas for 3D objects the imaging process is singular. This is a result of the fact that the depth of a 3D object is lost under projection. The non-singular plane-to-plane imaging map can be inverted relatively easily and the original shape recovered; this is not true for singular maps. Thus, the loss of depth information through the difference in the imaging processes for 2D and 3D objects has suggested the requirement for an alternative approach for the construction of indexes for 3D shapes compared to that taken for those that are planar.

Much of the recent work on computing invariants for 3D objects has relied on recovering some measure of the geometry of the original 3D object prior to computing its invariants. However, one is still sometimes able to measure the invariants directly in a scene. This chapter discusses a number of recent advances in 3D invariant shape extraction that have appeared in the literature. Even so, the results are intended to provide suggestions for future research directions; the descriptions that follow have not been used within reliable and automatic recognition systems such as LEWIS1 or

LEWIS2. It is however the hope that they can be used within the LEWIS framework once more is understood about how they can be extracted efficiently from scenes.

The invariants described within this chapter complement the theory of Burns, *et al.* (19):

Only trivial invariants can be formed from single views of 3D point sets in general position.

This result has also been stated by Clemens and Jacobs (24), Moses and Ullman (89), and Huttenlocher and Kleinberg (60). By general position we mean that *no* constraints can be placed on the features used to compute the invariants. The reason that invariants can be computed for all of the examples in this chapter is because constraints can be applied to the features of interest. In fact, features on real objects are infrequently in general position as they lie on real surfaces or edges; hence the non-existence theorem is of little interest within the context of object recognition.

Existence of invariants can be proved for 3D objects under a number of different circumstances demonstrated by example in the following sections: first, the butterfly construction[32] is introduced which demonstrates the simplicity with which invariants for 3D objects can be formed using the invariants of 1D or 2D structures; secondly it is shown how invariants can be computed for solids of revolution using a similar principle; then, a detailed derivation of the invariants for a more general class of 3D points is proposed, that is for those lying on vertices of polyhedra; and finally it is shown how symmetry can be exploited so that two-view invariants can be employed in single images. Note that none of the constructions in this chapter assume that there is enough information in any single object plane for the measurement of plane projective invariants.

Three areas of significant research have been explored elsewhere within the domain of 3D projective invariant representation. The first relies on the measurement of independent invariants within 1D or 2D structures and then using these to form 3D Euclidean invariants through pose. This reconstruction process relies on Euclidean knowledge of the lower-dimensional features and is described by Forsyth, *et al.* in (42). One example of this class would be an object containing a pair of circles on different planes (such as a piece of piping). From a single view, a pair of ellipses will be observed; backprojecting these onto world planes defines the slant and tilt of the original object planes up to a two-fold ambiguity (as the ellipses are required to project to circles). From these planes the (invariant) angle between the original object planes can be determined. If extra information such as the radii of the circles is known, a complete Euclidean construction is possible and then distance invariants can be computed.

---

[32]The existence of an invariant for this configuration was realized by Joe Mundy.

The second area covers the measurement of invariants and projective structure from multiple images. The processes involved are directly analogous to those used in more conventional stereo algorithms; however, there has been an interest in being able to provide shape reconstructions without the need for camera calibration. Currently it appears that freedom from calibration, or even just the use of the camera parameters that can be relied upon, results in a much more robust representation of the world. However in doing so there is usually a penalty in that initially only a projective or an affine reconstruction of the world can be achieved rather than a full Euclidean one. Examples of this form of *uncalibrated stereo* have been demonstrated by Faugeras (36), and Hartley, *et al.* (54), who have extracted projective structure from views of general 3D point sets. Both of these build on the affine reconstruction due to Koenderink and Van Doorn (66) which has also been used by Quan and Mohr (102), and Demey, *et al.* (28). Reconstruction in 3D allows the direct measurement of 3D invariant indexes. For more structured feature sets there are simpler ways of measuring the invariants: this has been shown by Mohr, *et al.* (86) and Beardsley (6). The symmetry construction in Section 8.4 that forms one of the examples we have examined exploits these invariants in a novel way.

The final approach involves the description of algebraic surfaces. Such objects are highly constrained and hence detailed information can be extracted from single views. Preliminary work by Forsyth, *et al.* (41) demonstrated how invariants may be computed for configurations of algebraic surfaces, with more recent work by Forsyth (44) showing that from a single generic view the entire surface can be reconstructed modulo a projective transformation of 3-space. It has yet to be proved, though, how effective these methods are for real object recognition. This last example highlights exceptionally well some of the problems that can be encountered in trying to understand the causes of observed image measurements. Although the world may place very tight constraints on what can be observed in images (in contrast to the theorem above of Burns, *et al.* (19)), the process of inverting the 3D to 2D imaging process is frequently made difficult due to the existence of errors in the image. Subsequently, certain routes to forming invariant shape descriptions may not prove fruitful from the point of view of the recognition system builder.

8.1   The butterfly configuration

The first example of an invariant measurement for a 3D shape is introduced due to its simplicity, though no results from images are reported. Recently Sparr (123) has used the same construction for the formation of invariants and has provided measurements from images.

Geometric configurations of 3D features can frequently be reduced to planar, or in this case linear, structures from which invariants can be measured. The butterfly construction is one simple example that indicates how

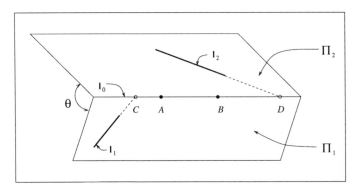

FIG. 8.1. The configuration consists of two planes (Π_1 and Π_2) each containing a single line (l_1 and l_2), and a pair of points A and B lying on the intersection line of the planes (l_0). A cross ratio can be formed by determining the positions of the points C and D where l_1 and l_2 intersect l_0, and then using the collinearity of $\{A, B, C, D\}$ to compute $\tau = \{A, B : C, D\}$. Obviously the cross ratio will be undefined if any of $\{A, B, C, D\}$ cease to be distinct.

easily 3D projective invariants can be measured directly in an image without the need for a reconstruction process. Another example is seen in Section 8.2 for the class of rotationally symmetric surfaces. The construction is demonstrated in Fig. 8.1, and is based on the cross ratio. In this case the required configuration is a pair of lines lying on different planes and two points on the intersection line of the planes; a full description of the construction is given in the figure. It is important to note there are not enough constraints in either plane to form a projective invariant (only one line and two points lie in either plane), but using both planes there are. Once the cross ratio $\{A, B : C, D\}$ for the four points has been measured it could be used to index into a model base and provides a shape description that can be employed within the LEWIS framework for recognition.

It should also be noted that the shape in Fig. 8.1 does not have to be rigid. The measured cross ratio will remain constant even if the planes Π_1 and Π_2 flex about their intersection line. This is one example of how parametrizations can be dealt with using invariant descriptions, though the general problem of designing parametric shape descriptions is too big a subject to be considered here.

8.2 Rotationally symmetric objects

Computing descriptions of curved surfaces from images has for a long time been considered to be a much harder problem than the analogous process for features such as points and lines. The reason is that the latter types of feature have infinite, or at least in real terms very high, curvature at

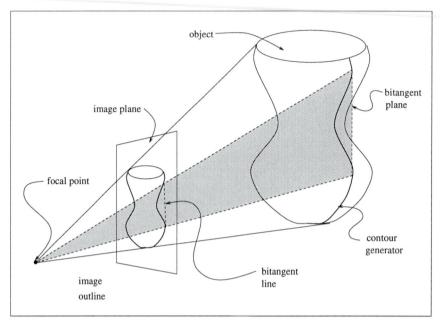

FIG. 8.2. The imaging geometry shows the contour generator, which is a
space curve on the object surface, projecting to a planar image curve.
The envelope of the contour generator is defined by planes through the
focal point that are tangent to the surface; the projection of any of
the tangent planes is a line tangent to the image curve. Subsequently
any plane that is bitangent to the object, and passes through the focal
point, will project to a line bitangent to the image curve.

their observed locations. Thus, as one moves viewpoint the position of the
observed point in three-space does not shift. Unfortunately this is not true
for surfaces. In practice one may find that the points observed on a surface
for two different viewpoints are extremely far apart for even a tiny change
in observation point.

The approach given in this section succeeds in finding an effective shape
representation because the symmetry of the surface is exploited. The class
of surfaces considered bound solids of revolution, or objects projectively
equivalent to them. The method for forming invariant indexes for such a
model class is described here briefly by restricting attention purely to solids
of revolution. Full details and extensions can be found in work by Forsyth,
et al. (43, 73).

The imaging geometry for solids of revolution is shown in Fig. 8.2. The
boundary curve of the object that projects into the image is called the
contour generator. It is defined as the set of points of tangency to planes
through the focal point that are tangent to the object. The image curve

is formed from the projection of each of these planes: each projects to a line tangent to the image curve forming the envelope of the outline. Any plane that is bitangent to the object and passes through the focal point will project to a line bitangent to the image curve (as shown in Fig. 8.2). Planes bitangent to the surface envelope right-circular cones that have their vertices on the axis of revolution of the object. Although these cones do not form physical surfaces, the generators of each cone (which are straight lines) are observed via the bitangent planes to the surface. These planes pass through the focal point and so project to lines bitangent to the image curve.

The images of the cone contour generators are shown in Fig. 8.3, where it is clear that when both sides of the object are visible, the complete images of the right-circular cones can be constructed. Measurement of these cones remarkably allows access to the geometry of the curve's surface from a single view. The projected locations of the vertices of the cones can be extrapolated (A and B) and these will lie on the projection of the axis of rotation of the object.[33] Because the world locations of the cone vertices lie on a straight line, as well as their images, the actual imaging model of interest has now been reduced to a line-to-line projectivity. Again, as in the butterfly case, the dimensionality of the descriptive task has been lowered. A cross ratio can be formed if four vertex positions can be measured in an image, and hence a projective description computed. Figure 8.3 shows only the measurement of two points, whereas Fig. 8.4 shows four pairs of bitangents which are used to compute the cross ratio. Its value for three different views are shown in Table 8.1: these are constant modulo noise.

This section has demonstrated how an index can be constructed for objects that are projectively equivalent to solids of revolution. In actual fact, richer descriptions can be formed using other surface features that are preserved under perspective projection such as creases, curve endings, and inflections. Full details are given in (43, 73), as well as examples of recognition from a large range of viewing situations for a larger model base than a single object. It has also been shown in (73) that the construction

---

[33]This construction yields a way of determining the axis of symmetry of a solid of revolution. An alternative method would exploit the fact that both halves of the image curve are projectively equivalent under an automorphism of the plane, and that the axis is preserved under the action of the automorphism. The proof that the two sides of the outline are projectively equivalent can be sketched as follows: from a given viewpoint rotate the camera about its focal point so that the optical axis intersects the axis of rotational symmetry of the object. There is a one-dimensional family of rotations that achieves this; any one of them may be used. This rotation causes a plane projectivity only of the observed features in the image plane, and the same projection affects both sides of the outline. Due to symmetry, after the rotation the two sides of the outline will be within a reflection of each other, and are thus related by a projectivity. Therefore, prior to the rotation they must also have been related by a projectivity.

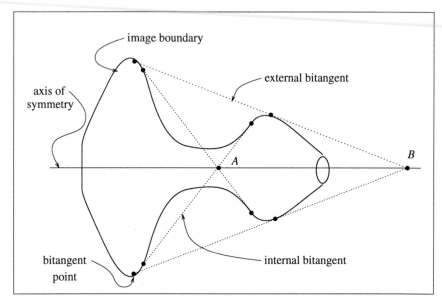

FIG. 8.3. The image of a solid of revolution can be considered to project
to two curves (separated by the axis of symmetry) that are projectively equivalent. The non-generic case of the curves having a reflectional symmetry is shown. This case corresponds to the optical axis
passing through the object's axis of revolution. By construction, corresponding bitangent lines (detected using the algorithms in Chapter 6)
intersect on the axis of symmetry at points A and B. All such intersections will be collinear and can be used to define a cross ratio; details
are in the text.

Table 8.1 *The cross ratios measured for the two
views of the lamp-stand in Fig. 8.4, plus one other
view, remain constant.*

view	cross ratio
a	-9.13
b	-9.12
c	-9.66

extends not only to objects that are projectively equivalent to surfaces of
revolution, but also to straight homogeneous generalized cylinders.

One final point to note with the rotationally symmetric construction is
that the features used to extract the cross ratio are based on $\mathcal{M}$ curves.
Subsequently, a lot of the machinery in LEWIS2 can be used within the
implementation employed for this shape description. Such a sharing of modules is not actually that rare and all of the examples given in this chapter

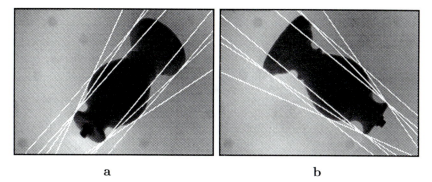

a   b

FIG. 8.4. For each view of a lamp-stand, which is a solid of revolution,
four stable bitangents can be found that are the projections of bitangent
planes. Each corresponding pair of bitangents intersect on the projection
of the axis of rotation of the lamp-stand, and the intersection points can
be used as a projectively invariant index for the shape; their values are
given in Table 8.1.

used the feature extraction processes of either LEWIS1 or LEWIS2.

8.3 Polyhedral cage

The third three-dimensional invariant shape descriptor considered is for
point sets lying on the vertices of polyhedra. The representation of such
feature sets using polyhedra is called *caging* in that we are interested only in
observing the vertices of a polyhedron and not either its edges or faces. Because these latter two types of feature do not have to be visible there is no
requirement for them even to exist. Thus, objects that have points lying at
the vertices of conceptual polyhedra can be caged by virtual polyhedra and
recognized through indexing as if they are the polyhedra. The construction
of the invariants is done via projectively reconstructing an imaged polyhedron within 3-space using a method analogous to that of Sugihara (126),
though a full perspective imaging model is assumed with an uncalibrated
camera. Again, not having the requirement for camera calibration means
that the results are frequently more stable. Once reconstructed, invariants
can be measured directly within 3D projective space.

The method is first described for actual polyhedra and is then extended
to non-polyhedral objects whose points coincide with the vertices of real
polyhedra. The key result of the method is that every non-degenerate member of the reconstruction solution space lies in the same projective equivalence class and hence all such solutions have the same projective invariants.
The computational process attempts to compute the plane equations of the
caging polyhedra within 3-space. Note that some of the planes of the caging
polyhedra are occluded by the object itself (self-occlusion is another feature

that makes 3D object recognition hard), and yet under certain assumptions the equations of these planes can be computed.

8.3.1   *Solid polyhedra*

Following the usual practice all vertices are assumed to be *trihedral*: these are points formed by the intersection of three world planes (that is planes in 3D Euclidean space). Trihedral junctions are *stable* because three planes generically meet in a single point; one can perturb any one of the planes and still form a single vertex close to the original vertex. This is not true for higher-order junctions. This assumption has little effect on the mathematics presented in Section 8.3.2, the difference being that if a point lies on n (rather than 3) planes $n - 1$ constraints on the plane parameters can be formed rather than the 2 for the trihedral case. However, it is impossible to infer structure from the self-occluded part of the viewed polyhedron unless the vertices are trihedral. A further assumption is that the polyhedra represent real solid objects, that is, a polyhedron is not just a polygon or a group of polygons embedded in 3-space.

8.3.2   *Forming the constraint equations*

The input is a set of unknown planes that are bounded by an arbitrary number of edges (at least three) and a set of points whose image locations are known. Using the trihedral assumption the points always lie on three given planes. The derivation is similar to that given by Sugihara in (126) except that a perspective imaging model is used and that the camera is uncalibrated.

The coordinate frame used to develop the theory has the world X and Y axes in a plane parallel to the image plane with directions shown in Fig. 8.5 and centred at the focal point. The Z axis lies along the principal axis of the camera. A polyhedron is made up of a set of planes:[34]

$$a_j X_i + b_j Y_i + c_j Z_i + 1 = 0, \qquad (8.3.1)$$

where (X_i, Y_i, Z_i) is a point known on the plane, $\mathbf{v}_j = (a_j, b_j, c_j, 1)^T$ is the homogeneous representation of the plane in projective 3-space, and $j \in \{1, ..., n\}$ where n is the number of planes on the object. Note that n is the sum of the observed planes in an image and the inferred occluded planes. For example, for a cube one would often observe three planes and be unable to see three of the planes due to self-occlusion; however, for this case $n = 6$. In the sequel it is assumed that the world points (X_i, Y_i, Z_i) can all be observed uniquely in an image and so must be formed by the polyhedral vertices.

---

[34]Planes that pass through the focal point are not represented as these project to a single line in the image.

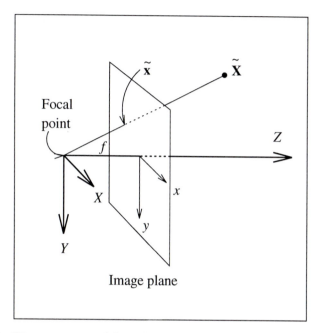

Focal point

f

X

x

y

Z

Y

Image plane

FIG. 8.5. The camera model used with the world and camera coordinate frames shown. A perspective imaging model is used to project the world point $\tilde{\mathbf{X}}$ to the camera plane point $\tilde{\mathbf{x}}$. Note that image coordinates only can be measured, rather than the camera coordinates of an image point (these two frames are linked by an affine map).

Under a pinhole projection model projection onto the plane $Z = 1$ maps the point (X_i, Y_i, Z_i) to (x_i, y_i) where:

$$x_i = \frac{X_i}{Z_i} \qquad \text{and} \qquad y_i = \frac{Y_i}{Z_i}.$$

Substituting these into eqn (8.3.1), dividing through by Z_i and setting $t_i = 1/Z_i$ gives:

$$a_j x_i + b_j y_i + c_j + t_i = 0. \qquad (8.3.2)$$

Note that this equation is linear in the unknowns $\{a_j, b_j, c_j, t_j\}$. In practice one does not measure (x_i, y_i) because of the image plane translation and scaling of the image points (for an uncalibrated camera). However, the image points $(x'_i, y'_i) = (fx_i/\alpha + c_x, fy + c_y)$ can be measured, with the camera focal length and aspect ratio being f and α respectively, and camera centre at (c_x, c_y). Rewriting eqn (8.3.2) gives:

$$\frac{a_j\alpha}{f}x_i' + \frac{b_j}{f}y_i' + c_j - \frac{\alpha c_x + c_y}{f} + t_i = 0$$

$$\implies \quad a_j'x_i' + b_j'y_i' + c_j' + t_i = 0, \tag{8.3.3}$$

where,

$$\begin{pmatrix} a_j' \\ b_j' \\ c_j' \\ 1 \end{pmatrix} = \begin{bmatrix} \alpha/f & 0 & 0 & 0 \\ 0 & 1/f & 0 & 0 \\ 0 & 0 & 1 & -(\alpha c_x + c_y)/f \\ 0 & 0 & 0 & 1 \end{bmatrix} \begin{pmatrix} a_j \\ b_j \\ c_j \\ 1 \end{pmatrix}.$$

Consequently, from the linearity of the above expression, the assumed plane equation is a projectivity of the actual plane equation, $\mathbf{v}_j' = \mathbf{C}\mathbf{v}_j$. Equation (8.3.3) is used in the sequel. Note that a very simple distortion on the image plane has been assumed, that is a scaling and a translation. As $\mathbf{C}$ represents a general projectivity any linear map may in reality be applied to the image.

From the trihedral assumption it is known that each image point lies on three planes, say $j \in \{p, q, r\}$. Eliminating the t_i term in eqn (8.3.3) between pairs of equations (one equation for each of the three planes) yields two linear equations per observed image point:

$$(a_p' - a_r')x_i' + (b_p' - b_r')y_i' + (c_p' - c_r') = 0,$$
$$(a_q' - a_r')x_i' + (b_q' - b_r')y_i' + (c_q' - c_r') = 0. \tag{8.3.4}$$

For the m observed image vertices a set of $2m$ equations are formed (which may or may not be independent) in the $3n$ unknowns:

$$\mathbf{A}(\mathbf{x}', \mathbf{y}')\,\mathbf{w}' = 0, \tag{8.3.5}$$

where $\mathbf{x}' = (x_1', \ldots, x_m')^T$, $\mathbf{y}' = (y_1', \ldots, y_m')^T$, $\mathbf{A}(\mathbf{x}', \mathbf{y}')$ is a $2m \times 3n$ array of constraints, and $\mathbf{w}' = (a_1', b_1', c_1', a_2', \ldots, c_n')^T$. The solution space of $\mathbf{w}'$ is the null space or kernel of the matrix $\mathbf{A}$ and represents the set of polyhedra that can be reconstructed from the image measurements. The dimension of the kernel is $d \geq 3n - 2m$. The '$\geq$' arises because the set of equations $\mathbf{A}$ may be linearly dependent. As long as the object is *position free* (as defined by Sugihara (126) and in Section 8.3.4), the dimension of the kernel immediately gives the number of degrees of freedom of the family of polyhedra that satisfy the image constraints. If this is the case, d is exactly the number of parameters required to define the solution set.

8.3.3   Interpretation of the kernel

The kernel of $\mathbf{A}$ is spanned by the vectors $\mathbf{b}_i'$, $i \in \{1, \ldots, d\}$. Therefore, the solution of eqn (8.3.5) is $\mathbf{w}' = \sum_{j=1}^{d} \mu_j' \mathbf{b}_j'$; this represents a d-dimensional subspace of the $3n$-dimensional polyhedral space. This basis set can be transformed to any linearly independent combination of the vectors to give a new basis $\mathbf{b}_i = \sum_{j=1}^{d} \lambda_j \mathbf{b}'_j$, with λ_j real. The chosen transform basis is such that:

$$\mathbf{b}_1 = (1, 0, 0, 1, \ldots, 1, 0, 0)^T,$$
$$\mathbf{b}_2 = (0, 1, 0, 0, \ldots, 0, 1, 0)^T,$$
$$\mathbf{b}_3 = (0, 0, 1, 0, \ldots, 0, 0, 1)^T.$$

A basis of this form always exists as will be explained. The motivation for this is as follows (now with $\mathbf{w}' = \sum_{i=1}^{d} \mu_i \mathbf{b}_i$): a plane solution for the polyhedron can always be constructed; this is easily accounted for by arbitrary choices for the μ_i's, $i \in \{1, \ldots, 3\}$, and $\mu_i = 0, i > 3$ (for this situation all the planes will have the form $\mathbf{v}'_i = (\mu_1, \mu_2, \mu_3, 1)^T$). Although only an arbitrary non-degenerate solution is needed to form the invariants (see later), this formulation prevents the mistake of choosing a degenerate solution as one can insist on a solution with $\mu_i \neq 0, i > 3$. A degenerate solution places all of the 3D features on a single plane and so the reconstructed object has no real depth; this is not a real polyhedron and so contradicts the prior assumptions. Furthermore, as the plane case is always a possible interpretation (the polyhedron may be the actual polygon drawn on top of the image features), it follows that for $d = 3$ the *only* possible interpretation is the plane solution.

Therefore, the dimension of the kernel immediately provides information as to whether the line drawing can be constructed as a real polyhedron or a planar object, in particular this process acts as a further filter in the interpretation of line drawings.[35] The following two cases are of interest:

1. $\mathbf{d} = \mathbf{3}$: The drawing can only be interpreted as a plane polygon (not a polyhedron), and is generically not position free.

2. $\mathbf{d} \geq \mathbf{4}$: It represents a d-dimensional class of solid polyhedra.

Understanding of the invariants for $d > 4$ is not considered here but is of current interest. In the sequel the case for $d = 4$ is considered and we also restrict our attention to shapes for which $n = 6$ (for such a polyhedron, which has certain similarities to a cube, m is generically equal to 7).

8.3.4   *Position-free polyhedra*

Real polyhedra can be segregated into two distinct classes: those that are *position free*; and those that are not. If a polyhedron similar to the original

---

[35] Much work has previously been done in determining the consistency of line drawings of polyhedra in images. The interested reader should consult: Huffman (56), Clowes (25), Waltz (138) and Mackworth (75). The goal of the consistency checks is to determine whether a single 3D structure could cause the observed image features.

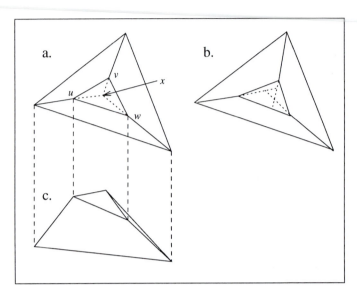

FIG. 8.6. (a) shows a plan view of a truncated tetrahedron which is not
    position free but can be realized as a 3D object. A different view of
    the same figure is shown in (c). If the point v is perturbed as in (b),
    the point x defined by the intersection of three lines in (a) is no longer
    defined and so the polyhedron can be interpreted only as a plane figure
    (such as the one lying on this page). In real images all vertices are
    perturbed by errors and so for a non-position-free object such as a
    truncated tetrahedron one can never recover a full 3D interpretation.

object can be reconstructed from any generic view even under small perturbations of the image vertex points, then the original object is defined
as being *position free*. In many cases this is not the case, such as the truncated tetrahedron shown in Fig. 8.6. For most perturbations of the image
vertices of this class of object the only realization of the polyhedron is as
a plane figure. Basically, for non-position-free objects the theory given in
Section 8.3.2 does not provide a genuine reconstruction of the object. For
such an object the generic rank of the matrix **A** will be higher than the
rank of the matrix for the exact imaging case (which can never be observed
due to image noise), and so the computed kernel will have fewer dimensions than expected. For the case of the truncated tetrahedron the kernel
is generically only of dimension $d = 3$ and so the only polyhedron that
can be reconstructed is a polygon. If useful information is to be extracted
from the images of non-position-free objects one must be able to spot this
non-degeneracy and remove its effects (generally by ignoring or massaging
one of the 'superfluous' constraints). A similar observation was made by
Sparr in (122).

The non-degenerate behaviour of A can be interpreted as a number of the original equations becoming independent when they should be dependent. This event is hard to spot by observing any property of A, and so one must observe the non-position-free case by another method.[36] Currently graph techniques are being investigated to achieve this (111). Once the erroneous regions of the image (those that cause the independent behaviour) have been found, chosen constraints may be deleted or adapted.

8.3.5 *Forming the invariants*

The route taken to forming the invariants for the position-free class of objects is through reconstructing the caging polyhedra of the points in 3-space and then measuring the projective invariants for the planes of the polyhedra. In Appendix D it is shown that all of the solutions represented by the kernel are equivalent up to a projectivity of 3-space and hence are equivalent to the actual object in the camera frame. Therefore, any one non-degenerate solution may be chosen and its invariants measured. The solution used is the one represented by the fourth basis vector (for a four-degree-of-freedom (dof) figure) as this has already been computed in the kernel computation. Proof that the invariants are also invariant to Euclidean actions in the world is trivial. Briefly, in 3D point space Euclidean actions are a subgroup of 3D projective actions. Using the duality of points and planes in projective 3-space and the group properties of projectivities, it follows that Euclidean actions on points will result in actions that are at most projectivities on the plane parameters. Therefore, the plane projective invariants measured through the reconstruction are equal to those that would be measured on the object itself.

For a simple 4 dof figure such as a cube three independent projective invariants can be formed. This results from the counting argument in Forsyth, *et al.* (42): six planes have $3 \times 6 = 18$ dof; the 3D projective group has 15 dof and so there are $18 - 15 = 3$ invariants. A possible set is:

$$I_1 = \frac{|\mathbf{I}_{3561}| \cdot |\mathbf{I}_{3542}|}{|\mathbf{I}_{3564}| \cdot |\mathbf{I}_{3512}|}, \quad I_2 = \frac{|\mathbf{I}_{3562}| \cdot |\mathbf{I}_{3142}|}{|\mathbf{I}_{3512}| \cdot |\mathbf{I}_{3642}|}, \quad I_3 = \frac{|\mathbf{I}_{3564}| \cdot |\mathbf{I}_{5612}|}{|\mathbf{I}_{3561}| \cdot |\mathbf{I}_{5642}|}, \quad (8.3.6)$$

where $\mathbf{I}_{abcd} = [\mathbf{v}_a, \mathbf{v}_b, \mathbf{v}_c, \mathbf{v}_d]$. The vectors $\mathbf{v}_i$ are the homogeneous representations of the planes. Considering the fourth basis vector to be composed of a set of three-vectors $\mathbf{m_i}$, one for each plane, gives:

$$\mathbf{b}_4 = (\mathbf{m}_1^T, ..., \mathbf{m}_n^T)^T.$$

Thus, each homogeneous plane vector is defined as $\mathbf{v}_i = (\mathbf{m}_i^T, 1)^T$.

---

[36]It may be possible to do this by noting small eigenvalues computed from the singular value decomposition of A. However, under projectivities it is hard to quantify what is 'small'.

An interesting case of the invariant is when the four planes $\{a, b, c, d\}$ forming I_{abcd} become concurrent, such as a cycle of faces on a cuboid. In this case the planes cease to be linearly independent and so $|I_{abcd}| = 0$; thus the invariants may become zero, unity or undefined. Note that the values will, modulo noise, still be invariant. Problems can arise though when error is added to the invariant measures as some independency may be observed, that is the determinants may take on a small but finite value. However, it is impossible to quantify a 'near zero' value as under a projectivity any determinant can be made arbitrarily large and so placing firm bounds on the possible invariant values for this class of objects is impossible.

8.3.6   *Examples*

In the following examples the polyhedral structure of the test objects is not used directly for the reconstruction. This avoids the intractable task of extracting labelled polyhedral line drawings from the image. Instead, only the observed vertex positions are used. These are grouped on virtual planes which may or may not be physical object planes. This process is termed *polyhedral caging*. Caging 3D points means that a larger class of objects can be recognized using the same construction, that is we are able to broaden the scope of the descriptor. In fact, any object for which points can be observed that lie at the vertices of a polyhedral structure can exploit the construction. Note that in the examples we have satisfied the requirement that there are a number of sets of (at least) four coplanar points, otherwise there is the situation of (19, 24, 89) where only non-trivial (constant) invariants can be formed.

In Fig. 8.7 a series of five images of a punch is shown with the same seven points marked on each image. These points are the images of vertices of the virtual polyhedron for which the invariants are computed. The images are processed using a Canny (22) edge detector and straight lines fitted to the edge data using an orthogonal regression routine. Vertex positions are found by intersecting pairs of lines (by hand) and the points are then grouped into planes to form a six-sided polygon. The invariants for (a), (b) and (d) should be equal, and those for (c) and (e) the same, though, not necessarily equal to those of the three former views. This is because a different set of points was used to compute the invariants for (c) and (e). However, because of the reflectional symmetry of the object the invariants are equal for all five views.[37]

The measured invariants for the five views are given in Table 8.2 and are essentially constant over the change in viewpoint. In the table the standard deviations are given, as well as the value of the standard deviation as a percentage of the mean invariant value (except for the first invariant which

---

[37]The symmetry is equivalent to a projective automorphism on the object and so will not affect the measured invariants.

Table 8.2 *The invariants computed for the views in Fig. 8.7, with their mean and standard deviations. In the last row the standard deviation is shown as a percentage of the mean for I_2 and I_3. The value is not computed for I_1 because in this case the mean is ideally zero. In fact, the punch is projectively equivalent to a cube and so the invariants should be $\{I_1, I_2, I_3\} = \{0, 1, 1\}$. From these values it is also evident that the invariants remain constant over a change in viewpoint (see also the graph in Fig. 8.8).*

	I_1	I_2	I_3
view a	-0.0141	0.9862	-1.0586
view b	-0.0356	0.9657	-0.9770
view c	-0.0189	0.9796	-1.0446
view d	-0.0400	0.9619	-0.9247
view e	-0.0012	0.9988	-1.0043
mean	-0.0219	0.9784	-1.0018
σ	0.0143	0.0135	0.0482
σ (%)	-	1.4	4.8

is meant to be zero[38]), and these are below 5%. The values are also plotted in the graph in Fig. 8.8.

In Fig. 8.9 a second example is shown with two views of a calibration table. The measured invariants are given in Table 8.3; they remain constant over the change in viewpoint but are different from the invariants computed for the punch in Fig. 8.7. This means that the invariants are both stable and give discrimination between different objects. Note that different invariants provide differing amounts of discrimination between objects; for example between the punch and the calibration table I_3 provides the only discrimination. Note that these invariants can again be used as indexes within a recognition system such as LEWIS; the rest of this section details how one might perform two different verification steps that would qualify first the initial polyhedral assumptions and then the hypotheses resulting from indexing.

8.3.7 *Verifying the polyhedral assumption*

So far only the projective structure has been computed for the point set represented by the seven visible points in the images. This ignores other image

---

[38]The reason for the invariant being zero is that four of the planes form a star and so the planes are not algebraically independent; this gives rise to a zero determinant. An alternative way to see this is that the edges of the caging polyhedron between the four planes intersect at a single point which lies on the world ideal plane.

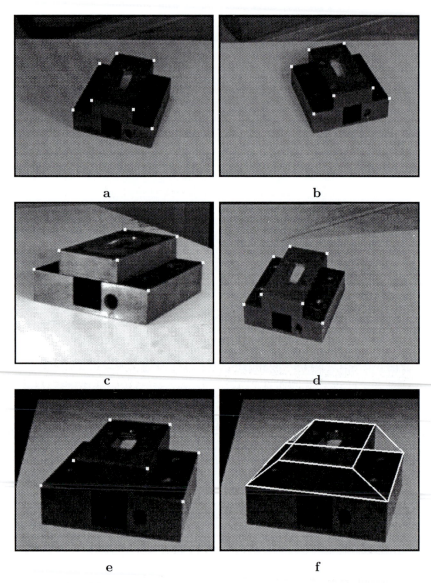

FIG. 8.7. (a)–(e) shows five views of a punch and the points used to compute the invariants. These points are caged by a polyhedron whose bounding planes are not actual object planes; the caging polyhedron for (e) is shown in (f). The computed invariants are given in Table 8.2.

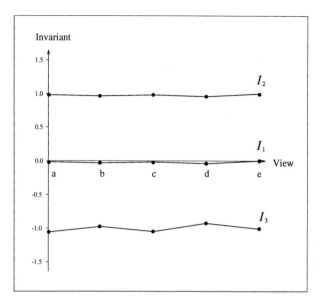

FIG. 8.8. The measured invariants for Fig. 8.7 and Table 8.2 remain unchanged over the change in viewpoint.

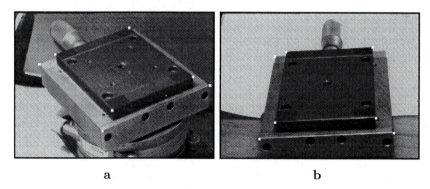

FIG. 8.9. Two views of the calibration table used to test the invariants.
The seven points used to compute the invariants are marked in white.
In the right image the eighth point is also visible; this could be used to
overconstrain the solution, but in this case it is ignored.

information that can be used to elaborate or confirm the hypothesis that
a caged polyhedron is really being observed (this should be compared with
the verification process in Section 4.2.6). The polyhedral assumption pre-
dicts the positions of other points in the image (in this case the eighth point
forming the caging polyhedron). If other points are visible, the predicted
and actual image positions provide an independent check on the validity of
the polyhedral assumption. The positions of the remaining points can be

Table 8.3 *The invariants measured for the two views of the calibration table in Fig. 8.9. The invariants stay fairly constant even under image noise. In this case I_3 can be used to discriminate between the calibration table and the punch in Fig. 8.7; again $\{I_1, I_2\} = \{0, 1\}$ for the calibration Table.*

	I_1	I_2	I_3
view 1	-0.00146	0.991	-6.30
view 2	0.00117	1.007	-6.44

determined either algebraically or geometrically as shown for a six-sided figure in the following sections.

8.3.7.1 *Algebraic approach* This is carried out by intersecting the three virtual planes that bound the eighth point. Note that the equations of planes that are totally occluded are being used to predict the position of an unobserved point.

When all of the solutions represented by the basis $\mathbf{w}'$ are considered the locus of the eighth point is seen to be a line in space passing through the centre of projection. If this line is projected into the image a single point is recovered that is the predicted position of the eighth point. This point is the same for all of the solutions of the caging polyhedra. Its position is shown in Fig. 8.10 for the examples given in Fig. 8.7. Instead of just showing the extra point, the complete polyhedra that were used to cage the data points are outlined. The good agreement between where the eighth points are expected (which are visible in some of the images) and the predicted positions highlights the accuracy of the method. Again the positions of the eighth points and the caging polyhedra for Fig. 8.9 are shown in Fig. 8.11.

8.3.7.2 *Geometric approach* The position of the eighth point can also be predicted geometrically; often geometric manipulations provide a much more intuitive understanding of the imaging process than purely algebraic analysis. In this case, one does not explicitly have to compute the 3D projective structure of the polyhedra but can do the construction in the image. Details of the construction are given in Fig. 8.12.

8.3.8 *Extending 3D knowledge*

Unlike any of the invariants described up to now in this book the polyhedral invariants are recovered from a reconstruction of the object in projective 3-space. As 3D information has already been computed it may as well be used for other tasks than just recognition, for example pose determination that could be used for gripping or navigation. If extra 3D information is

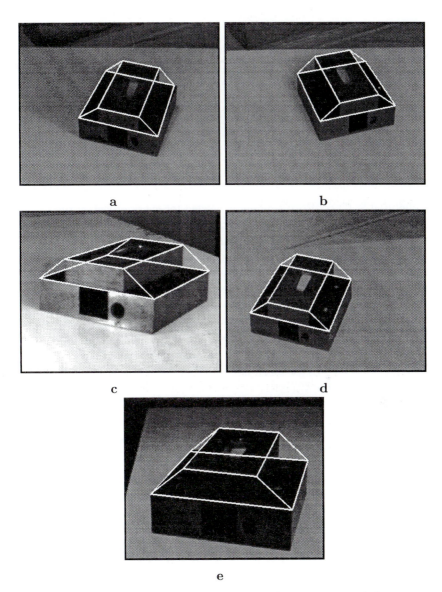

FIG. 8.10. The eighth point for each view is shown as part of the caging polyhedron. Note that at no stage has the position of the eighth point been measured in the image, but its location has been computed from the other seven points.

a   b

Fig. 8.11. The caging polyhedra for the examples in Fig. 8.9.

to be used a 3D projective model is needed for every object in the library. There are a number of ways that such a model can be constructed: one is by using a 3D CAD type model that directly provides Euclidean information about the object. An alternative is to use projective structure gained from two views, such as demonstrated in (28, 36, 54). However, as the actual objects are available the former is used.

Once the matching invariants have provided a correspondence between a set of eight points on the model and in the world, the entire model can be mapped into a 3D projective camera frame by a 3D projectivity (such a transform has 15 degrees of freedom and is thus determined by five pairs of corresponding points; eight points provide an overconstrained system). The transformed model then rests in the actual pose of the object in projective 3-space. The information can be projected into the original image to show registration on the measured features (for instance for verification). This is demonstrated for sample images taken from Figs 8.7 and 8.9 in Fig. 8.13. The good correspondence of the model to the image features exemplifies the performance of the process.

8.4   Objects with bilateral symmetry

The final class of objects that are considered are those containing a plane of bilateral symmetry (or that are projectively equivalent to one). For these objects invariants can be measured from single views using adaptations of multiple-view invariants. The key observation is that the plane of symmetry implies that two mirror views of half of the object are available from a single view (a reflection is a specialized projectivity), and so a construction forming the invariants from a view of each half of the object can be exploited. The same observation was made previously by Gordon (49) and Mitsumoto, *et al.* (84) who used a calibrated camera system to simulate stereo from a single viewpoint.

First we show how to derive multiple-view invariants for a certain feature configuration and then their application is demonstrated to real im-

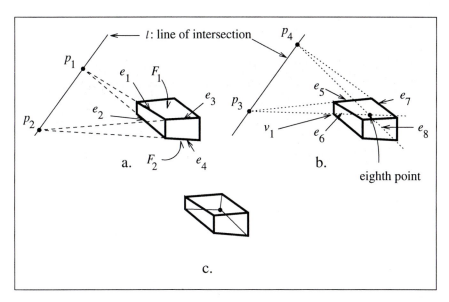

FIG. 8.12. The geometric construction for finding the eighth hidden point of a six-sided polyhedron. Note that all of the properties of interest are projective (hence pairs of planes will always intersect). (a) first find the intersection of planes F_1 (the top plane) and F_2 (the bottom plane): edges e_1 and e_2 both lie on the left-hand side plane of the object and so they will intersect at point p_1. As e_1 and e_2 lie respectively on planes F_1 and F_2 the two planes also intersect at p_1. By a similar argument with edges e_3 and e_4 construct the point p_2 which also lies on both F_1 and F_2. Two planes intersect in projective 3-space in a line; this is given by the points p_1 and p_2 and denoted by l. In (b) reverse the process to find the hidden eighth point. This point must lie on the plane defined by e_5 and e_6. The edge e_6 is not observable, but it can be computed: e_5 and e_6 both lie on the rear plane and so must intersect (at a point p_3). As they lie on F_1 and F_2 respectively, p_3 must lie on l. Therefore p_3 is defined as the point at which e_5 intersects l. Edge e_6 must pass through v_1 as well as p_3 and so e_6 is defined. The eighth point lies on e_6, and so its locus is restricted to a line. The argument can be repeated for e_7 and e_8 to restrict the eighth point to lie on e_8. Thus, the point is defined by the intersection of e_6 and e_8. This is shown in (c) with the reconstruction of the hidden lines.

ages. For this class of objects invariants can either be computed directly in the image or as is shown, the original object can be reconstructed projectively and then invariants measured as for the polyhedra in the previous example.

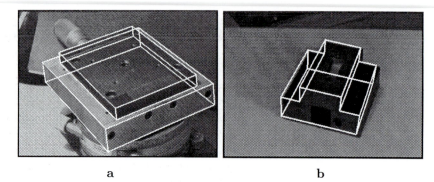

a   b

FIG. 8.13. The registration of 3D models onto the test images. To perform this task one has to compute the position of the objects in 3D projective space. This type of information is useful not only for recognition, but also for navigation.

8.4.1 *Two-view projective invariants*

First a construction for measuring invariants from two views for four coplanar points and a single line lying out of the plane is described; alternative derivations have been given previously by Quan and Mohr (102) and Beardsley (6). The construction is shown in Fig. 8.14, with (b) and (c) views of (a) using an uncalibrated camera. In (b) the four points and the projection of the world line (seen as l_1) are observed. In (c) the line is observed as l_2. As the line lies out of the plane, and the world space is projective, the extended line of which the segment is part (shown dotted) intersects the plane at a single point. In the sequel the terms l_1 and l_2 will be used to mean the infinite extensions of the lines. The aim is to determine the location of the intersection point, so yielding a total of five points in the plane and hence a pair of projective invariants.

First, the plane projectivity T is computed between the two of planes containing the points in views (b) and (c). This is done using the four coplanar points observed in each view. Generically T maps only points between (b) and (c) that lie on the world plane correctly. Therefore, if we map the image of l_1 using T into (c) to form l_3, the only points that project to locations that would have been observed in (c) through viewing the world directly are those that lie on the world plane. In practice only one point will satisfy this constraint; this is the single point given by the intersection of the line with the plane. Subsequently, only one point on l_3 actually lies on the world plane. Likewise, we know that l_2 intersects the plane at a single point and the point is thus constrained uniquely by the intersection of l_2 and l_3. Once the intersection point has been located it can be used with the four coplanar points to form a pair of projective invariants and subsequently an index for a model base.

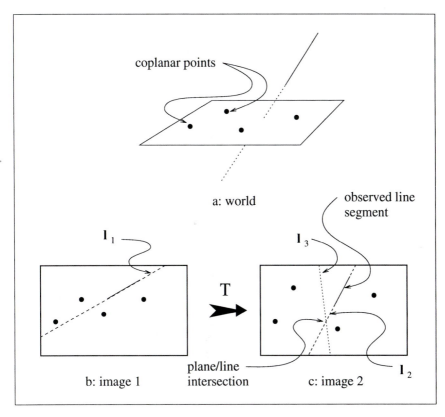

FIG. 8.14. A pair of projective invariants can be measured for two views
of four coplanar points and a line out of the plane. This is done by
computing the intersection point of the line and the plane yielding five
coplanar points. Details are given in the text.

Note that a genericity assumption was made about the properties of
T. These properties depend directly on the camera motion between the
two views. If the camera centre moves only within the plane defined by its
focal point in the first view and the world line then the construction breaks
down. This will be observed as l_3 mapping exactly onto l_2 and so a single
intersection point cannot be defined.

8.4.2 Exploiting symmetry

The task of computing projective structure for objects possessing a plane
of bilateral symmetry can be divided into two tasks. The first is the computation of a correspondence or epipolar structure for the given viewpoint,[39]

---

[39] Even though a single view is being employed the terminology used in stereo can be
used meaningfully.

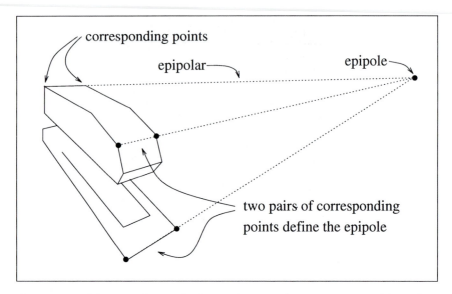

FIG. 8.15. The epipole can be located using the intersection of lines between two corresponding points on an object possessing a mirror symmetry (the points are marked by filled-in circles). Epipolars can then be constructed through the epipole to aid correspondence. Note that in the world all of the correspondence lines are parallel and intersect at a single point lying on the ideal plane. The image of this point is the epipole.

and the second is the actual recovery of structure. Computing the epipolar structure is simple, but the task is is important because it eases the problem of finding correspondences between points in each half of the object. All that is required to do the epipolar calibration is a pair of matching points lying on each side of the symmetry plane of the object. Drawing lines through the corresponding points yields epipolars, and the intersection of two such epipolar lines gives the location of the epipole. This is demonstrated in Fig. 8.15. Any line through the epipole is an epipolar that can be used to test for correspondence, as is shown in Fig. 8.16 for a real view of a stapler. In practice we do not at any time require the actual location of the epipole (even for computing the structure) but rather only the positions of the epipolar lines. Often we find that the epipolar can be constrained only poorly (maybe its location is known to within only a hundred or so pixels), but when it lies a long way off the image (a few thousand pixels) the errors in its position do not appear to affect the general epipolar structure.

Projective invariants can be computed from the four points employed to define the epipolar geometry using either a single additional line lying

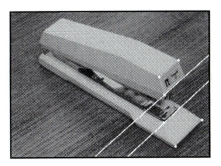

FIG. 8.16. The epipolars for two marked points are shown. Note that the corresponding points (by symmetry) lie on the epipolars. The four other marked points were used to determine the epipolar structure.

Table 8.4 *The measured invariants for each of the two views in Fig. 8.17 are given. The values remain reasonably constant under a change in viewpoint.*

	I_1	I_2
view 1	-4.85	-0.211
view 2	-5.01	-0.211

out of the plane of the points and its mirror correspondence, or using two more pairs of points that similarly define a corresponding pair of lines. The construction works by determining the intersection of either of the lines with the base plane and computing the invariants for the four points and the intersection point. The invariants are computed by applying the two-view invariants to each half-view of the object and follows directly from the description given above. Figure 8.17 demonstrates an example of symmetry being exploited for the formation of invariants: two views of a stapler are shown with the image features of interest superimposed in white. For each image the 3D invariants are computed. As shown in Table 8.4, the invariants remain fairly constant under change in viewpoint. These invariants could be used to index into a model base for a LEWIS style recognition system.

8.4.3   *3D projective reconstruction*

Rather than simply measuring invariants for objects with a plane of bilateral symmetry one is able to do a full three-dimensional reconstruction of the object from a single image. Obviously, once the 3D shape is known the invariants can be measured directly in 3-space. All that are required for the reconstruction are pairs of corresponding points from either side of the object. The reconstruction relies on finding four pairs of points and using these to construct a *canonical frame* in three-dimensional space. Once this

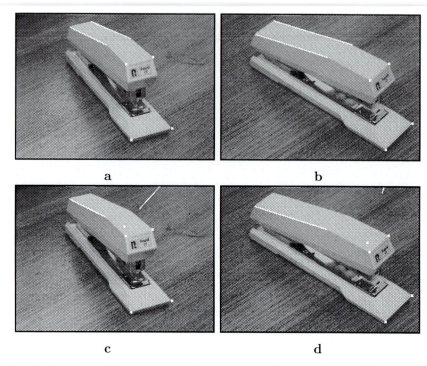

FIG. 8.17. Two different views of a stapler are shown in (a) and (b). From *each* view one can compute a pair of invariants. The process is as follows (just considering (a) and (c)): compute the projectivity that maps each of the four points marked onto its symmetrically corresponding point. Then, map one of the lines, in this case the right-hand one, using this projectivity onto the frame of the other half-object. This is marked in (c). By construction the intersection of the left line and the projected line lies in the plane of the four points. This yields a fifth point in the plane (which is marked in (c)) and hence the pair of projective invariants given in Table 8.4. The process can be repeated for (b) and (d) and the invariants compared. Note that invariants can also be computed by projecting the left line onto the right half-image; these invariants will be functionally dependent on the first two values.

frame has been formed, all other pairs of points can be assigned 3D projective coordinates. This frame is in fact exactly analogous to that used in Chapter 5 for the recognition of objects containing smooth planar curves.

In practice, two pairs of points only are required to initiate the construction; these are needed to deduce the epipolar construction. For example in Fig. 8.18a two pairs of points can be extracted from observable object markings on a teaspoon (the part of the spoon of interest is the space curve defined by its boundary). These can be used to determine the

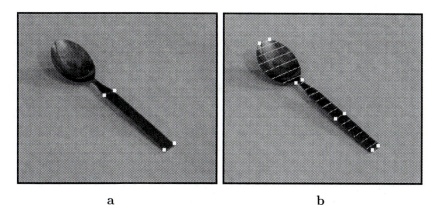

a   b

FIG. 8.18. (a) a single view of an object with a plane of bilateral symmetry
such as a teaspoon is sufficient to allow a full 3D projective reconstruction. Only two pairs of distinguished points are needed for the approach;
these are recovered from surface markings and can be used to determine
the epipolar structure of the image (b). Once the epipolar constraints
are available one can produce an arbitrary number of correspondences;
only eight points are required to constrain the reconstruction. Any other
pair of correspondences can be assigned 3D projective coordinates based
on the 3D locations of the first eight points. The projective coordinates
are themselves invariants for the shape.

position of the epipole and hence they define the epipolar structure given
in (b). From the epipolars the task of finding the second two pairs of corresponding points is trivial: choose two points on one side of the object
(ideally chosen to span the length of the object to yield better tolerance
to error), and then from their epipolars find their correspondences on the
other half of the object. This yields the four pairs of points needed for the
reconstruction (eight such points are shown in Fig. 8.18b).

The reconstruction proceeds by setting up a 3D coordinate frame based
on the image measurements (see Fig. 8.19):

1. Assign an XY coordinate frame in the plane of symmetry, and compute the X and Y coordinates of all pairs of points by projecting
   them onto this plane. Both of the elements of a pair will have the
   same X and Y coordinates.

2. Define the Z axis to be perpendicular to the symmetry plane; once
   the distance between the first pair of corresponding points has been
   defined one can compute the Z coordinates of any other point. A
   corresponding pair of points have equal but opposite Z coordinates.

As the Z axis is perpendicular to the XY frame, the projection of any
point onto the symmetry plane is given by intersecting its correspondence

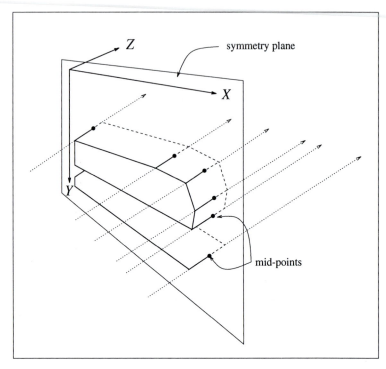

FIG. 8.19. The 3D reconstruction uses a coordinate frame with the X and Y axes in the plane of symmetry, and the Z direction perpendicular to the plane. The construction ensures that the Z axis is parallel to all of the correspondence lines. Thus, each correspondence line has constant XY coordinates and the mid-points of any corresponding pair of points has $Z = 0$.

line (epipolar) with the plane. By construction, this intersection point will be the mid-point of any pair of correspondences, therefore the first task is to determine the mid-points of pairs of points.

Under projection the mid-point of a pair can be computed using the construction shown in Fig. 8.20. Details are given in the caption. Note that this geometric construction does not rely on knowledge of the position of the epipole and so we achieve immunity from error in its location.

An alternative way to compute the mid-point uses the cross ratio and the position of the epipole:

The projections of two points, their mid-point, and the ideal point all lying on a straight line, have a *harmonic* cross ratio. More precisely, if the points are x_1 and x_2, with their mid-point x_m and projection of the ideal point x_∞, the cross ratio is constrained by $\{x_1, x_2 : x_m, x_\infty\} = -1$.

As the epipole is the projection of the ideal point along any correspondence

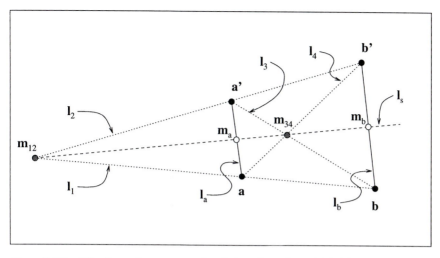

FIG. 8.20. The line of symmetry l_s of the plane $\{a, a', b', b\}$ can be determined geometrically as follows: compute the lines l_i, $i \in \{1, \ldots, 4\}$, and
then intersect as shown to give m_{12} and m_{34}; these constrain l_s. Then,
the mid-points of $\{a, a'\}$ and $\{b, b'\}$ are defined by the intersections of
l_s, l_a and l_b.

line the computation of the location of the mid-points is trivial. However,
we prefer to use the former geometric method for computing the mid-points:
their locations for the four spoon distinguished points is shown in Fig. 8.21.

The above construction constrains the mid-points to have the same
XY coordinates as the points themselves, therefore the aim is initially to
compute the coordinates of all of the mid-points of the pairs. First, compute
the locations all of the mid-points in the image and so conceptually we
have a view of the symmetry plane of the object. Then, define a coordinate
representation on the symmetry plane (that is align the XY axes by giving
X and Y coordinates to a number of points). As we are trying to achieve a
projective construction we can define a representation in the image plane
and then project it onto the symmetry plane. Again four points are required
to compute the projection and so the X and Y coordinates of four mid-
points have to be defined in the world. Therefore, the process is achieved
by giving four observed image points generic X and Y coordinates in a
canonical frame, computing the image-to-canonical-frame projectivity T_{33},
and then mapping all of the other observed mid-points to that frame. The
coordinates in the canonical frame become the coordinates of the final
reconstruction. Four such reference points have been marked in Fig. 8.21.
Note that these points should be chosen to be in general position; although
those shown in the figure are close to collinear the image locations of the

FIG. 8.21. The mid-point of any pair of points can be computed either geometrically, or using the cross ratio once the location of the epipole is known. The mid-points for the four pairs of points of Fig. 8.18b are marked. The mid-points have the same XY coordinates as the pairs of corresponding points, so the aim is to compute the coordinates for the mid-points, rather than the pair.

points are known with sufficient (subpixel) accuracy that the construction ultimately works well. As shown it is also wise to choose the points so that they effectively span the planar region containing the mid-points of the object.

So far we have defined the map T_{33} that sets up the representation in the symmetry plane. For convenience T_{33} is defined as the transformation that takes the world XY coordinates into the image xy coordinates rather than the other way around:

$$k_i \begin{pmatrix} x_i \\ y_i \\ 1 \end{pmatrix} = \begin{bmatrix} T_{11} & T_{12} & T_{14} \\ T_{21} & T_{22} & T_{24} \\ T_{31} & T_{32} & 1 \end{bmatrix} \begin{pmatrix} X_i \\ Y_i \\ 1 \end{pmatrix}.$$

The slightly unusual choice of subscripts is deliberate as is explained below. As stated T_{33} is defined uniquely by fixing the XY coordinates of four pairs of corresponding points in the world. From these the XY coordinates of any fifth pair of points can be computed directly by mapping their mid-point in the image onto the symmetry plane.

Having computed the XY coordinates we need to determine all of the Z values for the points. This is done using constraints provided by the 3×4 3D-to-image projective camera matrix T_{34} defined by Roberts (106):

$$k_i \begin{pmatrix} x_i \\ y_i \\ 1 \end{pmatrix} = \begin{bmatrix} T_{11} & T_{12} & T_{13} & T_{14} \\ T_{21} & T_{22} & T_{23} & T_{24} \\ T_{31} & T_{32} & T_{33} & 1 \end{bmatrix} \begin{pmatrix} X_i \\ Y_i \\ Z_i \\ 1 \end{pmatrix}. \qquad (8.4.7)$$

As yet this matrix is unknown, but note that by considering the map for $Z = 0$ we have the same projectivity as that which takes points on the symmetry plane into the image. The resulting map is just T_{33} and hence the choice of notation used previously. The consequence of this is that T_{34} contains only the three unknowns $\{T_{13}, T_{23}, T_{33}\}$. These can be fixed by placing a final constraint on the reconstruction in space. Assigning Z coordinates to any single pair of corresponding points that are observable in the image (in practice Z_0 and $-Z_0$) defines T_{34} uniquely: each of the two points provide a pair of linear constraints of the form of eqn (8.4.7). Therefore, for two points there are four constraints and yet only three unknowns. T_{34} is subsequently determined uniquely through a least squares minimization process.

Once T_{34} is known the final part of the reconstruction proceeds by computing the mid-point of any pair of points in the image and mapping these to the canonical frame using T_{33}. The coordinates in this frame give the XY coordinates of the pair of points in the world. Then T_{34} is used to provide two (overdetermined) constraints on the final unknown, the $\pm Z$ coordinates of the points.

Two different examples of the reconstruction are shown in Figs 8.22 and 8.24; full details are in the captions. Both have been rendered in believable Euclidean frames for clarity. The spoon was reconstructed using the base points shown in Fig. 8.21 and the stapler using the four points used to find the epipolar structure in Fig. 8.16 plus the two extremal pairs of points shown in Fig. 8.23. Note in both cases the credibility of the reconstructions.

The construction works well under any projective or affine distortion of the object so long as the camera focal point does not lie in the plane of symmetry of the object. Once the construction has been achieved we can again compute invariants for the shape and then use these to index into a model base for recognition.

8.5 Conclusions

This chapter has introduced four different procedures for forming invariants for 3D objects: the first one, the butterfly construction, was given to show how easy it can be to create 3D invariants; the others all form more detailed investigations into how larger structures can be described either with invariants measured directly in images, or through projective reconstructions. Frequently, there is no conceptual difference between being able to form invariants directly from images and a 3D reconstruction, though for some model classes the former can be done but not the latter (such as for solids of revolution). The goal of performing the constructions is to provide indexes that can be used within a LEWIS style recognition architecture for 3D object recognition.

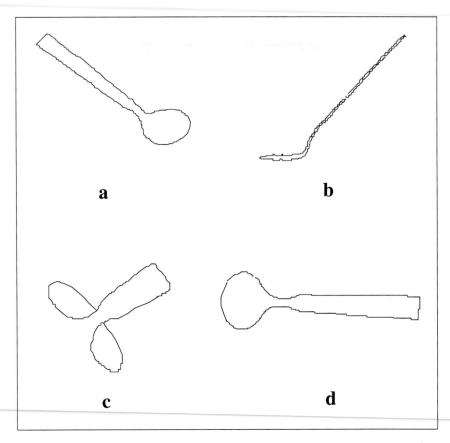

FIG. 8.22. Four different views of the 3D reconstruction gained from Fig. 8.18. The construction works very well: note the planarity of the handle recovered in (b), and the full 3D shape in all of the images.

As mentioned at the beginning of this chapter the constructions demonstrate that invariants can be formed for 3D objects, but the results fall short of proving that reliable recognition systems based on them can be developed. However, the fact that indexing can be achieved for three-dimensional objects is very encouraging. The following discussions highlight the need for future work not only within the framework of deriving a more complete range of invariants, but also in the need to engineer the descriptions so that they can work with the type of data that can be extracted from real images.

8.5.1 Rotational symmetry

A significant amount of work has been done on measuring the invariants for rotationally symmetric objects. This has involved the accurate extraction of

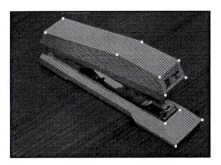

FIG. 8.23. The points used for the bilateral symmetry reconstruction in
    Fig. 8.24.

features using the segmentation algorithms of Chapter 6, and real system
building within the work covered by (43, 73). Fortunately the observed
outlines of rotationally symmetric objects are described by $\mathcal{M}$ curves.

An initial problem that emerged in the investigation was that pairing
the bitangents correctly is hard (pairs of bitangents had to be intersected
to locate the axis of symmetry and the cone vertices); this is due to the
vast numbers of bitangents that can be measured in an image. Yet again
this is an incarnation of the grouping problem. Fortunately, the structure of
the outlines of rotationally symmetric objects can be exploited in a novel
way: the curves making up the two sides of the outline are projectively
equivalent. Therefore, a simple curve matching algorithm can be used to
pair image curves as was done with the jigsaw puzzle matcher of (109).
Once matched, bitangents can be paired more easily and their intersections
determined. This has yet to be exploited, but the approach looks promising.

Furthermore, understanding of how such a highly constrained surface
can be reconstructed in 3-space once it has been recognized also needs to
be achieved: this is for verification. Again we intend to achieve verification through backprojection procedures similar to those used in LEWIS1.
Another important area of investigation is connected with how higher-level
ideas identifying the route required for breaking down limbed structures efficiently into subparts containing rotationally symmetry structures can be
used (as described by Marr (77)). Once these subparts have been recognized
hypothesis extension can be employed and the original shape reconstructed.
This emphasizes a major consideration required whenever a new shape cue
is designed, that is, the route to a local–global hierarchical description must
also be determined.

8.5.2   Caged point sets

One of the major drawbacks of the polyhedral construction is that it
assumes the presence of points grouped onto planes prior to constraint

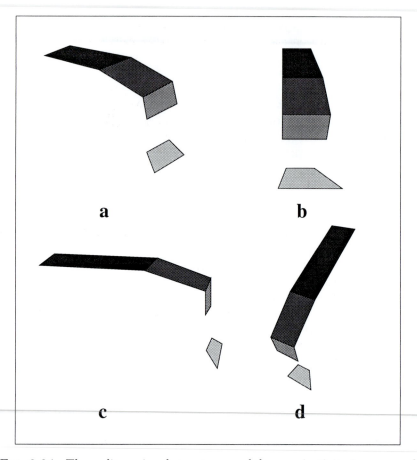

FIG. 8.24. Three-dimensional structure modulo a projectivity is recovered
for the points marked on the stapler in Fig. 8.23. Four typical views of
the reconstruction are shown: (a) the viewpoint is from a position close
to that of the original camera view; (b) the observer has moved round
to the front of the stapler to demonstrate the coplanarity of the points
on the left side of the stapler; (c) and (d) from other general viewpoints.
Note that the reconstruction did not constrain the points in (b) to be
coplanar, but only the width between a couple of corresponding points
is fixed. The fact that the genuine coplanarity is recovered is a measure
of the stability of the reconstruction method.

formulation.[40] This is itself a very hard problem, though useful ideas have

[40] Generally the world is not constructed of well-formed polyhedra and so any major
application would rely on caging. Even in cases in which actual polyhedra are visible,
the extraction of accurate and complete line drawings is currently infeasible and has
occupied a wealth of the literature in previous years.

been suggested by a number of authors (for example Beardsley (6)) as to how plane detection can be performed. Additionally, each point must be constrained to lie on multiple planes. This is a much harder problem: perhaps the solution lies in using invariants of lesser groups (such as affine (140) or *quasi-invariants*, Binford and Levitt (10)) to solve the grouping task before proceeding with full projective measures. This approach is in fact applicable to many of the invariant formulations discussed previously, and to a certain extent forms the basis of Lowe's grouping work (71). This approach to grouping will in fact be discussed in more detail in the next chapter.

Another problem evolves from the richness of the polyhedral description. To a certain extent, the invariants account for more global shape features than just the local vertex information used for example by Wayner (140). This develops into a problem with respect to the property of position freeness: generally, large structures are unlikely to be position free. Although a graph matching technique has been suggested to flag when polyhedra are not position free (111), developing a principled way to adjust the algebraic constraints remains very much an unsolved issue. An alternative approach would be to measure local descriptions and develop a hypothesis extension strategy as exploited in LEWIS1.

The one real benefit of the method is that exact projective information is yielded prior to recognition. This contrasts with the conclusions of Sugihara (126), who through using a Euclidean world model found that only parametrized families of shapes could be represented. Therefore, if the earlier parts of the process can be accomplished using workable grouping algorithms, it is clear the algorithm will actually provide a route to finding out the 3D information that is required for machine–world interaction.

8.5.3 *Objects with symmetry*

Two-view invariants are attractive because of their simplicity. Very few features are required, though again grouping (correspondence) must be solved between images. Grouping is simplified once the epipolar structure has been computed. However, with the single view invariants for symmetric objects, solving for epipolar structure is very easy. Once two pairs of matching symmetric points have been found the epipolar structure is defined and many other correspondences are available. When there are a sufficient number of correspondences full 3D projective structure can be recovered. The construction is also remarkably stable, though this still does not answer questions as to how to create the initial correspondences.

As symmetry is prevalent in many environments it is clear that the single view symmetry invariants have a broad scope. In fact, the construction can be applied to any repeated structures related by pure translations or reflections (or to systems projectively equivalent to these cases). Such objects all have the simple epipolar constraint provided by four points. It should also be noted that extensions are also possible to objects possessing discrete rotational symmetries if epipolar constructions can be derived for each half of the object (for this case each half of the object has its own epipole).

9

CONCLUSIONS

This book has considered one approach to object recognition, that is, a breakdown of the process into selection, indexing and finally correspondence. In particular, we have studied the importance of using invariant indexes for the efficient hypothesizing of the presence of objects in scenes. The approach has centred around the LEWIS recognition architecture; two different implementations of the architecture have demonstrated that planar objects can be recognized efficiently using invariant indexing. This has, however, thrown open a number of issues that have been mentioned briefly through the course of this book, but in practice remain as issues for further research. These are considered in more detail in the following discussion.

One important aspect of the research has been the building of actual working recognition systems. By doing this, theories can be tested, and their effects on recognition performance evaluated. As a result, aspects of system performance have not been sacrificed for the sake of gaining rapid access to the model libraries, or in fact, to the benefit of any other process. In the course of the discussion of the implementations, this book has also had to provide a substantial amount of detail on the entire recognition process leading from the image to the final recognition hypotheses. Although none of these processes have been in any way optimized, together they have produced a satisfactory solution to recognition.

9.1 Invariant shape description

We have concentrated on a very specific class of index function; that is, those constructed out of invariants. Although indexing processes can be developed that do not use invariants, such approaches tend to employ methods that index onto low-dimensional surfaces; these surfaces represent the geometric constraints between the different object parameters and also the object's pose, Jacobs (62). In contrast, invariant indexes are represented by single points in the index space. For the non-invariant approach, each object feature group requires a different surface and so the index space can fill up relatively quickly. This results in a reduction of indexing efficiency. Although there is value in using this method when invariants cannot be constructed, it appears that for a wide range of objects their geometry is sufficiently well constrained that invariants can be formed (note that the non-existence of invariants applies only due to the lack of object constraints, Burns, *et al.* (19)). Ultimately, invariants have demonstrated their value by being able to represent local object features by small clusters in the index space.

Chapters 3 and 5 examined a range of planar shape descriptors that are invariant under projective transformations. Plane algebraic invariants have been common in the literature for a relatively long period of time, though only recently have they been put into context within computer vision. As shown in Chapter 3, each different invariant can be formulated in a number of different geometric or algebraic ways. Invariance may be either easier to observe or prove in one form, or in another, but it must also be realized that the different methods actually yield invariants with contrasting performance characteristics. These characteristics can actually be stated as basic criteria for shape description such as discrimination, stability, and completeness.

The canonical frame construction has proved useful for the description of more general plane curves that cannot be represented reliably by algebraic features (it is also useful for three-dimensional shape description). Compared to algebraic invariants, this type of construction has been realized only recently, and yet it has already shown considerable descriptive power. We have reviewed only one construction that uses smooth portions of curve called $\mathcal{M}$ curves. The basis of the construction is the location of enough distinguished points for the computation of an image-to-canonical-frame projectivity. The canonical frame construction in LEWIS2 uses four distinct coplanar points that can be identified readily in the image (two bitangencies and two cast tangencies). However, in general any sufficiently rich combination of points of C^n discontinuity, or associated lines, could be used to the same effect. The possibility of using semi-differential invariants as local shape descriptors has also been suggested, as these can often provide an invariant representation that uses fewer distinguished points than a canonical frame. However, we have not actually implemented and tested such descriptions (the interested reader should follow-up the references by Van Gool, et al. (21, 87, 136) who have made a more detailed study of semi-differential invariants).

Ultimately, the world is not composed of planar shapes, but rather those that are three-dimensional. Although many 3D objects are composed of planar surfaces that contain a rich enough set of features to be recognized using planar descriptions, invariant descriptions are definitely required for more general 3D shapes. Such descriptions can be obtained either using uncalibrated stereo and multiple views, or as shown in the penultimate chapter of this book, they can even be extracted from single views for certain classes of object. The descriptors we have reported (those for rotationally symmetric surfaces, polyhedra or various other symmetries) represent only preliminary research in 3D shape description, and there is a definite need for a much deeper investigation. This should take two forms: firstly, these invariants have not been used to any degree within an automatic recognition system and so we are currently unsure of their real value for object recognition. Secondly, the scope of these 3D invariants is at present limited; consequently, the representations that can currently be extracted from the world are very sparse. However, the rapid progress with which 3D invariant shape description is being developed is very encouraging.

9.2   Grouping

Much research in object recognition has taken the pessimistic view that one is unlikely to recover any object structure prior to recognition. This is perhaps why there has been such an intense investigation into the use of interpretation trees, and other search methods such as hypothesize and test or the generalized Hough transform. However, there are many constraints available that can be used to suggest the presence of unified object structure in regions of an image. These are properties such as the topology and proximity of scene features. These measures have previously fuelled the research into selection and grouping that has dramatically enhanced the recognition performance of current systems. Unfortunately, the use of invariants places an increased burden on grouping, though it is our belief that combining a grouping process with indexing enhances the overall recognition efficiency as it allows the model base to be expanded without an excessive detriment to recognition performance. Certainly, LEWIS has demonstrated one instance of this approach being effective.

Additionally, many grouping methods do not make maximal use of the image information. There are certain benefits that can be observed if the image features are made to match the intensity surface more closely. So far, we have used only edge data for the extraction of lines, conics and $\mathcal{M}$ curves. It is well known that edge detectors perform poorly near corners which is precisely where we have required the connectivity information for grouping. We suggest that other feature detectors should be used in conjunction with edge detection to provide a much better initial understanding of the scene. For instance, image structure in the locality of line junctions would be understood better through the use of corner detectors, and so a pair of lines should be connected together only if a corner is found in the locality of their intersection.

There is an alternative approach that we might use to ease grouping. This would involve the use of geometric invariants to subgroups of the projective group, or the use of quasi-invariants, Binford and Levitt (10). The extra invariants offered by these groups might provide further clues to image structure; for instance, if the imaging model is represented by the affine group the observation of a pair of parallel image features could suggest a pair of parallel features in the world. A number of such invariants are know to exist and are derived from length, areas, angles, and their ratios. Such invariants can be used for indexing in the same way that LEWIS used projective invariants, although they would provide less discrimination between objects. This is because their measurement has to account for errors resulting from using a non-perspective imaging model. Beneficially, they require smaller feature groups and so the cost of selection and grouping would become somewhat smaller. After an initial indexing stage, hypothesis extension would be used to group features together into configurations possessing projective invariants; these can then be used to index more precisely.

9.2.1 *Hypothesis extension*

Hypothesis extension, or joint hypothesis formation, has a very important rôle to play within grouping. We have used extension to join together local image cues into more global descriptions subsequent to indexing. As the local descriptions are smaller than global ones, both tolerance to occlusion is enhanced and the grouping algorithms are allowed to concentrate their attention in smaller regions of the image (as subparts are by necessity smaller than entire objects). This means that the extent to which grouping algorithms have to search is reduced and so efficiency is improved.

Most objects contain local feature groups that are described by a variety of different invariants (for example one part of an object might be polyhedral and another part possesses a bilateral symmetry). The extension process allows different descriptions to be combined, thus providing a richer geometric understanding of scenes, as well as enhanced confidence in recognition hypotheses. Although we have developed only a two-layer object structure, that of subpart and object, the process can easily be adapted to allow for multi-layer hierarchical object descriptions.

Extension will play an important part in the construction of invariants for three-dimensional objects. Currently, grouping is hard for these structures, and the examples of Chapter 8 all required manual assistance in their computation. Again, we expect to exploit either invariants of smaller groups or quasi-invariants whilst grouping. For instance, many polyhedral objects possess trihedral vertices of distinctive shapes that can be recognized using the affine invariants of Wayner (140). Once individual vertices have been recognized as belonging to a specific class (in the nature of the $\mathcal{M}$ curve classes of Chapter 5), measures can be combined into more global three-dimensional structures for polyhedral or symmetric object reconstruction. These ideas are discussed in more depth in (113).

9.3 Scene consistency

The ultimate way to judge the performance of a recognition system is to evaluate the numbers of false positives and negatives that it produces. LEWIS has been tuned to ensure that a minimal number of false negatives are expected, though some do arise due to the presence of shadows or specularities that cause segmentation problems. Another important problem area is excessive occlusion. Performing recognition within this domain of operation means that an excessive burden is placed on the verification process; as noted in Chapter 4 this shows through with as many false positives being reported as correct hypotheses. Although other modules within the entire process can be altered to improve performance, there is a definite need to improve verification within LEWIS. Note that verification is simply a form of correspondence, and has thus been studied in depth within a number of other systems.

The lowest level of consistency that verification checks for is with the edgel data in the image. The current test is very simple:

Does a projected model feature have the same orientation as a proximal image feature?

This test is really quite naive in that is does not ensure consistency between neighbouring model features. For instance, if one model feature finds an image match, but an adjacent one does not, then there is likely to be some sort of occlusion event present in the image data between the features. Observing one of these events, for instance a 'T' junction, would improve the explanations of the different correspondences. Although the drop-out may not necessarily have been caused by occlusion, but rather by the presence of shadows or specularities, in many cases misinterpretations might be corrected using this information.

We have already suggested that including object pose within the scene interpretation will improve the effectiveness of verification. Such pose information requires Euclidean, equiform, or at least affine object models. To the large part, LEWIS makes use only of projective models. Chapter 4 detailed some ways in which information about object horizon lines (affine models) can be used to remove a significant proportion of the false positives. We are currently investigating to what extent other models (especially Euclidean) can be used to check for global scene consistency (46). These considerations aim to answer the following types of question:

1. Do two objects occupy the same region in space?
2. Do they share a common ground-plane?
3. Is the object pose stable with respect to the rest of the world?
4. Does one object correctly occlude another?
5. Is the camera pose believable with respect to the world?

Similar questions have appeared before within the domain of object recognition research and artificial intelligence. However, they have not been used to a sufficient extent within large automated object recognition systems. Thus, it is currently hard to say whether they are in fact an effective constraint in improving scene understanding.

9.4   Architecture

LEWIS has a straightforward bottom-up flow of control with no genuine feedback. Although the verification process makes use of segmentation information, it has no influence on the segmentation methods or on any other procedure below it. More communication between the different processing modules is required if recognition performances are to be improved. Furthermore, the higher processing levels should be permitted to drive recognition. Another drawback of the LEWIS architecture is that there is a lack of interaction between different recognition hypotheses. Note that a single scene feature should be assigned only to one object identity, and yet this is not employed in LEWIS due to caution triggered by the large numbers of false positives.

Future research in object recognition should ensure that every level in the process is able to interrogate the modules to which it is connected (both above and below). For instance, a line fitter should question whether the edge data it is using is reliable; the nearby presence of a shadow or a corner would draw attention to the fact that the edgels are likely to be poorly localized, and perhaps initiate a scheme for their amelioration. We have already had some success in doing this using snakes that are fitted directly to the intensity surface, Kass, *et al.* (64). Although we do not require much geometric sophistication in the snakes (the features we are looking for are lines, conics or $\mathcal{M}$ curves), they are reasonably reliable at locating feature terminations (corners) and providing global constraints on edgel geometry above the local constraints yielded by the edge detector. A consequence of this is that feedback to the edge detector would cause a re-evaluation of the local measurements, and hopefully an improvement in understanding of the scene. In this way the processing will be neither entirely bottom-up or top-down In addition, the feature grouping process should not just combine lines together if their endpoints are close together but should check that an image event (a corner) actually exists near to their proposed intersection. There are many examples of this type of interaction process that we intend to develop within the successor architecture to LEWIS. This is called MORSE: Multiple Object Recognition by Scene Entailment (150).

At a higher level, all hypotheses should be consistent with the current scene interpretation. If not, and if the contradictory evidence is convincing enough, the current search path (developed depth first) should be pruned and a new branch investigated. In this case, interactions between the processing modules must ensure that different object hypotheses are compatible both with the image and with each other. In doing this, we have to cease to accept each module within the recognition process as a black box which provides certain types of output. Rather, they are processes that can be assisted in their tasks by information gathered dynamically during search.

APPENDIX A

PLANE PERSPECTIVITIES AS A 3 BY 3 MATRIX

This appendix proves the following theorem:

Theorem A.1 *A pinhole perspective map between a set of homogeneous planar world points $\mathbf{X_i} = (X_i, Y_i, 1)^T$ and their images $\mathbf{x_i} = (x_i, y_i, 1)^T$ is represented by a plane projectivity.*

Proof A point in a 3D Euclidean world coordinate frame is represented by $\mathbf{X_4} = (X, Y, Z, 1)^T$. The world coordinate frame is linked to the camera frame by a 4×4 matrix:

$$\mathbf{X'} = \begin{bmatrix} R & t \\ 0 & 1 \end{bmatrix} \mathbf{X_4},$$

$$= G\mathbf{X_4},$$

where the matrix $R = [\mathbf{u} \; \mathbf{v} \; \mathbf{v}]$ is a 3D world rotation (a 3×3 matrix), and $\mathbf{t}$ a 3D translation vector. As the world points are planar the world frame can be orientated so that $Z = 0$, thus world points are represented by $\mathbf{X} = (X, Y, 1)^T$. Therefore:

$$\mathbf{X'} = \begin{bmatrix} \mathbf{u} & \mathbf{v} & \mathbf{t} \\ 0 & 0 & 1 \end{bmatrix} \mathbf{X}.$$

Under projection with a pinhole camera the point $\mathbf{X'}$ projects to $\mathbf{x} = (x, y, 1)^T$ by:

$$x = \alpha f \frac{X'}{Z'} + c_x \quad \text{and} \quad y = f \frac{Y'}{Z'} + c_y,$$

where f is the focal length of the camera, α its aspect ratio, and (c_x, c_y) the location of the camera centre (at this stage it has been assumed that the optical axis of the camera is perpendicular to the image plane). This may be written in matrix form as:

$$\mathbf{x} = \begin{bmatrix} \alpha f & 0 & c_x \\ 0 & f & c_y \\ 0 & 0 & 1 \end{bmatrix} \begin{bmatrix} 1 & 0 & 0 & 0 \\ 0 & 1 & 0 & 0 \\ 0 & 0 & 1 & 0 \end{bmatrix} \mathbf{X'},$$

$$= A [I \; 0] \mathbf{X'}.$$

Subsequently:

$$
\begin{aligned}
\mathbf{x} &= A\,[I\ 0]\begin{bmatrix}\mathbf{u}\ \mathbf{v}\ \mathbf{t}\\ 0\ 0\ 1\end{bmatrix}\mathbf{X},\\
&= A\,[\mathbf{u}\ \mathbf{v}\ \mathbf{t}]\mathbf{X},\\
&= T\mathbf{X},
\end{aligned}
$$

where T is a 3×3 matrix and hence a plane projectivity.   □

There are two useful consequences of this theorem:

1. Above it was assumed that the optical axis must be perpendicular to the image plane. This need not actually be the case as any skews in the image produced by moving the axis can be accounted for in the *calibration matrix* A, and this does not therefore affect the general form of T.

2. If the world points are not coplanar the world-to-image map is represented by a 3×4 matrix which can easily be shown to take the form $T_{34} = A[R\ t]$.

APPENDIX B

COMPUTATION OF PROJECTIVE TRANSFORMATIONS

This appendix builds on the theory given in Section 3.1.3 that showed how a 3×3 projective transformation matrix $\mathbf{T}$ is determined between correspondences of four or more points in a plane. Within the following sections the basic construction is extended for a variety of geometric configurations; the way that this is done is to reduce the problem to one of matching sets of points or lines and then computing the projectivity for them.

The motivation for determining the projective map is to enable the verification process detailed in Section 4.2.6. The configurations considered are therefore those that emerge out of using the invariants of LEWIS1. Because the recognition process has used invariants to provide a correspondence between model and image features it will almost always be the case that there are enough constraints to define the model-to-image projectivity. In fact the formulation is generally overconstrained; the only time this is not true is when an isotropy is present.

B.1 Points and lines

If the model and image features are the points (X_i, Y_i) and (x_i, y_i), $i \in \{1, \ldots, n\}$, with a known correspondence, a set of linear algebraic equations that constrain the parameters of the plane-to-plane projectivity can be derived of the form:

$$x_i(T_{31}X_i + T_{32}Y_i + 1) = T_{11}X_i + T_{12}Y_i + T_{13},$$
$$y_i(T_{31}X_i + T_{32}Y_i + 1) = T_{21}X_i + T_{22}Y_i + T_{23}. \qquad \text{(B.1.1)}$$

These result from the definition of the model-to-image map, $\mathbf{x}_i = k\,\mathbf{T}\,\mathbf{X}_i$, k non-zero, with[41] $\mathbf{T}$:

$$\mathbf{T} = \begin{bmatrix} T_{11} & T_{12} & T_{13} \\ T_{21} & T_{22} & T_{23} \\ T_{31} & T_{32} & 1 \end{bmatrix}.$$

---

[41] Note that $T_{33} \neq 0$, which is not a general property of a projectivity. In practice, no problem has been encountered in making this assumption because, as can be seen from Appendix A, this form of $\mathbf{T}$ is realized only when the world coordinate frame lies in the camera plane $z = 0$ (that is the z component of translation is zero). This scenario is unlikely to occur.

From eqn (B.1.1) a matrix equation of the form:

$$\mathbf{A}\,\mathbf{p} = \mathbf{v}, \qquad\qquad (\text{B.1.2})$$

is constructed where $\mathbf{p} = (T_{11}, T_{12}, \ldots, T_{32})^T$ and $\mathbf{v} = (x_1, \ldots, y_1, \ldots)^T$. The solution for $\mathbf{p}$ is found either by the direct inverse of $\mathbf{A}$, or for cases in which $n > 4$ by finding its pseudo-inverse; both of these procedures involve computing an 8×8 matrix inverse. This method of computing T should be compared to that of Sinclair, et al. (119) which requires the computation of only 3×3 inverses. The problem with this second formulation is that it does not adapt to overconstrained situations. Note that the overconstraining of T is achieved through a rather unintuitive minimization of errors; that is the minimization of the distance between the projected $\mathbf{p}$ and $\mathbf{v}$ vectors. Although this makes the pseudo-inverse convenient, it certainly does not provide the correct constraint. One may question what the best form of the error model is (note that it may not necessarily be the Euclidean distance measured in one of the planes).[42]

Using a dual construction, the projectivity linking sets of lines can be computed. The relation between the dual projectivity for lines and that for points is:

$$T_{\text{lines}} = T_{\text{points}}^{-T},$$

where T^{-T} is the inverse transpose of T. This can be seen from the image line and point incidence relationship:

$$\mathbf{l}^T \mathbf{x} = 0,$$
$$\Rightarrow \mathbf{l}^T\, T\mathbf{X} = 0.$$

Comparing this to the model line and point relationship $\mathbf{L}^T.\mathbf{X} = 0$ yields:

$$\mathbf{L}^T = \mathbf{l}^T\, T,$$
$$\Rightarrow \mathbf{l} = T^{-T}\, \mathbf{L}.$$

Normally one solves directly for T^{-T} when lines only are involved (i.e. perform the whole computation on the dual plane). An interesting case arises when there is a mixture of points and lines: for points the constraints given by eqn (B.1.1) are used, whereas for lines the constraints are derived from $\mathbf{L} = k\, T^T\, \mathbf{l}$. This provides constraints on $\mathbf{p}$ according to:

$$A_i(T_{13}a_i + T_{23}b_i + 1) = T_{11}a_i + T_{21}b_i + T_{31},$$

---

[42]Alternatively, one can express T as a 3×3 matrix with nine free parameters, and derive an equation equivalent to eqn (B.1.2) of the form $\mathbf{A}\,\mathbf{t} = 0$, where $\mathbf{t} = (T_{11}, T_{12}, \ldots, T_{33})^T$, and $\mathbf{A}$ a 8×9 matrix. One can then solve for T by finding the null-space of $\mathbf{A}$ subject to some constraint on $\mathbf{t}$, say $|\mathbf{t}| = 1$.

$$B_i(T_{13}a_i + T_{23}b_i + 1) = T_{12}a_i + T_{22}b_i + T_{32}, \qquad \text{(B.1.3)}$$

where the model and image line parametrizations are[43] $(A_i, B_i, 1)$ and $(a_i, b_i, 1)$. Using the combined constraints of eqns (B.1.1) and (B.1.3), a matrix equation of the form of eqn (B.1.2) is constructed for the matching points and lines. This is then solved to compute the model-to-image point projectivity. An interesting case arises for a configuration of two points and two lines: matrix A can be shown algebraically to be singular and so there is no unique solution to T. This arises due to the presence of an isotropy group for the configuration.

There are three important points to be noted for the algorithm implementation when there is a variety of algebraic features: the first is that points are not produced by segmentation and so lines are normally used to compute T; secondly, when there is a mixture of lines and conics, and there are at least four lines, then only the lines are used to compute T. This is done for efficiency reasons; as will be seen in the following sections inclusion of the conic requires extra unnecessary computation. The third issue is the use of the overconstrained solution for T. For incorrect hypotheses it is often impossible to construct a T that provides an accurate correspondence between the lines in the image frame and the projected model lines (verification is done in the image frame). For these cases the hypotheses can be ruled out before full verification is done (see Section 4.2.6 for details).

B.2   A conic and three lines

If an object has been indexed using the invariant of a conic and three lines, but with no additional index, it will be necessary to compute the model-to-image projectivity with the matching lines and conic. This can be done by reducing the configuration to one of five lines and then solving for T directly. The extra two lines are found by intersecting lines l_1 and l_2 to give a point $\mathbf{p}_1$, and l_2 and l_3 to give $\mathbf{p}_2$ (see Fig. B.1). The polars of $\mathbf{p}_1$ and $\mathbf{p}_2$ with respect to the conic C are the lines $l_4 = C\mathbf{p}_1$ and $l_5 = C\mathbf{p}_2$. T is then computed from the lines l_i, $i \in \{1, \ldots, 5\}$ (the solution is overdetermined).

Note that this way of computing T uses only $2 \times 5 = 10$ constraints. For a conic and three lines there are $5 + 2 \times 3 = 11$ constraints that can be used; an extra constraint line could be formed by computing the polar of the intersection of lines l_1 and l_3. This is not used because the intersection point can often be a long way off the image and would therefore be unreliable (if l_1 and l_3 are parallel).

---

[43] Note that the non-generic situation for which any number of the lines pass through the origin cannot be accounted for. However, applying a random translation to all of the features will prevent lines from passing through the origin; then T can be computed, and the random translation removed. The dual situation for points lying on the line at infinity in the image plane has been ignored because these points will not be observed in an image.

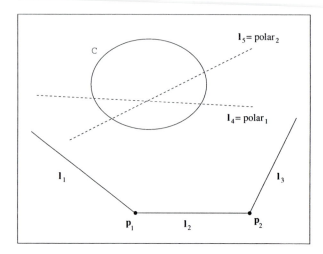

FIG. B.1. A conic and three lines can be transformed into a configuration of five lines using a polar construction. Construct p_1 the intersection of l_1 and l_2, and p_2, that of l_2 and l_3. Then, compute the polars of p_1 and p_2 by $l_4 = Cp_1$ and $l_5 = Cp_2$. This now gives the five lines l_i, $i \in \{1, \ldots, 5\}$, from which T can be computed using the formulae in Section B.1.

Again, as the computation of T is overdetermined it is used as an initial filter for verification. This is reported in detail in Section 4.2.6, though instead of just comparing lines the model and image conics can be used as well.

B.3   A pair of conics

The computation of the projectivity between a pair of model and image conics is much harder than the cases considered above. The reason for this is that the correspondence problem cannot be solved uniquely without the ordering provided by the lines.

The geometrical constraints provided between the model and image conics, C_i and c_i, $i \in \{1, 2\}$, are of the form (this is eqn (3.1.6)):

$$c_i = \kappa \cdot T^{-T} C_i \, T^{-1}.$$

This provides ten quadratic constraints on T; a solution by least squares is impractical. An alternative scheme would be to solve eight of the equations (a system of eight polynomial equations in eight variables), yielding 256 solutions in the generic case (Bezout's Theorem (117)). Most of these solutions could be eliminated by testing them against the other two equations. This again is impractical. The rest of this section explores a more practical solution.

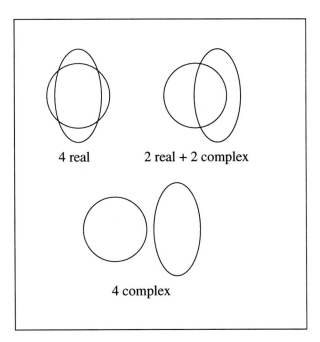

4 real   2 real + 2 complex

4 complex

FIG. B.2. For a generic pair of conics there are always four points of intersection. These may all be real, or two real with a complex conjugate pair, or all complex as two complex conjugate pairs.

Again the aim is to find sets of four points or lines that are distinguished with respect to the conics. This means that the points or lines must be preserved by projection, and can be identified on the model and in the image. Such features are the intersection points of the conics (bitangents can also be used, as reported in (108)).

In general a pair of conics intersect at four points, though the intersections are not always real. Figure B.2 shows how the number of real intersection points varies with position for a pair of ellipses. Here the complex case is actually used, but there is little difference in the methods for real or complex intersections apart from combinatorics of matching.[44] There are 24 ways (i.e. 4!) to match 4 image points to 4 object points. However, for real points, knowing that the transformation is a perspectivity restricts the ordering of points around the conic (the only permutations are reflection and a cyclic change, see Section 3.3, though reflections are excluded). This means that the combinatorics are reduced from 24 to 4 (the choice of which point to start from on the chosen conic). In fact, for the exact case of no image noise there are always at least four projective mappings that map one pair of conics onto another pair. This can be seen by consider-

[44]The constraints of eqn (B.1.1) apply equally well for complex points as real ones.

ing the isotropy group for a pair of conics: a pair of conics can always be represented in a *canonical frame* as:

$$C_1 = \begin{bmatrix} -1 & 0 & 0 \\ 0 & -1 & 0 \\ 0 & 0 & 1 \end{bmatrix} \quad \text{and} \quad C_2 = \begin{bmatrix} \lambda & 0 & 0 \\ 0 & \mu & 0 \\ 0 & 0 & 1 \end{bmatrix}.$$

This frame is reached by diagonalizing the first conic (by eigenvalue decomposition), and then scaling the major and minor axes to give the form given above. Then, put the second conic into diagonal form by a second eigenvalue decomposition (this will leave the first conic unchanged). Once in this frame it is clear that a transformation of the form:

$$T = \begin{bmatrix} \pm 1 & 0 & 0 \\ 0 & \pm 1 & 0 \\ 0 & 0 & \pm 1 \end{bmatrix},$$

will leave both conics unchanged (T is in fact the square root of the identity matrix). As the scale of T does not affect the projectivity it represents there are in fact only four different transformations that leave the conics C_1 and C_2 unchanged:

$$T = \begin{bmatrix} \pm 1 & 0 & 0 \\ 0 & \pm 1 & 0 \\ 0 & 0 & 1 \end{bmatrix}.$$

There is no way to order complex points. However, the combinatorics can be reduced to 8 by the following argument: the intersections are found by solving a real quartic, hence all complex intersections will appear in complex conjugate pairs. All complex world points map to complex image points by the same T matrix that transforms real world points. Therefore if a real projection has occurred the T matrix found by mapping complex points to complex points is real. Furthermore, all complex conjugate pairs project to conjugate pairs.[45] That is if:

$$[X_1, X_2, X_3] \rightarrow [x_1, x_2, x_3],$$

then:

$$[\bar{X}_1, \bar{X}_2, \bar{X}_3] \rightarrow [\bar{x}_1, \bar{x}_2, \bar{x}_3],$$

where $\bar{x}_i$ is the complex conjugate of x_i. Thus, the only possibilities for world points $[A, \bar{A}, B, \bar{B}]$ mapping to image points $[a, \bar{a}, b, \bar{b}]$, are:

[45] If the T matrix is real complex conjugate points project to complex conjugate points by linearity.

$$
\begin{bmatrix} A \\ \bar{A} \\ B \\ \bar{B} \end{bmatrix} \rightarrow \left\{ \begin{bmatrix} a \\ \bar{a} \\ b \\ \bar{b} \end{bmatrix}, \begin{bmatrix} a \\ \bar{a} \\ \bar{b} \\ b \end{bmatrix}, \begin{bmatrix} \bar{a} \\ a \\ b \\ \bar{b} \end{bmatrix}, \begin{bmatrix} \bar{a} \\ a \\ \bar{b} \\ b \end{bmatrix}, \begin{bmatrix} b \\ \bar{b} \\ a \\ \bar{a} \end{bmatrix}, \begin{bmatrix} b \\ \bar{b} \\ \bar{a} \\ a \end{bmatrix}, \begin{bmatrix} \bar{b} \\ b \\ a \\ \bar{a} \end{bmatrix}, \begin{bmatrix} \bar{b} \\ b \\ \bar{a} \\ a \end{bmatrix} \right\}.
$$

Any correspondence outside this set will produce a complex projective transformation matrix. For each correspondence T is computed. If the projectivities are to be used for verification each one has to be tested in turn, first to check that the model and image conics correspond under projection, and secondly that the rest of the model and image features match.

With all of the above methods for computing T there will be certain configurations for which the problem is ill-posed. Example cases are:

- For sets of points and lines, should three of the points approach collinearity, three lines concurrency, or incidence between points and lines then the solution for T will be inaccurate.
- If any of the line intersection points for the conic and three line case become close to, or are incident on the conic.
- Should a pair of conics be projectively equivalent to concentric circles the intersection and tangency points will be unstable.

APPENDIX C

LINE AND CONIC FITTING

This appendix contains the straight line fitting algorithm (by orthogonal regression) and the conic fitting algorithm (using Bookstein's method (13)).

C.1 Closed form fitting of a straight line by orthogonal regression.

The straight line fitting method used minimizes the sum of squared perpendicular distances from data points to the fitted line. Fitting is reduced to an eigenvector problem, and is done in closed form. The perpendicular distance from a point (x_i, y_i) to the line $ax + by + c = 0$ is:

$$q_i = \frac{ax_i + by_i + c}{\sqrt{a^2 + b^2}}.$$

If the line is normalized so that $\sqrt{a^2 + b^2} = 1$, the fitting cost for all n data points reduces to:

$$Q^2 = \frac{1}{n}\sum_n q_i^2 = \frac{1}{n}\sum_n (ax_i + by_i + c)^2.$$

Writing $\mathbf{v} = (a, b, c)^T$, and:

$$S = \begin{bmatrix} X^2 & XY & X \\ XY & Y^2 & Y \\ X & Y & n \end{bmatrix},$$

where $X^2 = \sum_n x_i^2$, $Y^2 = \sum_n y_i^2$, $XY = \sum_n x_i y_i$, $X = \sum_n x_i$ and $Y = \sum_n y_i$, gives:

$$Q^2 = \frac{1}{n}\mathbf{v}^T S\mathbf{v}.$$

The centre of mass of the point set, (x_c, y_c), is at $(X/n, Y/n)$. Minimizing the Langrangian with respect to c:

$$L = \frac{1}{n}\mathbf{v}^T S\mathbf{v} - \lambda(a^2 + b^2 - 1),$$

$$\Rightarrow \frac{\partial L}{\partial c} = \frac{2}{n}(aX + bY + cn),$$

$$= 2 \ (ax_c + by_c + c),$$
$$= 0 \quad \text{at the minimum,}$$

and hence the centre of mass lies on the line. Translating the coordinate frame so that the centre of mass is at the origin, and fitting the line $a_c x + b_c y + c_c = 0$ to the data set $(x - x_c, y - y_c)$, where $c_c = 0$ because the line passes through the origin of the translated frame, gives the Langrangian:

$$L_c = \frac{1}{n} \mathbf{v}_c^T S_c \mathbf{v}_c - \lambda (a_c^2 + b_c^2 - 1),$$

where:

$$S_c = \begin{bmatrix} X_c^2 & X_c Y_c & 0 \\ X_c Y_c & Y_c^2 & 0 \\ 0 & 0 & n \end{bmatrix},$$

$\mathbf{v} = (a_c, b_c, c_c)^T$. The elements of S_c are: $X_c^2 = \sum_n (x_i - x_c)^2$, $Y_c^2 = \sum_n (y_i - y_c)^2$ and $X_c Y_c = \sum_n (x_i - x_c)(y_i - y_c)$. Within the incremental algorithm the values of $\{X, Y, X^2, XY, Y^2\}$ are stored from which the translated parameters can be computed:

$$X_c^2 = X^2 - X.X/n,$$
$$X_c Y_c = XY - X.Y/n,$$
$$Y_c^2 = Y^2 - Y.Y/n.$$

Minimizing the Langrangian with respect to a_c and b_c gives:

$$\frac{\partial L_c}{\partial a_c} = 2 \ (a_c X_c^2 + b_c X_c Y_c - \lambda a_c),$$

and $\quad \dfrac{\partial L_c}{\partial b_c} = 2 \ (a_c X_c Y_c + b_c Y_c^2 - \lambda b_c).$

Setting:

$$\frac{\partial L_c}{\partial a_c} = \frac{\partial L_c}{\partial b_c} = 0,$$

gives:

$$\begin{bmatrix} X_c^2 & X_c Y_c \\ X_c Y_c & Y_c^2 \end{bmatrix} \begin{pmatrix} a_c \\ b_c \end{pmatrix} = \lambda \begin{pmatrix} a_c \\ b_c \end{pmatrix},$$

which is an eigenvector problem. Taking $(a_c, b_c)^T$ corresponding to the smallest eigenvalue minimizes Q^2: if the fitting cost in the translated frame is Q_c^2, and as the translation does not change the values of the distances from the line:

$$Q^2 = Q_c^2,$$
$$= \frac{1}{n} \mathbf{v}_c^T S_c \mathbf{v}_c,$$
$$= \frac{1}{n} (a_c, b_c) \begin{bmatrix} X_c^2 & X_c Y_c \\ X_c Y_c & Y_c^2 \end{bmatrix} \begin{pmatrix} a_c \\ b_c \end{pmatrix}, \quad \text{as } c_c = 0,$$
$$= \frac{1}{n} (a_c, b_c) \lambda \begin{pmatrix} a_c \\ b_c \end{pmatrix},$$
$$= \frac{\lambda}{n}, \quad \text{as } (a_c, b_c) \begin{pmatrix} a_c \\ b_c \end{pmatrix} = 1.$$

As the move of coordinate frame is a translation, $(a_c, b_c)^T = (a, b)^T$, and so $\mathbf{v}$ has been solved for in closed form.

This outlines the basic fitting algorithm for n points. Fitting can be performed incrementally in the following manner (incrementally means that a line can be refit to $n + 1$ points using the result of the fit to n points without having to repeat the entire operation):

1. From the fit to n points store the values of $\{X^2, XY, Y^2, X, Y\}$.
2. Increment each of these terms by $\{x_{n+1}^2, \ldots, y_{n+1}\}$.
3. Compute the position of the centre of mass from X and Y, and determine $\{X_c^2, X_c Y_c, Y_c^2\}$ from $\{X^2, \ldots, Y\}$.
4. Perform the eigenvalue computation.

This provides an efficient algorithm for updating the fit after each extra point is extracted from an edge chain; alternatively points can be deleted if required.

C.2 The Bookstein algorithm

The Bookstein algorithm for fitting a conic to point data is given in (13). It is a closed form fitting method requiring the evaluation of eigenvectors and eigenvalues. Let $\mathbf{v} = (A, B, C, D, E, F)^T$ be the vector of coefficients of the conic:

$$f(x, y) = Ax^2 + Bxy + Cy^2 + Dx + Ey + F,$$

where $f(x, y) = 0$ defines a point (x, y) on the conic. The algebraic distance of a point (x_i, y_i) is defined as:

$$q(x_i, y_i) = Ax_i^2 + Bx_i y_i + Cy_i^2 + Dx_i + Ey_i + F.$$

The fit minimizes the mean square algebraic distance over all the points:

$$Q^2 = \frac{1}{n} \sum_n q(x_i, y_i)^2.$$

This may be written in the form:

$$Q^2 = \frac{1}{n} \sum_n \mathbf{v}^T \mathsf{S}(x_i, y_i) \mathbf{v},$$

where $\mathsf{S}(x_i, y_i)$ is a 6×6 scatter matrix:

$$\mathsf{S}(x_i, y_i) = \begin{bmatrix} x_i^4 & x_i^3 y_i & x_i^2 y_i^2 & x_i^3 & x_i^2 y_i & x_i^2 \\ x_i^3 y_i & x_i^2 y_i^2 & x_i y_i^3 & x_i^2 y_i & x_i y_i^2 & x_i y_i \\ x_i^2 y_i^2 & x_i y_i^3 & y_i^4 & x_i y_i^2 & y_i^3 & y_i^2 \\ x_i^3 & x_i^2 y_i & x_i y_i^2 & x_i^2 & x_i y_i & x_i \\ x_i^2 y_i & x_i y_i^2 & y_i^3 & x_i y_i & y_i^2 & y_i \\ x_i^2 & x_i y_i & y_i^2 & x_i & y_i & 1 \end{bmatrix}.$$

Writing $\mathsf{S} = 1/n \sum_n \mathsf{S}(x_i, y_i)$, where S is real symmetric, gives:

$$Q^2 = \mathbf{v}^T \mathsf{S} \mathbf{v}.$$

The fit will minimize Q^2, but to rule out the trivial solution of $\mathbf{v} = \mathbf{0}$ the conic must be normalized. The normalization used is that $\mathbf{v}^T D \mathbf{v} = 2$ where D is the diagonal matrix of elements $\{1, \frac{1}{2}, 1, 0, 0, 0\}$. It is shown in (13) that the resultant fit is invariant up to a similarity transform of the original data when this normalization is used. Thus the Langrangian:

$$L = \mathbf{v}^T \mathsf{S} \mathbf{v} - \lambda(\mathbf{v}^T D \mathbf{v} - 2),$$

is minimized. Splitting S up into four 3×3 matrices:

$$\mathsf{S} = \begin{bmatrix} \mathsf{S}_{11} & \mathsf{S}_{12} \\ \mathsf{S}_{21} & \mathsf{S}_{22} \end{bmatrix},$$

with $\mathsf{S}_{21} = \mathsf{S}_{12}^T$. Both S_{11} and S_{22} are symmetric. Writing D_1 as the diagonal matrix $\{1, \frac{1}{2}, 1\}$, and letting $\mathbf{v}_1 = (A, B, C)^T$, $\mathbf{v}_2 = (D, E, F)^T$, gives:

$$L = \mathbf{v}_1^T \mathsf{S}_{11} \mathbf{v}_1 + 2\mathbf{v}_2^T \mathsf{S}_{21} \mathbf{v}_1 + \mathbf{v}_2^T \mathsf{S}_{22} \mathbf{v}_2 - \lambda(\mathbf{v}_1^T D_1 \mathbf{v}_1 - 2).$$

Minimizing this with respect to $\mathbf{v}_2$, where $\partial L / \partial \mathbf{v}_2$ represents ∇L with respect to the elements of $\mathbf{v}_2$:

$$\frac{\partial L}{\partial \mathbf{v}_2} = 2\mathsf{S}_{21} \mathbf{v}_1 + 2\mathsf{S}_{22} \mathbf{v}_2 = \mathbf{0},$$

$$\Rightarrow \mathbf{v}_2 = -\mathsf{S}_{22}^{-1} \mathsf{S}_{21} \mathbf{v}_1.$$

Substituting for $\mathbf{v}_2$:

$$L = \mathbf{v}_1^T(\mathbf{S}_{11} - \mathbf{S}_{12}\mathbf{S}_{22}^{-1}\mathbf{S}_{21})\mathbf{v}_1 - \lambda(\mathbf{v}_1^T\mathbf{D}_1\mathbf{v}_1 - 2),$$
$$= \mathbf{v}_1^T(\mathbf{S}_{11.2} - \lambda\mathbf{D}_1)\mathbf{v}_1 + 2\lambda,$$
$$\Rightarrow \frac{\partial L}{\partial \mathbf{v}_1} = (\mathbf{S}_{11.2} - \lambda\mathbf{D}_1)\mathbf{v}_1 = \mathbf{0} \qquad \text{at the minimum,}$$
$$\Rightarrow \lambda\mathbf{v}_1 = \mathbf{D}_1^{-1}\mathbf{S}_{11.2}\mathbf{v}_1.$$

This is an eigenvalue problem. The eigenvector of $\mathbf{v}_1$ which corresponds to the smallest eigenvalue of $(\mathbf{D}_1^{-1}\mathbf{S}_{11.2})$ gives the best conic fit to the data, and thus the minimum value of Q^2:

$$Q^2 = \mathbf{v}^T\mathbf{S}\mathbf{v},$$
$$= \mathbf{v}_1^T\mathbf{S}_{11.2}\mathbf{v}_1,$$
$$= \lambda\mathbf{v}_1^T\mathbf{D}_1\mathbf{v}_1,$$
$$= 2\lambda.$$

As the eigenvalue computation is for a 3×3 matrix it can be solved in closed form. $\mathbf{v}_2$ is determined from $\mathbf{v}_1$.

In its basic form the Bookstein algorithm can be implemented incrementally in a way similar to the orthogonal regression algorithm in Appendix C.1. Storage must simply be allocated for the fourteen differing elements of $\mathbf{S}$ dependent on each (x_i, y_i).

APPENDIX D

PROJECTIVE EQUIVALENCE OF ALL THE KERNEL SOLUTIONS

The derivations in this appendix show that the measures taken for 3D point sets in Chapter 8 are in fact invariant to 3D projective actions. First we prove the following theorem:

Theorem D.1 *With regard to the reconstruction of a polyhedral object, the solutions formed by the 4 dof kernel $\mathbf{w}'$ of the constraint matrix $\mathbf{A}(\mathbf{x}', \mathbf{y}')$ in eqn (8.3.5) are projectively equivalent.*

Proof Let $\mathbf{w}' = \sum_{i=1}^{4} \mu_i \mathbf{b}_i$. Consider the fourth basis vector to be composed of a set of three-vectors $\mathbf{m_i}$, one for each plane:

$$\mathbf{b}_4 = (\mathbf{m}_1^T, ..., \mathbf{m}_n^T)^T.$$

A description of the camera frame plane equations, $\mathbf{v}_i$, $i \in \{1, \ldots, n\}$ is required, or at least the $\mathbf{v}_i'$, $i \in \{1, \ldots, n\}$. Let $\mathbf{v}_i' = (\mathbf{u}_i'^T, 1)^T$, where $\mathbf{u}_i'$ is a 3-vector. Knowing that the correct Euclidean interpretation of the shape can be constructed modulo camera calibration:

$$\begin{pmatrix} \mathbf{u}_1' \\ \vdots \\ \mathbf{u}_n' \end{pmatrix} = \mu_1 \mathbf{b}_1 + \mu_2 \mathbf{b}_2 + \mu_3 \mathbf{b}_3 + \mu_4 \begin{pmatrix} \mathbf{m}_1 \\ \vdots \\ \mathbf{m}_n \end{pmatrix}, \qquad (\text{D.0.1})$$

and letting $\lambda = 1/\mu_4$, $\mathbf{a} = -\lambda \left(\mu_1, \mu_2, \mu_3 \right)^T$, gives (note the choice of $\mathbf{b}_i$, $i \in \{1, \ldots, 3\}$, is as in eqn (8.3.6)):

$$\mathbf{m}_i = \lambda \mathbf{u}_i' + \mathbf{a}.$$

Writing $\mathbf{I}_3$ as the 3×3 identity matrix yields:

$$\begin{pmatrix} \mathbf{m}_i \\ 1 \end{pmatrix} = \begin{bmatrix} \lambda\, \mathbf{I}_3 & \mathbf{a} \\ 0 & 1 \end{bmatrix} \begin{pmatrix} \mathbf{u}_i' \\ 1 \end{pmatrix},$$

$$\text{or,} \qquad \mathbf{M}_i = \mathbf{P}\, \mathbf{v}_i',$$

$$= \mathbf{P}\, \mathbf{C}\, \mathbf{v}_i. \qquad (\text{D.0.2})$$

Therefore, each choice of $\mathbf{M}_i$ is a projectivity of the actual world planes $\mathbf{v}_i$.

$\square$

Now we can derive the invariants: in 3-space the mapping from points in the object frame to the camera frame is a 3D Euclidean action. As points and planes are dual in projective 3-space, and Euclidean actions form a subgroup of projectivities, it follows directly that the mapping relating model planes to planes in the camera frame is a projectivity of space. This can be represented by:

$$\mathbf{v}_i = k_i \, \mathbf{Q} \, \mathbf{V}_i.$$

Therefore, the kernel basis elements and the plane parameters are related by:

$$\mathbf{M}_i = k_i \, \mathbf{P} \, \mathbf{C} \, \mathbf{Q} \, \mathbf{V}_i,$$
$$= k_i \, \mathbf{T} \, \mathbf{V}_i. \tag{D.0.3}$$

If the matrices $\mathrm{I}_{abcd} = [\mathbf{V}_a, \mathbf{V}_b, \mathbf{V}_c, \mathbf{V}_d]$ and $\mathrm{I}'_{abcd} = [\mathbf{M}_a, \mathbf{M}_b, \mathbf{M}_c, \mathbf{M}_d]$, are formed it becomes apparent that:

$$\mathrm{I}'_{abcd} = T(\mathrm{I}_{abcd}),$$

hence, $\quad |\mathrm{I}'_{abcd}| = k_{abcd} \, |\mathbf{T}| \, . \, |\mathrm{I}_{abcd}|, \quad$ where $\quad k_{abcd} = k_a k_b k_c k_d.$

Therefore an invariant measured either in the object frame or from the kernel $\mathbf{w}'$ can be formed:

$$I_1 = \frac{|\mathrm{I}'_{abcd}| \cdot |\mathrm{I}'_{abef}|}{|\mathrm{I}'_{abce}| \cdot |\mathrm{I}'_{abdf}|} = \frac{|\mathrm{I}_{abcd}| \cdot |\mathrm{I}_{abef}|}{|\mathrm{I}_{abce}| \cdot |\mathrm{I}_{abdf}|}. \tag{D.0.4}$$

This is not the only index that can be measured. Using the counting argument of Forsyth, et al. (42), six planes have 18 parameters, the 3D projective group has 15 degrees of freedom, and so there are $18 - 15 = 3$ independent invariants.

REFERENCES

1. Åström, K. "Affine Invariants of Planar Sets," *TR,* Department of Mathematics, Lund Institute of Technology, Sweden, 1993.
2. Asada, H. and Brady, M. "The Curvature Primal Sketch," *IEEE Trans. PAMI,* Vol. 8, No. 1, p.2-14, January 1986.
3. Ayache, N. and Faugeras, O.D. "HYPER: A New Approach for the Recognition and Positioning of Two-Dimensional Objects," *IEEE Trans. PAMI,* Vol. 8, No. 1, p.44-54, January 1986.
4. Ayache, N. and Faugeras, O.D. "Building a Consistent 3D Representation of a Mobile Robot Environment by Combining Multiple Stereo Views," Proceedings IJCAI, p.808-810, 1987.
5. Barrett, E.B., Payton, P.M. and Brill, M.H. "Contributions to the Theory of Projective Invariants for Curves in Two and Three Dimensions," Proceedings 1st DARPA-ESPRIT Workshop on Invariance, p.387-425, March 1991.
6. Beardsley, P.A, "Applications of Projective Geometry to Robot Vision," D.Phil. Thesis, Department of Engineering Science, Oxford University, 1992.
7. Besl, P.J. and Jain, R.C. "Three-Dimensional Object Recognition," *ACM Computing Surveys,* Vol. 17, No. 1, p.75-145, March 1985.
8. Besl, P.J. and Jain, R.C. "Segmentation Through Symbolic Surface Descriptions," Proceedings CVPR86, p.77-85, 1986.
9. Binford, T.O. "Inferring Surfaces from Images," *Artificial Intelligence,* Vol. 17, p.205-244, 1981.
10. Binford, T.O. and Levitt, T.S. "Quasi-Invariants: Theory and Explanation," Proceeding Darpa IUW, p.819-829, 1993.
11. Bolles, R. and Cain, R. "Recognising and Locating Partially Visible Objects: The Local-Feature-Focus Method," *IJRR,* Vol. 1, No. 3, p.57-82, 1982.
12. Bolles, R.C. and Horaud, R. "3DPO: A Three-Dimensional Part Orientation System," *Three Dimensional Vision,* Kanade, T. editor, Kluwer Academic Publishers, p.399-450, 1987.
13. Bookstein, F. "Fitting Conic Sections to Scattered Data," *Computer Vision Graphics and Image Processing,* Vol. 9, p.56-71, 1979.
14. Borgefors, G. "Hierarchical Chamfer Matching: A Parametric Edge Matching Algorithm," *IEEE Trans. PAMI,* Vol. 10, No. 6, p.849-865, November 1988.
15. Brady, M. "Criteria for Representation of Shape," in *Human and Machine Vision,* Beck, Hope and Rosenfeld editors, Academic Press, 1983.

16. Brady, M. and Yuille, A. "An Extremum Principle for Shape from Contour," *IEEE Trans. PAMI*,-6, No. 3, p.288-301, May 1984.

17. Brooks, R.A. "Model-Based Three-Dimensional Interpretations of Two-Dimensional Images," *PAMI*-5, No. 2, March 1983.

18. Burns, B.J. and Kitchen, L.J. "Rapid Object Recognition From a Large Model Base Using Prediction Hierarchies," Proceedings DARPA Image Understanding Workshop, p.71-719, April 1988.

19. Burns, J.B., Weiss, R.S. and Riseman, E.M. "The Non-Existence of General-Case View-Invariants," in (92), p.120-131, 1992.

20. Carlsson, S. "Projectively Invariant Decomposition of Planar Shapes," in (92), p.267-273, 1992.

21. Carlsson, S., Mohr, R., Moons, T., Morin, L., Rothwell, C., Van Diest, M., Van Gool, L., Veillon, F. and Zisserman, A. "Semi-Local Projective Invariants for the Recognition of Smooth Plane Curves," In preparation, 1994.

22. Canny J.F. "A Computational Approach to Edge Detection," *IEEE Trans. PAMI,* Vol. 8, No. 6, p.679-698, 1986.

23. Cass, T.A. "Polynomial-Time Object Recognition in the Presence of Clutter, Occlusion, and Uncertainty," Proceedings ECCV2, p.834-842, 1992.

24. Clemens, D.T. and Jacobs, D.W. "Model Group Indexing for Recognition," Proceedings CVPR91, p.4-9, 1991, and *IEEE Trans. PAMI,* Vol. 13, No. 10, p.1007-1017, October 1991.

25. Clowes, M.B. "On Seeing Things," *Artificial Intelligence,* Vol. 2, p.79-116, 1971.

26. Connolly, C.I., Mundy, J.L,. Stenstrom, J.R. and Thompson, D.W. "Matching From 3-D Range Models into 2-D Intensity Scenes," Proceedings ICCV1, p.65-72, 1987.

27. Cox, I.J., Rehg, J.M. and Hingorani, S. "A Bayesian Multiple Hypothesis Approach to Contour Grouping," Proceedings ECCV2, p.72-77, 1992.

28. Demey, S., Zisserman, A. and Beardsley, P. "Affine and Projective Structure from Motion," Proceedings BMVC92, p.49-58, 1992.

29. Dexter, C. *MORSE: The Riddle of the Third Mile,* Bantam Books, p.102, June 1988.

30. Dexter, C. *MORSE: The Silent World of Nicholas Quinn,* Bantam Books, 2nd Printing, p.189, July 1990.

31. Dhome, M., Lapreste, J.T., Rives, G. and Richetin, M. "Spatial Localization of Modelled Objects of Revolution in Monocular Perspective Vision," Proceedings ECCV1, p.475-485, 1990.

32. Dickson, J.W. "Image Structure and Model-Based Vision," D.Phil. Thesis, Department of Engineering Science, Oxford University, Oxford, 1991.

33. Duda, R.O. and Hart P.E. *Pattern Classification and Scene Analysis,* Wiley, 1973.

34. Ettinger, G.J. "Large Hierarchical Object Recognition Using Libraries of Parameterized Model Sub-Parts," Proceedings CVPR88, p.32-41, 1988.

35. Faugeras, O.D. and Hebert, M. "The Representation, Recognition, and Locating of 3-D Objects," *International Journal of Robotics Research,* Vol. 5, No. 3, p.27-52, 1986.

36. Faugeras, O. "What can be Seen in Three Dimensions with an Uncalibrated Stereo Rig?" Proceedings ECCV2, p.563-578, 1992.

37. Fisher, R.B. *From Surfaces to Objects: Computer Vision and Three Dimensional Scene Analysis,* John Wiley and Sons, 1989.

38. Flynn, P.J. and Jain, A.K. "CAD-Based Computer Vision: From CAD Models to Relational Graphs," *IEEE Trans. PAMI,* Vol. 13, No. 2, p.114-132, February 1991.

39. Forsyth, D.A., Mundy, J.L., Zisserman, A.P. and Brown, C.M. "Projectively Invariant Representations Using Implicit Algebraic Curves," Proceedings ECCV1, p.427-436, 1990.

40. Forsyth, D.A., Mundy, J.L., Zisserman, A.P. and Brown, C.M. "Invariance - A new framework for vision," Proceedings ICCV3, p.598-605, 1990.

41. Forsyth, D.A., Mundy, J.L., Zisserman, A.P. and Rothwell, C.A. "Invariant Descriptors for 3-D Object Recognition and Pose," Proceedings 1st DARPA-ESPRIT Workshop on Invariance, p.171-208, March 1991.

42. Forsyth, D.A., Mundy, J.L., Zisserman, A.P., Coelho, C., Heller, A. and Rothwell, C.A. "Invariant Descriptors for 3-D Object Recognition and Pose," *IEEE Trans. PAMI,* Vol. 13, No. 10, p.971-991, October 1991.

43. Forsyth, D.A., Mundy, J.L., Zisserman, A.P. and Rothwell, C.A. "Recognising Curved Surfaces from their Outlines," Proceedings ECCV2, p.639-648, 1992.

44. Forsyth, D.A. "Recognizing Algebraic Surfaces from their Outlines," Proceedings ICCV4, p.476-480, 1993.

45. Forsyth, D.A. and Rothwell, C.A. "Recovering Extruded Surfaces from a Single Image," Proceedings 2nd ARPA/NSF-ESPRIT Workshop on Invariance, p.411-426, October 1993.

46. Forsyth, D.A., Mundy, J.L., Zisserman, A.P. and Rothwell, C.A. "Using Global Consistency to Recognise Euclidean Objects with an Uncalibrated Camera", to appear, CVPR, 1994.

47. Ganapathy, S. "Decomposition of Transformation Matrices for Robot Vision," Proceeding ICRA, p.130-139, 1984.

48. Goad, C. "Special Purpose Automatic Programming for 3D Model-Based Vision," Proceedings Image Understanding Workshop, p.371-381, 1983.

49. Gordon, G. "Shape from Symmetry," Proceedings SPIE Intelligent Robots and Computer Vision VIII, Algorithms and Techniques, Vol. 1192, 1989.

50. Grimson, W.E.L. and Lozano-Pérez, T. "Localizing Overlapping Parts by Searching the Interpretation Tree," *IEEE Trans. PAMI,* Vol. 9, No. 4, p.469-482, July 1987.

51. Grimson, W.E.L. "Recognition of Object Families Using Parameterized Models," Proceedings ICCV1, p.93-101, 1987.

52. Grimson, W.E.L. and Huttenlocher, D.P. "On the Sensitivity of the Hough Transform for Object Recognition," *IEEE Trans. PAMI,* Vol. 13, No. 3, p.255-274, March 1990.

53. Grimson, W.E.L. *Object Recognition by Computer, The Role of Geometric Constraints,* MIT Press, 1990.

54. Hartley, R.I., Gupta, R. and Chang, T. "Stereo from Uncalibrated Cameras," Proceedings CVPR92, p.761-764, 1992.

55. Hopcroft, J.E., Huttenlocher, D.P. and Wayner, P.C. "Affine Invariants for Model-Based Recognition," in (92), p.354-374, 1992.

56. Huffman, D.A. "Impossible Objects as Nonsense Sentences," *Machine Intelligence,* Vol. 6, Meltzer, B. and Michie, D. editors, Edinburgh University Press, 1971.

57. Huttenlocher, D.P. and Ullman, S. "Object Recognition Using Alignment," Proceedings ICCV1, p.102-111, 1987.

58. Huttenlocher, D.P. "Three-Dimensional Recognition of Solid Objects from a Two-Dimensional Image," Ph.D. Thesis, Department of Electrical Engineering and Computer Science, MIT, 1988.

59. Huttenlocher D.P. "Fast Affine Point Matching: An Output-Sensitive Method," Proceedings CVPR91, p.263-268, 1991.

60. Huttenlocher, D.P. and Kleinberg, J.M. "On Invariants of Sets of Points or Line Segments Under Projection," *TR-92-1292,* Cornell University, 1992.

61. Illingworth, J. and Kittler, J. "A Survey of the Hough Transform," *CVGIP,* Vol. 44, p.87-116, 1988.

62. Jacobs, D.W. "Space Efficient 3D Model Indexing," Proceedings CVPR-92, p.439-444, 1992.

63. Kalvin, A., Schonberg, E., Schwartz, J.T. and Sharir, M. "Two-Dimensional, Model-Based, Boundary Matching Using Footprints," *International Journal of Robotics Research,* Vol. 5, No. 4, p.38-55, 1986.

64. Kass, M., Witkin, A. and Terzopoulos, D. "Snakes: Active Contour Models," Proceedings ICCV1, p.259-268, 1987.

65. Keren, D., Subrahmonia, J. and Cooper, D.B. "Robust Object Recognition Based on Implicit Algebraic Curves and Surfaces," Proceedings CVPR92, p.791-794, 1992.

66. Koenderink, J.J. and Van Doorn, A.J. "Affine Structure from Motion," *J. Opt. Soc. Am. A.* Vol. 8, No. 2, p.377-385, 1991.

67. Kriegman, D.J. and Ponce, J. "On Recognizing and Positioning Curved 3-D Objects from Image Contours," *IEEE Trans. PAMI,* Vol. 12, No. 12, p.1127-1137, December 1990.

68. Lamdan, Y., Schwartz, J.T. and Wolfson, H.J. "Object Recognition by Affine Invariant Matching," Proceedings CVPR88, p.335-344, 1988.

69. Lee, C.H. and Huang, T. "Finding Four Point Correspondences and Determining Motion of a Rigid Object from two Weak Perspective Views," Proceedings CVPR88, p398-403, 1988.

70. Lei, G. "Recognition of Planar Objects in 3-D Space from Single Perspective Views Using Cross Ratio," *IEEE Trans. Robotics and Automation,* Vol. 6, No. 4, p.432-437, August 1990.

71. Lowe, D.G. *Perceptual Organization and Visual Recognition,* Kluwer Academic Publishers, 1985.

72. Lowe, D.G. "The Viewpoint Consistency Constraint," *International Journal of Computer Vision,* Vol. 1, No. 1, p.57-72, 1987.

73. Liu, J., Mundy, J.L., Forsyth, D.A., Zisserman, A. and Rothwell, C.A. "Efficient Recognition of Rotationally Symmetric Surfaces and Straight Homogeneous Generalized Cylinders," Proceedings CVPR93, p.123-128, 1993.

74. McLauchlan, P.F., Reid, I.D. and Murray, D.W. "Coarse Image Motion for Saccade Control," Proceedings BMVC92, p.357-366, 1992.

75. Mackworth, A.K. "Interpreting Pictures of Polyhedral Scenes," *Artificial Intelligence,* Vol. 4, p.99-118, 1973.

76. Mao, J., Jain, A.K. and Flynn, P.J. "Integration of Multiple Feature Groups and Multiple Views into a 3D Object Recognition System," Proceedings 2nd ARPA/NSF-ESPRIT Workshop on Invariance, p.267-286, October 1993.

77. Marr, D. "Analysis of Occluding Contour," *Proc. R. Soc. Lond.* Series B, Vol. 197, p.441-475, 1977.

78. Marr, D. *Vision,* Freeman, 1982.

79. Masciangelo, S. "3-D Cues from a Single View: Detection of Elliptical Arcs and Model-Based Perspective Backprojection," Proceedings BMVC90, p.223-228, 1990.

80. Maxwell, E.A. *The Methods of Plane Projective Geometry based on the use of General Homogeneous Coordinates,* Cambridge University Press, 1963.

81. Maybank, S.J. "The Projective Geometry of Ambiguous Surfaces," *Proc. R. Soc. Lond.* , Series A, Vol. 332, p.1-47, 1990.

82. Maybank, S.J. "Probabilistic Analysis of the Application of the Cross Ratio to Model Based Vision," *TR,* GEC Hirst Research Centre, 1993.

83. Maybank, S.J. and Beardsley, P.A. "Applications of Invariants to Model Based Vision," to appear *Journal of Applied Statistics,* 1994.

84. Mitsumoto H., Tamura S., Okazaki K., Kajimi N. and Fukui Y. "3D Reconstruction Using Mirror Images Based on a Plane Symmetry Recovery Method", *IEEE Trans. PAMI,* 14, 9, 941-945, 1992.

85. Mohr, R. and Morin, L. "Relative Positioning from Geometric Invariants," Proceedings CVPR91, p.139-144, 1991.

86. Mohr, R. "Projective Geometry and Computer Vision," in *Handbook of Pattern Recognition and Computer Vision,* Chen, Pau and Wang editors, 1992.

87. Moons, T., Pauwels, E., Van Gool, L. and Oosterlinck, A. "Viewpoint Invariant Characterization of Objects Composed of Different Rigid Parts: a Mathematical Framework," in *Geometry and Topology of Submanifolds,* Vol. 5., Verstraelen, P. and Dillen, F. editors, World Scientific, 1993.

88. Morgan, A.P. *Solving Polynomial Systems Using Continuation for Scientific and Engineering Problems,* Prentice-Hall, Englewood Cliffs, N.J., 1987.

89. Moses, Y. and Ullman, S. "Limitations of Non Model-Based Recognition Systems," Proceedings ECCV2, p.820-828, 1992.

90. Mukherjee, D.P. Zisserman, A. and Brady, J.M. "Shape from Symmetry - Detecting and Exploiting Symmetry in Affine Images," *TR,* Department of Engineering Science, Oxford University, Oxford, 1993.

91. Mundy, J.L. and Heller, A.J. "The Evolution and Testing of a Model-Based Object Recognition System," Proceedings ICCV3, p.268-282, 1990.

92. Mundy, J.L. and Zisserman, A.P. *Geometric Invariance in Computer Vision,* MIT Press, 1992.

93. Mundy, J.L. "Repeated Structures: Image Correspondence Constraints and Ambiguity of 3D Constructions," Proceedings 2nd ARPA/NSF-ESPRIT Workshop on Invariance, p.51-64, October 1993.

94. Murray, D.W. "Model-Based Recognition using 3D Structure from Motion," *Image and Vision Computing,* Vol. 5, p.85-90, 1987.

95. Murray, D.W. and Cook, D.B. "Using the Orientation of Fragmentary 3D Edge Segments for Polyhedral Object Recognition," *IJCV,* Vol. 2, No. 2, p.153-169, 1988.

96. Murray, D.W., Du, F., McLauchlan, P.F., Reid, I.D., Sharkey, P.M. and Brady, J.M. "Design of Stereo Heads," *Active Vision,* Blake, A. and Yuille, A. editors, MIT Press, p.155-172, 1992.

97. Nielsen, L. "Automated Guidance of Vehicles using Vision and Projective Invariant Marking," *Automatica,* Vol. 24, p.135-148, 1988.

98. Olver, P. *Applications of Lie Groups to Differential Equations,* Springer, 1986.

99. Pavlidis, T. *Structural Pattern Recognition,* Springer-Verlag, 1977.

100. Pollard, S.B, Pridmore, T.P, Porrill, J., Mayhew, J.E.W. and Frisby, J.P. "Geometrical Modelling from Multiple Stereo Views," *International Journal of Robotics Research,* Vol. 8, No. 4, p.132-138, 1989.

101. Pridmore, A.P., Porrill, J. and Mayhew, J.E.W. "Segmentation and Description of Binocularly Viewed Contours," *Image and Vision Computing,* Vol. 5, No. 2, p.132-138, May 1987.

102. Quan, L. and Mohr, R. "Towards Structure from Motion for Linear Features through Reference Points," Proceedings IEEE Workshop on

Visual Motion, 1991.

103. Quan, L., Gros, P. and Mohr, R. "Invariants of a Pair of Conics Revisited," Proceedings BMVC91, p.71-77, 1991.

104. Reid, I. "Recognising Parameterized Models from Range Data," D.Phil. Thesis, Department of Engineering Science, Oxford University, Oxford, 1991.

105. Reiss, T.H. and Rayner, P.J.W. "Object Recognition using Algebraic and Differential Invariants," *CUED/F-INFENG/TR.97*, Department of Engineering Science, Cambridge, 1992.

106. Roberts, L.G. "Machine Perception of Three-Dimensional Solids," *Optical and Electro-optical Information Processing,* Tippett, *et al.* editors, MIT Press, p.159-197, 1965,

107. Rothwell, C.A., Zisserman, A. Forsyth, D.A. and Mundy, J.L. "Using Projective Invariants for Constant Time Library Indexing in Model Based Vision," Proceedings BMVC91, p.62-70, 1991.

108. Rothwell, C.A., Zisserman, A., Marinos, C.I., Forsyth, D.A. and Mundy, J.L. "Relative Motion and Pose From Arbitrary Plane Curves," *Image and Vision Computing,* Vol. 10, No. 4, p.250-262, May 1992.

109. Rothwell, C.A., Zisserman, A., Forsyth, D.A. and Mundy, J.L. "Canonical Frames for Planar Object Recognition," Proceedings ECCV2, p.757-772, 1992.

110. Rothwell, C.A., Zisserman, A., Mundy, J.L. and Forsyth, D.A. "Efficient Model Library Access by Projectively Invariant Indexing Functions", Proceedings CVPR92, p.109-114, 1992.

111. Rothwell, C.A., Forsyth, D.A., Zisserman, A. and Mundy, J.L. "Extracting Projective Information from Single Views of 3D Point Sets," *TR OUEL 1927/92*, Department of Engineering Science, Oxford University, Oxford, 1992.

112. Rothwell, C.A., Forsyth, D.A., Zisserman, A. and Mundy, J.L. "Extracting Projective Information from Single Views of 3D Point Sets," Proceedings ICCV4, p.573-582, 1993.

113. Rothwell, C.A. "Hierarchical Object Descriptions using Invariants," Proceedings 2nd ARPA/NSF-ESPRIT Workshop on Invariance, p.287-302, October 1993.

114. Sampson, P.D. "Fitting Conic Sections to 'Very Scattered' Data: An Iterative Refinement of the Bookstein Algorithm," *Computer Graphics and Image Processing,* Vol. 18, p.97-108, 1982.

115. Semple, J.G. and Kneebone, G.T. *Algebraic Projective Geometry,* Oxford University Press, 1952.

116. Sha'ashua, A. and Ullman, S. "Structural Saliency: The Detection of Globally Salient Structures Using a Locally Connected Network," Proceedings ICCV2, p.321-327, 1988.

117. Shafarevich, *Basic Algebraic Geometry,* Springer, 1977.

118. Shapiro, L.S. and Brady, J.M. "Rejecting Outliers and Estimating Errors in an Orthogonal Regression Framework," *TR OUEL 1974/93*, Department of Engineering Science, Oxford University, Oxford, 1993.

119. Sinclair, D.A., Blake, A., Smith, S. and Rothwell, C.A. "Planar Region Detection and Motion Recovery," Proceedings BMVC92, p.59-68, 1992, and *Image and Vision Computing*, Vol. 11, No. 4, p.229-234, 1993.

120. Sinclair, D.A. "Experiments in Motion and Correspondence," D.Phil. Thesis, Department of Engineering Science, Oxford University, Oxford, 1993.

121. Slama, C.C. *Manual of Photogrammetry*, American Society of Photogrammetry, 4th edition, 1980.

122. Sparr, G. "Depth Computations from Polyhedral Images," Proceedings ECCV2, p.378-386, 1992.

123. Sparr, G. "Notes on Geometric Invariants in Vision," *TR*, University of Lund, 1993.

124. Springer, C.E. *Geometry and Analysis of Projective Spaces*, Freeman, 1964.

125. Stockman, G. "Object Recognition and Localization via Pose Clustering," *Computer Vision Graphics and Image Processing*, Vol. 40, p.361-387, 1987.

126. Sugihara, K. *Machine interpretation of Line Drawings*, MIT Press, 1986.

127. Swain, M. "Object Recognition from a Large Database Using a Decision Tree," Proceedings DARPA Image Understanding Workshop, p.690-696, April 1988.

128. Sutton, M., Stark, L. and Bowyer, K. "Function-Based Generic Recognition for Multiple Object Categories," in *Three-Dimensional Object Recognition Systems*, Jain, A.K. and Flynn, P.J. editors, Elsvier, 1993.

129. Syeda-Mahmood, T.F. "Data and Model-driven Selection using Color Regions," Proceedings ECCV2, p.115-123, 1992.

130. Taubin, G. and Cooper, D.B. "Object Recognition Based on Moment (or Algebraic) Invariants," *IBM TR-RC17387*, IBM T.J. Watson Research Centre, P.O. Box 704, Yorktown Heights, NY 10598, 1991.

131. Taubin, G., Cukierman, F., Sullivan, S., Ponce, J. and Kriegman, D. "Parameterizing and Fitting Bounded Algebraic Curves and Surfaces," Proceeding CVPR92, p.103-108, 1992

132. Taubin, G. "An Improved Algorithm for Algebraic Curve and Surface Fitting," Proceedings ICCV4, p.658-665, 1993.

133. Thompson, D.W. and Mundy, J.L. "Three-Dimensional Model Matching from an Unconstrained Viewpoint," Proceedings ICRA, p.208-220, 1987.

134. Tsai, R.Y. "An Efficient and Accurate Camera Calibration Technique for 3D Machine Vision," *Journal of Robotics and Automation*, Vol. 3 No. 4, p.364-374, 1987.

135. Turney, J.L., Mudge, T.N. and Volz, R.A. "Recognizing Partially Occluded Parts," *IEEE Trans. PAMI,* Vol. 7, No. 4, p.410-421, July 1985.

136. Van Gool, L. Kempenaers, P. and Oosterlinck, A. "Recognition and Semi-Differential Invariants," Proceedings CVPR91, p.454-460, 1991.

137. Walker, D.F.J. and Chatwin, C.R. "Fast Object Recognition using a Hybrid Optical/Digital Processor," Proceedings BMVC90, p.413-419, 1990.

138. Waltz, D. "Understanding Line Drawings of Scenes with Shadows," *The Psychology of Computer Vision,* Winston, P.H. editor, McGraw-Hill, p.19-91, 1975.

139. Wang, H., Bowman, C., Brady, M. and Harris, C. "A Parallel Implementation of a Structure-from-Motion Algorithm," Proceedings ECCV2, p.272-276, 1992.

140. Wayner, P.C. "Efficiently Using Invariant Theory for Model-Based Matching," Proceedings CVPR91, p.473-478, 1991.

141. Weiss, I. "Projective Invariants of Shapes," Proceedings DARPA Image Understanding Workshop, p.1125-1134, April 1988.

142. Weiss, I. "Noise Resistant Projective and Affine Invariants," Proceedings CVPR92, p.115-121, 1992.

143. Weyl, H. *The Classical Groups and their Invariants,* 2nd edition, Princeton University Press, 1946.

144. Wilczynski, E.J. *Projective Differential Geometry of Curves and Ruled Surfaces,* Teubner, Leipzig, 1906.

145. Witkin, A.P. "Scale-Space Filtering," *Readings in Computer Vision - Issues, Problems, Principles and Paradigms,* Morgan Kaufmann, p.329-332, 1987.

146. Wolfson, H.J. "Object Recognition by Transformation Invariant Indexing," Proceedings Invariance Workshop, Second European Conference in Computer Vision, 1992.

147. Yuan, J.S-C. "A General Photogrammetric Method for Determining Object Position and Orientation," *IEEE Transactions of Robotics and Automation,* Vol. 5, No. 2, p.129-142, July 1989.

148. Zisserman, A.P., Marinos, C.I., Forsyth, D.A., Mundy, J.L. and Rothwell, C.A. "Relative Motion and Pose from Invariants," Proceedings BMVC90, p.7-12, 1990.

149. Zisserman, A.P, Blake, A., Rothwell, C.A., Van Gool, L.J. and Van Diest, M. "Eliciting Qualitative Structure from Image Curve Deformations," Proceedings ICCV4, p.340-346, 1993

150. Zisserman, A.P., Forsyth, D.A., Mundy, J.L., Rothwell, C.A. and Liu, J. "3D Object Recognition using Invariance", submitted for publication, 1994.

INDEX